edited by Gary Lane W9-BPE-018

Sylvia Plath
New views on the poetry

The Johns Hopkins University Press
Baltimore and London

15327

The frontispiece for this book, entitled "The spirit of blackness is in us," is from a
lithograph by Louis Lubbering and was commissioned by the author for this work.

Manufactured in the United States of America

The Johns Hopkins University Press, Baltimore, Maryland 21218
The Johns Hopkins Press Ltd., London

Library of Congress Catalog Card Number 78-20515
ISBN 0-8018-2179-7

Library of Congress Cataloging in Publication data will be found on the last
printed page of this book.

For Franny and Bart

Contents

Introduction

Sylvia Plath is one of the most controversial poets of our time—and she is more. Plath has grown into a cult figure, a dramatic presence whose dramatic absence—her suicide at thirty—shrouded the woman and her work in conjecture's cloak of holes. For some she became the symbol of woman oppressed, albeit by cultural forces rather than the physical brutality she sometimes invokes; others saw her as the triumphant victim of her own intensity, the authentic poet pursuing sensation to that ultimate, exciting uncertainty, death; for still others she became in retrospect the doomed innocent, undone by a sensibility too acute for our gross physical world. But the list of projected Plaths might go on for pages: everyone, it seems, has his own version of the Sylvia Plath myth.

Such mythologizing affects everything about the poet, including criticism of her work. In 1970 Mary Kinzie found Plath criticism divided sharply into two periods, with the poet's death, on 11 February 1963, marking the turning point. The early criticism, "reviews of *The Colossus and The Bell Jar*[,] had been brief, reserved, entirely conventional."[1] The next period, through and beyond the book in which Kinzie's remarks appeared, was devoted to revaluation and canonization.

Plath's suicide and the publication two years later of *Ariel* evinced something very like poetic sainthood, recoloring the earlier work and lending the whole enterprise an austere pallor of immortality. Critics who, lacking the evidence of the later poems, had *of course* not heard all that lay submerged beneath *The Colossus*, now found the overlooked meanings embarrassingly plain. Even so acute a reader as Richard Howard, in an essay that remains one of the most perceptive discussions of Plath, found himself beginning with a public confession of earlier blindness: "The first review I ever wrote of a book of poems was of *her* first book of poems, that breviary of estrangement..., *The Colossus*..., and in my account...of these well-behaved, shapely poems by a *summa cum laude* graduate of Smith who had worked as a guest editor of *Mademoiselle* and won a Fulbright to Newnham, the wife of Ted Hughes and the mother of two children, I missed a lot—I had no premonition of what was coming."[2] Plath ascended. We need but mark Howard's italicized *"her,"* his recitation of biographical details, to gauge the tenor of that second period of Plath criticism.

The past five or six years have seen the emergence of more measured consideration and the arrival of several book-length studies, but the balanced appraisal Plath needs has not yet appeared. Edward Butscher's gossipy, oversimplifying "critical biography," *Sylvia Plath: Method and Madness*, is at best cursory in its criticism and nowhere captures a poet. David Holbrook's reductive psychoanalytic study, *Sylvia Plath: Poetry and Existence*, conceals its occasional insights among a forest of Freudean trees; there are so many more pricks than kicks that we lose track of the kicks almost entirely. Even the most informative scholarly study to appear, Judith Kroll's *Chapters in a Mythology: The Poetry of Sylvia Plath*, considerably overextends its quite useful research, fitting all of Plath's poems to a thesis that can cover only some of them.

There is a strong calling, then, for the present collection. Not yet the unified, full, and just evaluation that Plath deserves, it is nevertheless a movement by committee to that end, a diversity of carefully formulated praise and blame, analysis and contextualization, from which serious students and later evaluators can usefully draw. The book is divided into three parts, Achievement and Value, Process and Influence, Personal and Public Contexts; by no means hermetic, these sections nevertheless represent the broadly differing approaches of aesthetic overview, technical examination, and biographical and historical connection. With a single exception, all of the essays were commissioned for this book. And all of them were able to draw on materials that most earlier commentators lacked: a substantial body of Plath's poems and prose, a moderately detailed biographical record, and an important selection of the poet's correspondence.

2

Because the essence of this book lies in the demonstration of its writers' claims, which, I think, are carried out in exceptionally rich and diverse ways, little of these essays' thunder will be stolen by summarizing and introducing them. Such a summary has its uses: it will serve as a process of abstracting for those readers who are determined to pursue only certain inquiries; it will suggest both the shape and the voices of the book; and it may help the thoroughly involved reader, laboring to assimilate many, sometimes unfamiliar examples, keep the arguments straight.

Part one begins with Calvin Bedient's admiring demonstration of Plath's romanticism. Bedient finds Plath's thought unimportant and her sensibility —exhaustingly consumed in contradiction, overvulnerable—primarily useful in helping us recognize our own complicity in it. He locates Plath's importance in intensity—"she became our second queen (poor queen, mad queen) of subjectivity"—and his essay is an exceptionally sensitive characterization of the subjective drama of Plath's poetry.

J. D. McClatchy's valuation is also high, but somewhat different. For him, Plath is a period poet, one "whose sensibilities uniquely captured —and whose work continues to recover for later readers—[her] contemporary culture's tone, values, and issues." Like Bedient, McClatchy sees little importance in Plath's subjects; for him, however, her importance resides in a "rapidly evolving relationship to style," and he traces that evolution from the traditionalism of the *Colossus* poems to the taut new purity of *Ariel*, with its "abundance and abandon," its "sense of autopsy." Plath, he concludes, is an innovator as important as Lowell or Roethke in her "experiments with voice and the relationships among tone and image and address."

Hugh Kenner puts a damper on the enthusiasm for Plath. Marking the precision and control of the early poems, he finds that the intricate formalism of *The Colossus* "detained her mind upon the plane of craft, and so long as it was detained there it did not slip toward what beckoned it." Kenner sees great promise in that first book—had she developed its ways of working, "it is a plausible guess that the arc of her development might have easily exceeded Lowell's"—but finds the promise betrayed by the "bogus spirituality" of the *Ariel* poems. Made to seem a new and final sincerity, these poems, he argues, manipulate us as consciously as, and far more dangerously than, their predecessors. These "death poems—say a third of *Ariel*—are bad for anyone's soul. They give a look of literary respectability to voyeurist passions: no gain for poetry, nor for her."

The section's final essay and strongest task-taking is by David Shapiro. Shapiro sees Plath's work as melodramatic and exaggerated, a "flight into performance." He mourns its overdetermination—"a constant program of the referential in an age of degraded public realisms"—and misses "the whole delicious sense of the nondiscursive in poetry." His is the committed voice of a fine young poet, and his judgments and examples will give pause to the staunchest of Plath enthusiasts.

Part two opens with Richard Blessing's examination of certain techniques of style, tone, and structure in the late poems. Linking the later, rapid method of composition with his sense that "Plath's great and underlying terror is always the nausea of movement itself," Blessing finds velocity and venom the qualities that distinguish *Ariel* from *The Colossus* and explores some of the ways Plath generated these qualities: through deliberate ambiguity and the manipulation of images, through a calculated impurity of tone, and through a structural pattern of dominance and submission. The essay is particularly rich in examples, offering expanded readings of many familiar lines.

J. D. O'Hara's essay begins with a theoretical discussion of comedy, and of incongruity in particular. The theory leads him to see Plath's poems as reflexive: their subject matter is neither objective nor external but is instead the highly subjective consciousness of their own poetic speakers. This is the basis for Plath's indecorous, disturbing comedy, a detached, existential gallows humor that in the absence of tragedy, of felt human significance, can exploit "the disparity between pain and appearance, [or] a woman's irrationally inflated obsession with her dead father, [or] a desperate attempt to understand what has gone wrong with a marriage."

The next three essays are more narrowly focused. Sister Bernetta Quinn examines Medusan imagery in Plath, concentrating on a close and revealing reading of the difficult "Medusa" and radiating from it to related references. The poem's image is multileveled—Medusa moves from "(1) jellyfish to (2) Gorgon to (3) the lunar Muse over art conceived of as 'sculpted form' to (4) the 'false heaven' of drugs"—and Sister Quinn offers not only an explication but also a background for each level.

My own discussion of influence and originality in Plath attempts two things: "to track the early, imitative phase, marking borrowings as they appear in the poems and suggesting a logic to their appropriation, and to characterize the originality of the voice Plath finally made her own." Thomas, Roethke, Stevens, and Yeats are invoked as her special poetic fathers, and I suggest how each was able to fill a particular defensive need in the poet. In the later poems, I see Plath subsuming influence, and I try to articulate her new intensity in considerations of "Cut," "Contusion," and "Morning Song."

A more specialized influence study concludes this section, Barnett Guttenberg's essay on Plath and Yeats. Guttenberg argues that Plath, who died in a house Yeats had once lived in, "builds a complete system, with a Yeatsian antithetical vision and consistent clusters of Yeatsian imagery. In addition, she seems to offer a series of rejoinders on various points of disagreement." He shows us a dialectical Plath whose vision, though patterned after Yeats's, was far darker than her master's.

Part three begins with two essays of personal context. Using *Letters Home* as a central document, a suggestive biography of the poetry, Marjorie Perloff considers the poetic consequences of Plath's relation to her mother. She sees the early poems as indicative of "Sivvy," the accommodating, all-American girl who conformed in her slick, "mature" imitations even as she conformed in her cheery, banal letters. By the time Plath recognized and rejected her mother in herself, the identification had become identity, and so the metaphorical "killing" of Aurelia Plath in "Medusa" became the inevitability of the poet's own suicide.

Suicide is also the concern of Murray M. Schwartz and Christopher Bollas, whose psychoanalytic examination of Plath's work leads them to explain the poet's death as a convergence of factors identifiable from the latent content of the poems: "She would merge with father, with mother. She would murder them. She would act out her murderous wishes. She would cope magically with the burden of actual mothering. She would end her physical pain. She would stop performing." Carefully documenting these factors with examples, they offer a convincing portrait of a psyche dominated by a complex absence of bridgeable others that can be traced back to a child's relations with her father and mother.

Two essays of a more public context follow. Carole Ferrier's feminist reading of Plath sees in the poetry a continual dialectic that embodies the alternative possibilities of "self-destruction or motivation toward social change," the results of alienation turned uselessly inward or helpfully outward on its causes within society. Ferrier argues that this dialectic suggests Plath's complicated relationship to patriarchy, and she examines its ambivalence and gradual clarification in a particularly interesting reading of the bee poems in *Ariel*.

Jerome Mazzaro concludes the book by placing Plath and her concerns into a rich historical tapestry and by reminding us of the cultural, scientific, literary, and political events that shaped and characterized her time. His eclectic essay ranges widely, now suggesting the impact of Lowell's "Memories of West Street and Lepke" on the structure of *The Bell Jar*, now noting the influence of Loren Eiseley's *The Immense Journey* on "Lorelei" and "Full Fathom Five"; and when we have finished the essay, Plath seems something less of a monolith, something more of a temporal being.

3

Plath would have liked, I like to think, the living friction of this welter of essays. "Perfection is terrible," she wrote, "it cannot have children." I hope for children from this collection, for response and discrimination and change, for "A disturbance in mirrors." These essays, in their variety of approach and valuation, offer provocative, often acute insights into a violently interesting poet, and the serious reader, whatever his initial opinion of Plath, is sure to find that opinion challenged, changed, or deepened. My final hope is that of every poetry critic: that the discussions here will stimulate not only a rethinking but also a reexperiencing of the poems, and that the reader will return to them wiser, warier, yet somehow more vulnerable.

Notes

1. Mary Kinzie, "An Informal Check List of Criticism," in *The Art of Sylvia Plath: A Symposium*, ed. Charles Newman (Bloomington: Indiana University Press, 1970), p. 283.
2. Richard Howard, "Sylvia Plath: 'And I Have No Face, I Have Wanted to Efface Myself...,'" in *The Art of Sylvia Plath*, p. 77.

1. Achievement and value

Calvin Bedient

Sylvia Plath, Romantic...

Sylvia Plath was a romantic of the most self-cancelling kind. She reduced romanticism to a fever, a scream of defiance; but romantic she was, and exactly to the degree that she was alive and struggling. Her romanticism was her wish to live, if at times only in that touchingly qualified transcendence (located on no one's map of earth or heaven) where she could be born once again as her father's little girl.

A romantic is an unhatched Platonist, one unable to renounce the beautiful heresy of matter. Loving the freedom of nonbody, the romantic yet instinctively shuns its lack of intimacy—the absence of a loved individual face or of what Rilke called "unique space, intimate space," a particularity of place that has spoken to the spirit. The romantic would happily melt time into aboriginal timelessness, but not if that meant (as it would) the deliquescence of space.

Sylvia Plath was made an impure Platonist of this kind at the precocious age of eight. Her father, "full of God," died, removing divinity from life. The absolute, power, love—if these then were absent, what was present? Confusingly, an absence. But so it was. One had only to put an ear to the body to hear the "black muzzles / Revolving, the sound / Punching out Absence!" To live is to be an unopened "letter" flying "to a name, two eyes."

Then to start over in freedom, only two to the world! And always, always to be seen. For the eyes that look on us with love corroborate our ineffable value. Plath felt a fury to be reflected, to see her own immensity (or, in default of that, her affliction) being seen.[1] She was raised in a "mentally ambitious" family in which worth was measured by accomplishment. How she wishes in *Letters Home* that her mother could "see" her now, in this or that moment of triumph. But the most missed eyes were elsewhere. The world was in fact barren and blind, death rocked a cradle and could see. A child bride, a wintered Persephone somehow left above ground, would she not have to enter the dark, to be made visible by love?

In this little girl's romantic version of death ("death includes the concept of love"), the ancient longing of mankind for a place where the soul will be made whole again is fitted to a single Massachusetts grave. Toward a human "face at the end of the flare" Plath redirected the sublime feelings of the great religions: quailing before omens, agonized waiting, the painful ecstasy of purification, anticipation of the "beyond," peace in a great and terrible will. Yet these are the same in the new name as in Christ's: the child's dependence on the mother and father and fear of the power or loss of either is the clay from which every heaven is made.

Crushing, nearly Kafkaesque as this father worship was, it is nonetheless moving. No embrace more longed for, more healing and validating than the father's. For so judgment gets a heart, distance takes us up and hugs us to the source of power. Plath is our scapegoat, the child who needed this blessing more, who would not give up asking for it until the effort killed her.

But her quest was by definition immature. And, except as the mote that provoked the splendid blindness of her poetry, what is its importance? Critics maunder about her vision, but as Irving Howe suggests,[2] she had none. She saw neither the next world nor this one; she saw only her distance from each. What her husband called her "free and controlled access to depths formerly reserved to the primitive ecstatic priests" was at best a private clairvoyance, as her romanticism was a private "salvation."

It is true that her sense of the horror of Creation was up to the minute. But her relation to this commonplace was private and tandem. If she saw entropy as an animistic terror, a piranha religion drinking from live toes, it was not simply because the scientific view of things had once again been dipped into a child's and a poet's primitivism. It was specifically because her heart was under her father's foot, "sister of a stone." What her "vision" of the dripping "mercuric / Atoms that cripple" shows is not insight but an instinct for self-justification.

4

And if she drank dismay from history as we all do, she has nothing of interest to say about it. Everyone knows her words, "I think that personal experience...should be generally relevant, to such things as Hiroshima and Dachau, and so on"; and at least one critic, Barbara Hardy, has underlined her mythical and historical "enlargements."[3] But how merely hopeful the term "enlargement" is. If a snapshot is blown up, the result is not a panorama but a bigger snapshot. Plath uses the historical and mythical as a vanity mirror. When she writes as if she were as abused as a Nazi victim she climbs to self-importance over the bodies of the dead. She enters a moral sphere that her amoral personal imagination cannot apprehend.

So her thought is not important. Nor, in a way, is her sensibility, for it was self-consumed in contradiction. Ambivalence afflicted her. For she did try to love life—how she tried. And, given her advantages, shouldn't she have found life a treat? But her splendid assets (her education, her brains, her creative energy, her looks) could suddenly seem worthless. Something kept "trashing" them. Was it her mistrust of men? Yet how the men in her life deserved mistrust! Otto Plath had hurt her, God had hurt her, Ted Hughes had hurt her—it is the male's way. How men would like to take everything from her—her gold fillings, her genius, her life! Yet there must be good in them, something repairing, or would she feel so much pain, such an awful lack? Ambivalence. . . .

At worst, and often, her sensibility was "childish," overvulnerable: a chest pounding in terror, blood boiling blackly. When told of her father's death she said, "I'll never speak to God again!" She was ever thus extreme. The whole strength of her sensibility lay in reaction, in the cry that, as Simone Weil says, is the innocence of the soul: "Why am I being hurt?" And reactive she was vindictive, reducing Ted Hughes, for instance, from the complete helpful gentle husband he had evidently been to his betrayal of her, as if betrayal were his true identity, exposed at last. Her imagination lacked justice. She used it as those backed against a wall use a knife, fingernails, anything.

Emotionally her work is a vicious circle of weakness and strength, the strength unstable because reactive. Her capacity for feeling injured and angry were equally awesome. Now she was a toadstool, her flesh falling apart at a nudge, now a lioness. Everything that enters her world seems either too strong to live with or too weak to live. How could she but disconcert us? Her sensibility has no horizon, no free space, no issue except extinction. Where Hughes in *Crow* flogs hackneyed horrors to get a sign of life from them, Plath had but to be herself to terrify.

Yet in a way her sensibility is useful, a monstrous dredging machine. Like the young woman in "The Tour" it addresses the maiden aunt in all of us and bids us look into our hearts:

Morning Glory Pool!
The blue's a jewel.
It boils for forty hours at a stretch.

O I shouldn't dip my hankie in, it *hurts!*

Plath takes us down to where familial and other fears and resentments crawl; she exercises a dark-of-the-basement fascination. And we may come to see that it's only honest to admit our complicity in these petty and unreasonable and serious and pathetic passions.

In *Letters Home*, Plath put her intention this way: "Don't talk to me about the world needing cheerful stuff! What the person out of Belsen —physical or psychological—wants is nobody saying the birdies still go tweet tweet, but the full knowledge that somebody else has been there and knows the *worst*, just what it is like. It is much more help for me, for example, to know that people are divorced and go through hell, than to hear about happy marriages. Let the *Ladies' Home Journal* blither about *those.*"

"Cheerful stuff!"—how singular this outbreak of scorn in *Letters Home*, that in the main so impenitently "sunny" volume. It sits amid the bright pages like a pin-hole leading to the enormous black energies of the poems. For the poetry is the inverse of the letters, their antimatter. This poet is not least curious in repudiating in her verse almost the whole of her daily consciousness, at any rate as her letters and reported conversations disclosed it. The letters mirror a lah-lahing Pollyanna whom the poetry, sneaking up behind, ruthlessly savages.

Plath *A*, the Plath people knew, not only struggled to "master" the fiction formulas of the slicks; she lived pulp dreams. At Smith she seemed to compete for the title "All-American Girl." Turning out for crew, singing songs in a group around the piano, having a "platinum summer," dating Princeton and Yale men, holding offices, copping scholarships, winning the *Mademoiselle* fiction contest, etc.—how she enjoyed the narcissistic pump-ups of the college years. It was all such a thrill. "Honestly, Mum, I could just cry with happiness."

Husband, children, house, fame—she was to go after them as one pursues the Fully Desirable, the Approved. The frequent superlatives in her letters—the quarters and half-dollars of "amazing," "marvelous," "happiest"—were part of the dues she paid to the American dream.

Where in *Letters Home* are a poet's slatted observations, a poet's accents and reserves? Banality, banality; it never lets up. "I am really regrettably unoriginal, conventional, and puritanical," she freely confesses at one point—only to run on without apparent regret.

Plath epitomized the great middle of her generation, taking to the whole system of competition and reward, "failure" vs. "success," true romance and good housekeeping, with gullible eagerness. She was not simply like everyone else, she was more so. What Ted Hughes called her "tremendous will to excel" sent her running to the longest lines, to be first in them. Of course she could not afford mistakes. Even her capacity for love (Hughes labeled it "genius") she managed like an efficiency expert. She "controlled" her "sex judiciously"; "graduate school and travel abroad" were not to be "stymied by any squalling, breastfed brats." When it appeared that she had "wasted" her junior year, putting herself behind in the great contest of Smith, she protectively broke down. "Six terrible months at McLean." Then again the engine was "killing the track."

This Sylvia who had been "a healthy, merry child," according to her mother, "the center of attention most of her waking time," this Sylvia who described herself as "an extremely happy and well-adjusted buoyant person" was at the same time a maelstrom of panics and aversions. Plath *B* saw through her—saw that she was thin air, the brilliance that bounces off mirrors. Plath *B* was Plath *A* when all the friendly mirrors were taken away. She was also a pointed retaliation against Plath *A*, against all that fulsome trust. For had not Plath *A* betrayed her, by leaving her so appallingly unprepared?

The common denominator of these two Plaths was personal energy. Plath *A* was *Mademoiselle* through and through, but a Daughter of Romantic Germany beside, a self-declared Overwoman charged like some combined David Herbert-Frieda with "magnificent" being. Her conceptions of herself, of her husband, and of her marriage were all overblown in a quite German way. She "must be one of the most creative people in the world." With her husband's help she would be "a woman beyond women for [her] strength." She would go "singing all the way, even in anguish and grief, the triumph of life over death and sickness and war." As for Hughes, that "big, unruly Huckleberry Finn," his energy was "amazing," he was a "genius" and "the male counterpart" of herself. "I have never felt so celestially holy," she says, "for the fury which I have and the power is, for the first time, met with an equal soul." Their union rested on the "faith" that "comes from the earth and sun," on harmony with "the creative forces of nature."

This curious soup of romantic dynamism and idealism, this romantic assertion of personality, this romantic belief in "the adventure of life," in the cosmic privilege of genius—was it this that flowed in the veins of the young Cambridge University student who wrote fashion articles illustrated by a professionally posed tall slender smiling model: herself? It was. Here her conventional optimism found its most overweening expression. And a real force lay behind it; for try to deny it and it would change into something "furious," boiling for forty hours at a stretch.

When she fell, the ground shook, she saw to that. Plath *A*, Plath *B*, each acted on the post-Hegelian romantic belief that true being lies in intense feeling. No mute renunciation, no neutered acceptance, for her. If a rock crushes your toe, will you inquire into the law of gravity or do a dance of pain? Plath danced then kicked the rock.

She became our second queen (poor queen, mad queen) of subjectivity. The first of course was Emily Dickinson, an early influence. Both poets told "all the Truth," meaning all it would be pretty to leave out, but told it "slant," through the amusement rides, terror rides, of metaphor. Neither questioned the sufficiency or even the supremacy of her own intensity as a subject for art. Hence their terrific concentration. That both may have written partly to "fill the awful longitude" scored by a departed man also explains the peculiar urgency of some of their work, work that seems the outlet for a great vehemence. Both exemplify romantic passion, an infinitude of force imprisoned in a mortal personality. And the over-charged feeling in each produced a similar poetic of bolts ("Flash," as Dickinson put it, "And Click—and Suddenness"). To be sure, Plath is the more discursive even though she lacks Dickinson's deep (if gust-ruffled) power of reflection. She does not reflect, she reacts.

What is it to be a queen, as I have both mockingly and respectfully put it, of subjectivity? In Plath's case, writing against a nominally Christian culture (and against its backdrop), it is to have at best a macabre magnificence. The small demons attend Plath. Then, too, her self-pity is like an enormous underground labyrinth in which she wanders as if raging for her lost diadem—but the labyrinth itself is the only domain permitted to her, and her subjects have all gone away.

Yet how impressive she is as she wails, "Why am I being hurt?" How absolutely she commits herself to what Kierkegaard called "the moment of individuality," subjective being conceived as a unique, irreducible nexus of reality. And how much yearning her pain and anger express for the romantic experience of a lyrical harmony with others and with the world.

Yet to us Plath's subjectivity would be nothing without her objectifying dramatic values. Her astonishing force lies in the way she performs her emotions. She invents and speaks from within para-objective scenes that give body to her intensity without diminishing her subjectivity. If she attacks her feelings from outside, it is not to allay them but, with a director's aural and visual sort of dreaming, to delight in staging the person in her passions.

True, like all modern poets, she was handicapped for writing drama. When culture was sent to the boards by the increasing industrialization of society (as Delmore Schwartz notes in his essay "The Isolation of Modern Poetry"), the poet lost a knowledge of other people and dramatic and narrative poetry fell away. What was left but to cultivate sensibility? Hence romantic lyricism. Yet, opposite though they tend to be, romanticism and drama share a common love: the blood-hot moment. It remained for the romantic poets — a Hopkins, a Yeats — to discover the dramatic values of the lyric itself.

Plath is one of the greatest of these inventors. It may be true that her only successful character creation was her imaginative exaggeration of her own. Still, how much drama this produced! Which of our other poets gives us so much of conflict, elliptical plot, eloquence under circumstantial stress? Plath is almost alone in the field. Her wounds forced her to her knees precisely at the center of all drama, what Karl Jaspers calls Communication, the struggle to love other persons. She could write only about herself, but she herself was the struggle of persons, she herself was drama.

To the intensity of her emotions Plath added the implicit intensity of fantasy, the piquancy of the peculiar, and turning-screw situations. The result was alarming, beautiful. And she was of it: her last poems could boast and wail with Captain Ahab, "A personality stands here." She was of it yet transformed. It was as if after a fateful sleep she had awakened fully herself but more concentrated, ignited by pressing circumstances, in a realm magic and terrible. Now she was a plotting woman in purdah, now a girl with a Nazi father, now Lady Lazarus. Thus was born Plath C in her many moments.

Plath's fantasy, with its magnifications, macabre distortions, violence and magic and foreboding, exaggerates, but on behalf of subjective truth. It is a graph of affliction. Nor is there anything would-be about it. What Octavio Paz says of Tantrism applies to it: it "acts out symbols literally. This literalness is naive and terrible."

Take these lines from "Purdah":

> Attendants of the eyelash!
> I shall unloose
> One feather, like the peacock.
>
> Attendants of the lip!
> I shall unloose
> One note
>
> Shattering
> The chandelier
> Of air that all day plies
>
> Its crystals,
> A million ignorants.

Who are these attendants so luxuriously devoted to single parts of their lady—a single eyelash, a lip? They do not exist except at the desperately imperious summons of the speaker. And just as they are less real than she is, since she invents them, so she is less real than the poet who invented her, and who uses her much as she uses them, for her liberation. In one way the speaker is not even apparently real: no one would take at face value this "cross-legged" figure. *Of course* her purdah state refers to the patriarchal suppression of women. All the same, the speaker is extraordinarily present and personal, the exigent breath of the poem. If too abstracted from probable experience to bear a name, she is too image- and emotion-specific to be a mask. Would not Plath herself have to struggle to possess so much being? Indeed, everything in the poem, no matter how figurative, is superreal. Though the unloosed feather refers to an eyelash, the eyelash the oppressive adornments of women, we can almost see the feather, it is like a peacock's; and could it be like a peacock's and not *be* a feather? Can the air be thus described as a chandelier and still be seen as mere air? So it is that her surroundings become as vivid as she is. This woman makes her own world as she goes.

As if by a sudden access of dramatic impulse, still other of the late poems combine momentum and momentousness—for instance, "Daddy," "Lady Lazarus," "Getting There," "Ariel," "Fever 103°." These poems simultaneously exhilarate and frighten by catching the moment just before, or just as, a tremendous tension peaks. Going over a hundred miles an hour and still on the road and getting there, Plath invents for the lyric a new urgency.

Of course her style of monologue (sometimes dramatic monologue) helps convey what Roethke called "the full spasm of human nature, not blankness and beauty." For the most part it is blocked in short sentences. Like tamps. And this sharp insistence of breath falls in with her visual startlingness. For she visualizes everything as if working from the very young child's assumption that to be at all is to be visible. Her whole content is shaped as for an appreciative and all but literal gaze; even the horrors enter as hypnotic objects of perception, as if winking light from a blade. Could it be that her father's disappearance created a certain optic desperation? With theater at any rate the poems share a fascination with the espial of human behavior under stress. Plath seems to have wanted above all to see what she felt—not to understand it but to see it, even if as in "terrible rooms / In which a torture goes on one can only watch."

Nor in taking note of Plath's dramatic inventiveness can we avoid the impression that her poems unfold what is in some sense a tragedy. The poet had read classical tragedy at Cambridge, and its glamorous fatalism staggered her mind. The "blood-spoor of the austere tragedies" crosses her pages. She notes "A blue sky out of the Oresteia" arching above herself and her father—indeed, she must have seen that family romance is at the heart of Greek tragedy and its tense air of the forbidden. And in her first poem about Hughes and herself, "Pursuit," she quotes from Racine's *Phedre*, "where," she remarks, "passion as destiny is magnificently expressed." Like Hughes in "Pursuit," her father seems in some of the poems to claim her life deliciously. And "Edge" projects the classical death of a young woman, the victim and beneficiary of an apparent "necessity." (Toward the end of *Letters Home* Plath writes, "I am seeing the finality of it all.") In sum, her immersion in tragic literature may have caused her to emulate a destiny of passion and an unnatural yet crowning end.

Since nothing is more undramatic than a life, how to make a drama of it except by fabrication? Plath fabricated not after the Greek pattern (she was too anarchic to share its view of transgression) but after the simple model of a destroying passion. She went to where the flesh met the blade, omitting an explanatory world picture.

For the sake of seeing her work as a story and as a whole, the tragedy may be imagined as having the following acts and scenes:

Act 1: She Finds Herself Married to Shadow. ("The Colossus," "Lorelei," "Full Fathom Five," "The Beekeeper's Daughter.")

Scene 1: Even dead, how colossal her father is. She never could put him "together entirely," and now that he is dead he seems all the more a thing of giant, broken parts over which she crawls confusedly, devotedly, "an ant in mourning." Elemental, his limits undiscoverable, in death he is a god. All the same she shelters in her sense of him, squatting nights "in the cornucopia" of his left ear, "out of the wind, / Counting the red stars and those of plum-color"—distant from blood and bruises, and from fruit and from the cosmos too, for this is a barren cornucopia and a cave of death. And if he is dead, so in a way is she, since he is her world: "My hours are married to shadow."

Scene 2: If he cannot come to her may she not go to him? Only look at the Lorelei floating up in the river, "their limbs ponderous / With richness." They know in those murky depths of permissive unions the voluptuousness of a forbidden consummation as well as the restful heaviness of marbly death. And if they, why not she? But they "sing / Of a world more full and clear / Than can be." How skeptical she is after all! The first line of the poem, "It is no night to drown in," though apparently forgotten, holds her back like a kindly hand. If only to be "Exiled to no good":

> Your shelled bed I remember.
> Father, this thick air is murderous.
> I would breathe water.

Act 2: Unable to Go Down, She Breaks Down. ("Who," "Dark House," "Maenad," "The Beast," "The Stones," "Witch Burning.")

Scene 1: She is hospitalized, "at home . . . among the dead heads." Her mind falls to Roethke's mad idiom of the ground: "Let me sit in a flowerpot, / The spiders won't notice." "Small," she has been reduced to the minimally conscious, "Without dreams of any sort." In a way she has joined her father, housekeeping as she is "Down here" in "Time's gut-end / Among emmets and mollusks, / Duchess of Nothing, / Hairtusk's bride." But how fallen he is, this fossil, who has made her suffer so ignobly. Well, she has been to the bottom and it isn't a "Drunkenness" or "sure harborage" as the Lorelei sang, but "rubbish."

Scene 2: She has been "intimate," she confesses, "with a hairy spirit." And only the devil can eat the devil out. She goes to electroshock therapy as a witch for burning: "My ankles brighten. / Brightness ascends my thighs. / I am lost, I am lost, in the robes of all this light." Now she is "ready to construe the days / [She] coupled with dust in the shadow of a stone." Yes, give her back her shape. She will live!

Act 3: She Reenters Life through Marriage and Childbearing, Renouncing her Union with Shadow. ("Faun," "Gulliver," "Man in Black," "Love Letter," "Moonrise," "Heavy Women," "You're," "Morning Song," "Small Hours," "Childless Woman," "The Other," "Stillborn," "The Munich Mannequins," "Candles," "Event," "Crossing the Water," "Nick and the Candlestick," "By Candlelight," "Mary's Song," "The Night Dances," "For a Fatherless Son.")

Scene 1: She meets a man who "fills somehow that huge, sad hole [she] felt in having no father." He, too, is a god, and a hairy spirit, but hot-blooded, of the ripe earth. She "Saw hoof harden from foot, saw sprout / Goat-horns. Marked how god rose" and she was won. A poet, let him transcend human identity altogether, his eye an eagle, the shadow of his lip an abyss. For only a dead male or a male of genius is stronger than the fatal weakness she knows in herself. Indeed, in his "dead / Black coat, black shoes" and "Black hair" he is already coded for the absolute. His very figure fixing the "vortex" of reality, he rivets "stones, air, / All of it together." Her dependence on a strong man is the price of her security. But how rigid that riveting! How sinister that black!

Scene 2: Like her father and husband, her first child (she will not identify it as a girl) is set "among the elements." Its cry is "bald." She is no more its mother "Than the cloud that distills a mirror to reflect its own slow / Effacement at the wind's hand." From all that we seem to give birth to, that seems to give birth to us, we are remote. Life gives and takes away indifferently. Its other name is death.

Scene 3: A second child miscarries. The "small hours" show what she is, this small flat woman of Gulliver's, "Worm-husbanded" still. To be so "nun-hearted" that life cannot spring from you! Even her poems (for she too is a poet) are "stillborn." "Perfection is terrible, it cannot have children." It is of the grave and the gods.

Scene 4: A son is born—another male the "spaces lean on." She delights in his transcendent innocence, his tabula-rasa purity. The blood blooms "clean" in this "ruby," this living element. Yet as with the original "baby in the barn," only the mother is with him. The "Black bat airs" in the room waft from the absent man in black. There has been some terrible "event." Someday the son will know, will touch "the small skulls, the smashed blue hills." Another child condemned to brokenness and smallness by the disappearance of a father, a god. This baby is a "golden child the world will kill and eat." No, he cannot save her; already his crib gestures fall "white" on her eyes, lips, hair, "Touching and melting / Nowhere."

Act 4: Deserted Wife and Daughter, She Attempts to Free Herself from Dependency of Men. ("The Detective," "Purdah," "Lady Lazarus," "Daddy," "Lesbos," "Stings.")

Scene 1: The men in her life have been fascists, intolerable! The villagers always knew it, she must have known it. Thirty years in her father's black shoe and then in her "valley of death," though the cows thrived, she vaporized while her husband smiled. Oh the smiles of men! Watson, if you see one, remark the "crow in a tree. Make notes."

Scene 2: She vows vengeance against men. They are narcissists? Let there be a "shriek in the bath." They hide their brute hearts? Let them wear a "cloak of holes." Let even Herr God beware!

Scene 3: She turns to women, the bitches, for love. Her friend still has a husband around, but as a man he is "just no good to her," the inversion of the man in black—despicable because weak. Still his wife hates women even more than men, as one feels more horror of the crushed bug than of the boot. "Every woman's a whore," she says, "I can't communicate." For speak of how hateful men are and they'll agree! Or they won't! Impossible, this feverish sisterhood. Time to pack the babies—the schizophrenic girl, the smiling boy—and leave.

Act 5: She Takes Her Farewell of Life. ("Apprehensions," "Sheep in Fog," "Fever 103°," "Ariel," "Getting There," "Totem," "Poppies in July," "A Birthday Present," "Death & Co.," "Edge," "Words.")

Scene 1: Her life is pure dilemma, "stopped dead." Men are necessary and impossible. No way out from the "self," that howl for approval, except into nothing. Even the everything of "Ariel" drives suicidally into a solar "red eye"—her father's eye in its murderous essence. Compared to this living death where the butcher's guillotine whispers, "How's this, how's this?" death itself would be a birthday, "a nobility." If only death did not come a piece at a time, each piece stamped "in purple," the slaughter all too official and regulated. Oh to step at last from "the black car of Lethe, / Pure as a baby"! At least there is a margin for illusion in a fever of 103°, when, shedding the males internalized in oneself, him, him, and him, one ascends, "a pure acetylene / Virgin...To Paradise."

Scene 2: She sees that she is "done for." It is males, of course, who come to take her: two, one an eater, the other a smiler—the old truth and trick. But too little protest remains, then none, for already she sees herself dead and laid out in the great tomb of Appearance. For better or worse the dead woman has attained perfection, that which can have no children. See, "She has folded // [her children] back into her body as petals / Of a rose close when the garden // Stiffens." Her child-bearing was a deviation into a realm where she had no license and no competence, that of the sweet impurities of love and fruitfulness. Her poems, too, were false lights, unable to alter the "fixed stars" that governed her. A word, a poem drops into the pool of the psyche only to become a "white skull / Eaten by weedy greens." Nun-hearted, she was meant to belong to death, she and all her progeny. Death was her father, what but death could be his child? Ancient in barrenness, the moon looks down and is not surprised.

Scarcely a classical action—a spin of a silver wheel in the mire of memory, down, back up, and down again, deeper. But (in Aristotle's terms) a "serious" and "complete" action it is, and also "of a certain magnitude": long enough to "admit in the sequence of events of a change from bad fortune to good, or vice versa."

Does this tragedy have a large meaning as well? We can deduce nothing from it, it leaves us darkened. In classical tragedy, necessity is a clear idea in a just world. The law above the gods themselves, it corrects a fatal excess of will or passion. But the fate of being intended for death, "perfected" in death alone, lies outside reason and makes us doubt. What is the necessitating principle? Not metaphysical, since for Plath there was no cosmos, only her father, herself, her father's substitute, her son, perhaps her daughter, her poems, and her mother, in that order. Crass casualty then? Doubtless her father's death, her husband's desertion, her fevers, helped make Plath herself suicidal. But a necessity made of accidents? In any case, unlike those graphed by Hardy these would seem to leave a margin for survival. Then, with the captious exception of "Daddy," the poems allow nothing so devastating to imagination as the Freudian view that a pursuing fate is the mere shadow of a neurotic compulsion to repeat. No, necessity is somehow sublime. The night, the laws of roses, the Gothic moon are implicated in it. The stars that govern us...sublime.

Far from being a tragedy of will, like classical tragedy, Plath's is a tragedy of weakness, of a fatal vulnerability to the sense of injury. If there is heroism here, it talks of putting a stake in the fat black heart of a vampire; it talks like a pouting child. We feel pity and even terror before such sensitivity, but it has nothing to teach us. It looks like an accident in the scheme of things, a senseless failure.

Yet with its extremes of feeling, its spasms, barbarism, surprises, her tragedy has romantic power. Even as her fear and bitterness attack the quick of romanticism, numbing the nerve of love and life, her imagination startles her experience into drama. She wrote as if vividness itself could soothe suffering, as if she could escape pain by increasing its intensity.

To her dramatic imagination Plath brought a sense of language unceremoniously her own but still in the reverberant classical line: traditional grandeur sped up with a corresponding gain in mass. "The Sunday lamb cracks in its fat. / The fat / Sacrifices its opacity": between the Emersonian gnome-snort of "cracks" and the English elegance of "sacrifices" stretches her taut but shaded style.

Her verbal and prosodic values blend with her dramatic values in being not only vivid in themselves but dramatic in their variety. From clauses as swift as Stevie Smith's to phrases as slow as Keats', dying into themselves of a swoon; from language tortuously lathed by lineation to sentences plopped down on the bartering counter of the line; from classical pentameter to the nude line "the nude" to spillaway lines of eighteen syllables; from a murmured chiming dialogue of vowels and consonants to vituperative repetitions; from slang to stunning metaphors—as a poet there was little she did not permit herself, and nothing she permitted herself to do that she did not do well.

She quickly burned through the elaborate prosody of her early poems. "Fair chronicler of every foul declension"—the fusty phrase tells how it was. She learned to get down into the foulness, to make foul itself fair. Her desperate force, her very ambition, made her drop her mouldy style and rush on 1961, 1962.

Romantic in its immediacy, her sharpened poetic was not quite typical of the sixties, and precisely to the extent that it was Poundian. Poundian in the first place as to eye. Her work unfolds perhaps for the first time the full dramatic potential of what T. E. Hulme called "the new visual art," an art depending "for its effect not on a kind of half sleep produced by meter, but on arresting the attention, so much so that the succession of visual images should exhaust one." (This rapid piling up of "distinct images" produces "the poet's state in the reader." Now, despite the avowed classicism of Hulme and Pound, Imagism was actually a centaur poetic of which the basic and stronger half was romantic sensation. To induce the poet's state in the reader when that state is visual ecstasy, a state in which the magic breath of metaphor ripples the dull surface of life, is to write romantically.) But though the new visual art set itself off from leisured

15

traditional description by rapid-fire figuration, it was notorious for being static, limitedly pictorial. The instant fixing of a single impression, as by a jeweled pin, was its convention. Still, there was nothing to prevent its being thickcoming and developmental; it could be galvanized.

Or so Plath, more than any other, was to prove. She made images burst forth and succeed one another under acute psychological pressure, the dramatic crisis of the poem a generating furor. In violent import, color, solidity, and velocity her images are unsurpassed. Even when her spirit ebbs, her imagery ferments. In "Words," for instance, one metaphor instantly gives rise to two others, which are then elaborated in quick succession, each giving way and coming in again, but without any effect of haste. Proliferation has perhaps never been more subtle and vigorous, more constantly deepening.

But the most "delicate and difficult" part of the new art, so Hulme implies, is "fitting the rhythm" to the image—fitting *all* the sound, I might amend. And Plath's ear is no less gifted than her imaginative eye. For instance, she rivals Pound's hearkening ear for the calling back and forth and expressive rightness of sounds. Consider "And daylight lays its sameness on the wall," with its quasi-tedious fly-buzz of *a* and *s* and same-same meter, the slight staleness of the pentameter form precisely supporting the feeling. Or the language of "Ariel," say "Then the substanceless blue / Pour of tor and distances." With what an accord "substanceless" fails of substance through its recurring inchoate breathless vowels and its sibilant repetition of thin air. And how the first line tilts for the pour at the line break, and how the blurring of sights is matched by the fusing sounds of "pour" and "tor" and the fleeting reference back of "distances" to "substanceless." In writing like this, the phrases are single beings made of rhythm and rhyme, inexhaustible to the emotional ear.

Her lineation sometimes shows the same headcocked quality. These beautiful lines from "Edge" display her mastery:

> The woman is perfected.
> Her dead
>
> Body wears the smile of accomplishment,
> The illusion of a Greek necessity
>
> Flows in the scrolls of her toga,
> Her bare
>
> Feet seem to be saying,
> We have come so far, it is over.

While the language is retiring (except in the fifth line), the structure composed by the spacing and lineation is contrastingly elegant and a form of heightening. It emphasizes and all but creates interplays of meaning and sound. For instance, ending where it does, the second line dies sympathetically and, further, makes a dead, horrifying, unexpected, and perverse rhyme with "perfected." "Body" then emerges starkly, uglily —insisted on by position as if raised to view on a tomb. Then "flows" takes its rightful place as the well for a line of liquid mingling l's and o's and falling rhythms. As for the breach after "bare," we may find it obvious yet in repeating every function of the break after "dead," it enhances the sense of repose and perfection. The analogical imagination and a feeling for tensions at once spatial and dramatic contribute to this exquisite craft. Such lineation is gesture and architecture as well as rhythm; the tensions are to be seen as well as heard.

With Pound, Plath also shared the decidedly modern ear for what she called the "straight out" rhythms and words of prose and colloquial speech; like Pound, if less ambitiously and more evenly, she assimilated them into poetry, creating new verse rhythms. For instance, in "you are here, / Ticking your fingers on the marble table, looking for cigarettes," from "The Rival," what could pass for prose becomes, in the context and through lineation, a rapid nervous verse eloquence. And poems like "A Birthday Present" are wonderfully speech excited. (Perhaps only Stevie Smith, whom Plath admired, could do loquacity better, having the advantage of a crazed note and a flawless ear.) The breathless doubling of a clause ("is it . . . is it . . . ?") is peculiarly Plathian. Although working free from meter Plath liked a rhyme or grammatical construction or beat that swung back even as it pounded on. She favored the piston rhythms of anxiety.

At times she may be too laboring in exposition, as in "Tulips" and "The Bee Meeting," though these poems have been much admired. "If I stand very still, they will think I am cow parsley, / A gullible head untouched by their animosity, / Not even nodding, a personage in a hedgerow" —here she goes on too long. But no one will question her general authority in the colloquial range of the art. She was even more inventive at spoken than at written effects and worked them for an equal if different intensity.

Of course, she often modulates between the poetic and the prosaic, her voice quick, alive in change:

> Love, love,
> I have hung our cave with roses.
> With soft rugs —
>
> The last of Victoriana.

Anonymously lyrical at first, this shades through two degrees (the discursive but buoyant second line; the softly grateful third) to a kind of editorial aside, a footnote: "The last of Victoriana." Yet even this prosy line fascinates in the way the flat *a* in "Victoriana" makes a coziness with the *a* in "last." Or consider a complex single line, the first in "Poppies in October": "Even the sun-clouds this morning cannot manage such skirts." "Even," "this," "manage," and "such" are "straight out," and "sun-clouds," if literary, suffers the prose-clutch of the hyphen: the line risks appearing undistinguished. Yet its sibilance and resonance hold the ear and the rhythm is mildly rapturous amid the workaday words. The idea itself is romantic, a visual and anthropomorphic conceit of intensity. The line satisfies formality and impulsiveness, voice and eye, equally.

Plath's poetic, then, is Poundian—romantic. True, classical simplicity shows up in passages, and classical grace and proportion sometimes govern whole poems. Then, too, her persistent use of stanzas reflects the same orderly habit of mind that made her list each morning what she wanted to accomplish during the day. Undeniably, moreover, certain associations of the word "romantic" shrivel when held up to her flame. The shriek of her ego, the sound of a tense holding on to little, drove off every softness. She maximized horror as if she lived on menace. All the same, her poetic is full of romantic presence. No retreat, no passivity, can harbor in it; it is the aggressive poetic of one buried alive but not ready to die. (Even in expressing revulsion from reality she reached obsessively and inconsistently for visual analogy, a language of rapport.) What is her struggle against fear, pain, isolation, if not romantic? Perhaps we would deny her reasons for writing at all to think of it as anything else or anything less.

Notes

1. See David Holbrook's stress, in *Sylvia Plath: Poetry and Existence* (London: Athlone Press, 1976), on the felt absence of "creative reflection" in her world, particularly in eyes.
2. Irving Howe, "The Plath Celebration: A Partial Dissent," in *The Critical Point* (New York: Horizon Press, 1973), pp. 158-69.
3. Barbara Hardy, "The Poetry of Sylvia Plath: Enlargement or Derangement?" in *The Survival of Poetry*, ed. Martin Dodsworth (London: Faber and Faber, 1970), pp. 164-87.

J. D. McClatchy

Short circuits
and folding mirrors

Read together, Aurelia Schober Plath's edition of her daughter's *Letters Home* and Edward Butscher's overheated, undiscriminating, yet interesting biography, *Sylvia Plath: Method and Madness*, remind one of the strong "period" quality of this poet's life and attitudes. McCartheyism, heavy petting, the military-industrial complex, *The New Yorker*, bomb shelters, the vocationalism and domesticity, the unfocused neuroses and emotional hyperbole—these suggest the era: Plath's ambitions and anxieties were redolent of the ruthless vanities and sad defenses of Eisenhower's America. Even the most extensive and convincing interpretations of Plath's work—Judith Kroll's elaborate, even pedantic *Chapters in a Mythology: The Poetry of Sylvia Plath*—reinforces this sense by reading the career in terms of the then fashionable murk of Robert Graves's White Goddess mythologies. In Plath's "mythicized biography," Kroll contends, the poet's confessional impulses were subsumed by archetypal patterns and strategies that at once revealed, organized, and articulated her experience in poetry. In impressive detail, Kroll traces through Plath's sources and imagery the poet's pursuit of the Muse as both the subject of her work

19

and its inspiration. There is no doubt that Plath resorted to and exploited various back-of-the-brain protocols as a ready-made source of images and plots that, at the same time, were resonant with and focused the facts of her own life.

Kroll's is a symptomatic response to this poet, though more intelligent than most. The establishment of a cult, with accompanying distortions of attention, inflated claims, and rapt explications, normally attends the appearance and aftermath of any "period" poet. (I do not mean that as a pejorative term; among others, Shelley and Arnold, Hart Crane and Frank O'Hara seem to me equally "period" poets, whose sensibilities uniquely captured—and whose work continues to recover for later readers—their contemporary culture's tone, values, and issues.) I suspect that, in retrospect, Plath will have emerged as the most distinctly "period" poet of her generation. Already she is viewed as a cultural, as well as a literary, phenomenon. Alternately heroine or victim, martyr or scapegoat, she has been symbolized and exploited so hauntingly in the cultural consciousness that it is difficult not to read her life—with its gestures of defiance, compulsion, and despair—rather than her work, in which those gestures are reflected or reimagined. But Plath is also an especially representative figure of the directions and dynamics of poetry in the early 1960s. And I think that can be seen nowhere more clearly than in a stylistic reading of her work, of the ways in which she absorbed and altered the poetic climate then prevailing. In the dedicatory poem to *Nones*, which was published at about the time Plath first began writing verse, Auden caught the official tone exactly when he spoke of a "civil style" vitiated by "the wry, the sotto-voce, / Ironic and monochrome." Her initiation into such a situation, her attempts to master it while achieving an individual voice, the methods she used to dismantle or energize such a polite inheritance, and her shift to a more daringly expressionistic and highly inflected verse—all of these are aspects of a larger trend then occurring in poetry. But in a poignantly foreshortened way, Plath got there first, so that her career remains paradigmatic. Its force and permanence reside less in her subjects than in her rapidly evolving relationship to style, and in her final accomplishment of a form that combines its prosody, imagery, and tone with a unique and abiding authority.

Plath was an assiduous apprentice, and put herself resolutely through the traditionalist paces and patterns. However predictably feeble or vapid the results were, she did acquire a degree of technical expertise and fluency, so that by the time she considered herself a professional she had ready answers to an interviewer's question about her sense of craft:

> Technically I like it to be extremely musical and lyrical, with a singing sound. I don't like poetry that just throws itself away in prose. I think there should be a kind of constriction and tension which is never artificial yet keeps in the meaning in a kind of music too. And again, I like the idea of managing to get wit in with the idea of seriousness, and contrasts, ironies, and I like visual images, and I like just good mouthfuls of sound which have meaning. . . . At first I started in strict forms—it's the easiest way for a beginner to get music ready-made, but I think that now I like to work in forms that are strict but their strictness isn't uncomfortable. I lean very strongly toward forms that are, I suppose, quite rigid in comparison certainly to free verse. I'm much happier when I know that all my sounds are echoing in different ways throughout the poem.[1]

What is curious in that hurried litany of modernist pieties is that her attention was as often fixed on the possibility of error as of achievement. And indeed, her early poetry consistently pursues and portrays her abilities rather than her experience; in fact, that is frequently the explicit subject of the poems themselves: "Hardcastle Crags," "The Ghost's Leave-taking," "Black Rook in Rainy Weather," "A Winter Ship," "Ouija," "Snakecharmer," "Moonrise," and the uncollected "On the Difficulty of Conjuring Up a Dryad." These are all poems that worry the difficulty of aligning reality and vision, and "vision" in *The Colossus* is a term with no mystical force. It is Plath's word for art itself—a transcendent, idealized heterocosm, ordered and self-reflexive. It is, in other words, the well-wrought poetics of the modernist masters and their New Critics: Yeats, Stevens, and Auden, as domesticated and institutionalized by Brooks-and-Warren. *The Colossus* is not merely the poetry of an ambitious but cautious beginner; it is a summary of the prevalent mode, and Plath's imagination, though equal to its forms and discretions, was not yet strong enough to assert a personality apart from the mimed voice. She followed the rules of the game, and generally set low stakes.

Her first collection betrays the novice's self-consciousness. It is a poetry of chosen words, of careful schemes and accumulated effects; its voice is unsteady, made up. It leans heavily on its models and sources; there are broad hints of help from Stevens, Roethke, even Eliot. The refinement of this poetry derives not only from its being influenced or allusive. There is also a kind of awkward delicacy to it—which may come from her identification of herself with what she thought was a genteel line of women poets like Marianne Moore or Elizabeth Bishop, or may be connected with her insistent academicism. Whatever the reasons, there is an inhibited quality to the verse's perspectives, as well as a distinctly literary cast to many of the poems that borrow Oedipus or Gulliver, Byron or Medea, Gabriel or Lucine for their authority. Another symptom is the stiff, stale diction that rattles around in so many of these poems: words like "cuirass," "wraith," "descant," "bole," "bruit," "casque," "ichor," "pellicle." This is a language found nowadays only in the columns of a Thesaurus—an underlined copy of which Ted Hughes remembers always on his wife's knee at the time, as if she were more interested in the unusual than in the appropriate word. One need only compare her "Sow" to "View of a Pig" by Hughes—who early became and always remained the strongest influence on her work—to sense the more natural ease with which he urges and controls his language and the power it draws from strangeness. His dead pig retains a menacing vitality, as Hughes narrows his regard, pares his description, and concentrates on essentials. Plath, on the other hand, fusses with piggy banks and parslied sucklings, a constantly shifting metric, long sentences, and a glut of adjectives—all of which dilute her argument and blur the poem's occasion and subject.

In 1958, at a time when she was as devoted to drawing as she was to verse, Plath wrote to her mother, "I've discovered my deepest source of inspiration, which is art"—not an unusual discovery for any young poet. But she was not referring only to the origins of poems, though she drew on Breughel's *The Triumph of Death*, Rousseau's *Charmeuse de Serpents*, and DeChirico's *The Disquieting Muses*, among others. I take her to have meant her method as well. It is not merely those expected *Gemäldegedichte* that would lead one to call most of the poems in this book *compositions*. Throughout, she is attracted to textures and shapes, to landscape, primary colors and gradated shades, grounded figures, and above all, to design. These are, of course, concerns and effects that enact the then dominant aesthetic, with its stress on correctness and perspicuity, on elaborated forms, on the observing eye and ordering mind.

The pictorial bias in *The Colossus* has, in turn, inevitable stylistic consequences. "Man in Black" is a convenient example:

> Where the three magenta
> Breakwaters take the shove
> And suck of the grey sea
>
> To the left, and the wave
> Unfists against the dun
> Barb-wired headland of
>
> The Deer Island prison
> With its trim piggeries,
> Hen huts and cattle green
>
> To the right, and March ice
> Glazes the rock pools yet,
> Snuff-coloured sand cliffs rise

> Over a great stone spit
> Bared by each falling tide,
> And you, across those white
>
> Stones, strode out in your dead
> Black coat, black shoes, and your
> Black hair till there you stood,
>
> Fixed vortex on the far
> Tip, riveting stones, air,
> All of it, together.

The poem is in the rhyme scheme that most frequently appears in Plath's early poetry, slanted terza rima. (It seems typical of this poet that she favored one of the most stylized and difficult verse forms in English, and then worked against its strictures. It is as if she wanted to take advantage of a tradition, but without ever seeming to do so.) The entire poem—and this is unusual for Plath—consists of just one long sentence. The careful, pointed exposition is clearly blocked in hard edges, not unlike those drawings by Plath I have seen that are heavy, dark, flat. This poem's "narrative" has preceded the opening stanza, its one character is outline and absence, and all its details converge toward the last, abstract stanza (which seems to echo Wordsworth), where the mysterious human figure alone establishes the relationships among the objects that, in random ensemble, comprise the scene. It is, in other words, a poem about the poet; a poem about itself, its single sentence containing the whole. But notice too that each of its shifts of direction or attention is signaled by "and." This is a characteristic of Plath's early poems—this, or her constant use of an appositional format, usually a metaphor per line. Such tactics count on a *succession* of ideas, objects, or equivalents to structure a poem, and not on their *interdependence*, relationships that a more complex syntax, for instance, would demonstrate. Plath's technique tends to give the same lexical value to the different parts of the poem, and thus produces a flattening or equalizing effect—like a painting with no perspective.

Instead of animating her poems by the intricacies of arrangement, she tries to invest them with a kind of verbal and metrical energy, almost as if to distract the reader from their meanings, to veil their deeper significance of subject and flourish instead their versified foreground. Levels of diction, from the colloquial to the exalted, are inexcusably jumbled. Parts of speech are regularly interchanged, forceful predicative words are especially favored as substitutes. And though rhyme schemes (or, occasionally, syllabics) are employed to steady a stanza, the metric of any one line within that stanza is erratic and aggressive. Accents may be

23

syncopated, but most often are just heaped up. Plath does the same thing with adjectives, which abound. The combination results in a blistered, hectoring line that lacks any real subtlety or persuasion. She doesn't like to play on or with words; she rarely uses enjambments successfully or ingeniously. She is concerned, then, primarily with the length, the intensity, and the patterning of her lines and poems, and not with their modulation or variety.

Ted Hughes thinks that most of Plath's early poems turn on "the opposition of a prickly, fastidious defence and an imminent volcano"—an antagonism, finally, between the disciplines of her art and the demands of her experience. "Poem for a Birthday," the sequence that concludes the British edition of *The Colossus*, seems her first calculated effort to discover rather than impose the form of her experience. Despite its reliance on Roethke, there is a new assurance and freedom to the verse that permits strong tonal effects and interesting elliptical cuts. Perhaps that is because these poems are not dominated by the representational eye but by the presentational vagaries of the unconscious. Again, I suspect the influence of Hughes. It was at about this time that he turned her attention away from studying poetry toward mystical and anthropological texts; away from formal literary exercises and more seriously toward horoscopes, the tarot, the ouija board, improvisations, meditational devices, and free association games. In its own way, each is a ritualistic yet unstructured procedure to release experience from the unconscious, to which one would give voice rather than shape. This corresponds with Plath's own sense of poetic strength, which was invariably bound up with the notion and sensation of release. After the birth of her two children, she began to write with an increasingly confident maturity, just as later her separation from her husband delivered her into a final creative fury—Judith Kroll notes that in October 1962, the month after her separation, she wrote at least twenty-six poems. *The Bell Jar* seems to have had a kind of purgative function for its author, and her simultaneous discovery of the confessional poetry of Robert Lowell and Anne Sexton—which provided her the necessary examples of how to include her life in poetry—she also described in terms of release.

Each is a release *into* the self, into emotional and psychological depths either cultivated by or thrust upon her. And at the same time, she was prompted to free her work of the inhibitions, both psychological and stylistic, that had restricted her first book. It is very difficult to analyze in clear, progressive detail a stylistic "development" such as Plath's, which matured in only a few years and could change radically over several months. (And the situation is further complicated by the incomplete and confusing editions of her work.) Still, her so-called "transitional" collection, *Crossing the Water*, can be read as a record of her experiments to secure the rapid advances she made over *The Colossus*. Take, for instance, the opening stanza of "Finisterre":

> This was the land's end: the last fingers, knuckled and rheumatic,
> Cramped on nothing. Black
> Admonitory cliffs, and the sea exploding
> With no bottom, or anything on the other side of it,
> Whitened by the faces of the drowned.
> Now it is only gloomy, a dump of rocks—
> Leftover soldiers from old, messy wars.
> The sea cannons into their ear, but they don't budge.
> Other rocks hide their grudges under the water.

Plath's use of a word like "cannons" is familiar enough, but those rocks that "hold their grudges under the water" are new; they mark a shift from the striking word to the startling image. And furthermore, this is an image whose occasion and impact are calculated, controlled, and coaxed from the opening line's clutching hand of land. The poem's effects, in other words, are less immediate and transient. The brace of a rhyme scheme is gone, and the lines are irregular in length. Both those decisions seem a part of Plath's desire to approximate the rhythms of speech. Her poetry is never exactly conversational, but "Finisterre," if not the "direct, even plain speech" that Hughes says she was soon striving for in an effort to escape the rhetoric of the official High Style, has at least the effect of a soliloquy's heightened naturalism—an effect that her radio script "Three Women" displays brilliantly, though it comes at the expense of the theatrical. In her last work, Plath intensified that voice, but it always remained a dialogue between the mind and itself.

Although several of the "transitional" poems—say, "The Babysitters" or "In Plaster"—are too prosaic, they are merely the failures of Plath's otherwise successful project to give her poems a more dramatic posture, not merely by manipulating a poem's rhythms and imagistic resources, but by providing a situation for its voice. "Face Life" and "Parliament Hill Fields" are fine examples of Plath's new awareness of plotting a poem, implying a character—of accumulating significance within the poem's own narrative. It was a necessary step toward the refracted events and mysterious presences in *Winter Trees* and *Ariel*. What, in the late poetry, seems blurred by psychic disjunctiveness is given its force by the hard exactness of tone, and the poems in *Winter Trees*—poems like "Purdah," "Childless Woman," "By Candlelight," and "Thalidomide" —have a heightened, penetrating force that her poems of mid passage lack. There is something more than the psychological realism of accommodating narrated facts into poetry, or of using the poem itself to discover her experiences rather than merely to record or fantasize her feelings about them. By the time one reads *Winter Trees*, one hears a voice grown markedly more inflected—usually with an angry irony:

> O maiden aunt, you have come to call.
> Do step into the hall!
> With your bold
> Gecko, the little flick!
> All cogs, weird sparkle and every cog solid gold.
> And I in slippers and housedress with no lipstick!

("The Tour")

And the tone of voice comes increasingly to determine the line breaks, now a collusion of image and breath:

> Do not think I don't notice your curtain—
> Midnight, four o'clock,
> Lit (you are reading),
> Tarting with the drafts that pass,
> Little whore tongue,
> Chenille beckoner,
> Beckoning my words in—
> The zoo yowl, the mad soft
> Mirror talk you love to catch me at.

("Eavesdropper")

Increasingly in her later work, as here, the voice becomes both the rhythmical principle and the context for meaning. In poems like "By Candlelight" or "The Other" the syntax of accusation or inquiry or reaction, the disjunctive details of private experience, and the spliced images of her surrealist tendencies, begin to merge into what can be called a characteristic poem. In *Crossing the Water*, for example, "Last Words" or "A Life" still display the tension of the will doing the work of the imagination. But in a later poem like "The Other," the willfulness yields to a purified, demonic energy, an insistent inevitability:

> You come in late, wiping your lips.
> What did I leave untouched on the doorstep—
>
> White Nike,
> Streaming between my walls!
>
> Smilingly, blue lightning
> Assumes, like a meathook, the burden of his parts.
>
> The police love you, you confess everything.
> Bright hair, shoe-black, old plastic,

Is my life so intriguing?
Is it for this you widen your eye-rings?

One way to approach and appreciate the stylistic breakthrough of *Ariel* is to trace some of the recurrences of a single concern—her father, The Father—to its treatment in the book's most famous poem, "Daddy." The plain-prose version is in *The Bell Jar*, whose narrator, Esther Greenwood, "was only purely happy until [she] was nine years old," when her father—who had come "from some manic-depressive hamlet in the black heart of Prussia"—had died. And Esther, on the psychotic verge of suicide, "had a great yearning, lately, to pay [her] father back for all the years of neglect, and start tending his grave." It is only a simple sense of loss, of the horrible distance between the living and dead, that is revealed:

> At the foot of the stone I arranged the rainy armful of azaleas I had picked from a bush at the gateway of the graveyard. Then my legs folded under me, and I sat down in the sopping grass. I couldn't understand why I was crying so hard.
> Then I remembered that I had never cried for my father's death.
> My mother hadn't cried either. She had just smiled and said what a merciful thing it was for him he had died, because if he had lived he would have been crippled and an invalid for life, and he couldn't have stood that, he would rather have died than had that happen.
> I laid my face to the smooth face of the marble and howled my loss into the cold salt rain.

Immediately after this scene, Esther returns from the graveyard, swallows the pills, hides in a cellar hole, and lies down to death: "The silence drew off, baring the pebbles and shells and all the tatty wreckage of my life. Then, at the rim of vision, it gathered itself, and in one sweeping tide, rushed me to sleep." Given the point of view, the emotion here is left distanced and unaccountable, and is told with the restraint that Plath uses throughout the novel to draw out slowly its cumulative effects of disorientation and waste. But the images of stone and sea, sleep and escape, quarry and fear, that structure her account are important. In a memoir written for a 1963 broadcast, "Ocean 1212-W," Plath broods on her relationship with the sea and her earliest self: the miracles of immersion and completion. The birth of her younger brother then defined for her, of her, "the *separateness* of everything. I felt the wall of my skin: I am I. That stone is a stone. My beautiful fusion with the things of this world was over. The tide ebbed, sucked back into itself." And later, at the end: "My father died, we moved inland. Whereon those nine first years of my life sealed themselves off like a ship in a bottle—beautiful, inaccessible, obsolete, a fine, white flying myth."

To watch this myth, these images, resumed in the poems discovers Plath, at first, refining and deepening her metaphor with the precisions of verse. In "The Colossus," the girl clambers in helpless self-absorption over the mammoth ruins of her father:

> Thirty years now I have laboured
> To dredge the silt from your throat.
> I am none the wiser.
>
> Scaling little ladders with gluepots and pails of lysol
> I crawl like an ant in mourning
> Over the weedy acres of your brow
> To mend the immense skull-plates and clear
> The bald, white tumuli of your eyes.
>
> A blue sky out of the Oresteia
> Arches above us.

The figure is right: its immense size symbolizing her incest-awe, its ruined fragments projecting her ambivalent feelings. But the mystery of loss and betrayal, the secretive sexual fantasies, the distortions of knowledge and memory, are left unexplored, dependent solely on the poem's figurative force:

> Nights, I squat in the cornucopia
> Of your left ear, out of the wind,
> Counting the red stars and those of plum-colour.
> The sun rises under the pillar of your tongue.
> My hours are married to shadow.
> No longer do I listen for the scrape of a keel
> On the blank stones of the landing.

It is *The Bell Jar's* suicidal darkness she curls into here, longing to be reborn into return; it is the same sea that threatens suitors. The same sea that washes through "Full Fathom Five": "Your shelled bed I remember. / Father, this thick air is murderous. / I would breathe water." The same stone in "The Beekeeper's Daughter," a poem addressed to "Father, bridegroom": "My heart under your foot, sister of a stone." The same dark exclusion that ends "Electra on Azalea Path":

> I am the ghost of an infamous suicide,
> My own blue razor rusting at my throat.
> O pardon the one who knocks for pardon at
> Your gate, father—your hound-bitch, daughter, friend.
> It was my love that did us both to death.

In all of these early poems, the images are retried to approximate the experience, but their equivalents cannot manage its depth and intricacies. But "Daddy"—the title alone indicates that she will write out of the experience directly—is suddenly, strikingly different, even as its details are finally aligned. The echoes we are meant to recall sound with a first force: "black shoe / In which I have lived like a foot / For thirty years, . . .Marble-heavy, a bag full of God, / Ghastly statue, . . .a head in the freakish Atlantic." The language and movement of "Daddy" are entirely new: instead of slow, careful gestures, the poem races its thickly layered and rhymed syncopation into some strange, private charm to evoke and exorcise a demon-lover. The short lines—which Plath reads with tremulous contempt in her recording of the poem—have a formulaic quality appropriate to the murderous ritual that the poem enacts: "Daddy, I have had to kill you. / You died before I had time." But what is most extraordinary about this poem is the amount and complexity of experience that it can convincingly include. If "The Colossus" deals with remorse, "Daddy" deals in guilt. The poem veers between love and hate, revenge and regret, Eros and Thanatos. Imagining herself as a Jew and her father as a Nazi, or her husband as a vampire and herself as a maiden, the poet languishes in the need for punishment to counter the loss of love. The ambivalence of identification and fear is used to reveal more than "The Colossus" even hints at:

> Every woman adores a Fascist,
> The boot in the face, the brute
> Brute heart of a brute like you. . . .
>
> At twenty I tried to die
> And get back, back, back to you.
> I thought even the bones would do.
>
> But they pulled me out of the sack,
> And they stuck me together with glue.
> And then I knew what to do.
> I made a model of you,
> A man in black with a Meinkampf look
>
> And a love of the rack and the screw.
> And I said I do, I do.

The paranoid's identification of the persecutor with the rejected father, the macabre *Liebestod*, the "model" marriage that confirms tortures finally felt in a real marriage, the degradation of her father (which doubles as the origin of guilt in the murder of the primal father) as a form of self-loathing, the loss of her father and husband like two suicides that leave the poet furiously fingering her scars—"Daddy" astonishes a reader by the subtle fury of its hurts.

The strong poetic personality that emerges in "Daddy" should remind a reader that the accomplishment of *Ariel* is first of all a stylistic one —what Ted Hughes calls its "crackling verbal energy." The exuberance is of a special sort. One would hesitate to term it "American," except that Plath herself did in a 1962 interview: "I think that as far as language goes I'm an American, I'm afraid, my accent is American, my way of talk is an American way of talk." The crucial dynamics, the sharp, quick tonal contrasts, the biting precision of word and image, the jaunty slang, the cinematic cutting, the high-power montage—these are what she is pointing to. Even in poems, like "Tulips," with quieter long lines, she sustains a new tension of menace and propulsion:

> My body is a pebble to them, they tend it as water
> Tends to the pebbles it must run over, smoothing them gently.
> They bring me numbness in their bright needles, they bring me sleep.
> Now I have lost myself I am sick of baggage—
> My patent leather overnight case like a black pillbox,
> My husband and child smiling out of the family photo;
> Their smiles catch onto my skin, little smiling hooks.

In the book's best poems, the lines are pared down, at times to a stark, private code, but always with purity and exactness. Paradoxically, this taut, new control often creates effects of singular primitivism—the sense we have when encountering language used for rituals that precede literature, that impersonally participate in something more than they are. The seeming impersonality of the surfaces of the *Ariel* poems, as distinct from their private or confessional origin, derives from Plath's abundance and abandon, from the sense of autopsy she creates. There are several ways this has been achieved.

Though there are a few strong poems that employ two-line, pistonlike stanzas, her favorite stanza remained the tercet. The *Ariel* stanza must have developed from her earlier habit of terza rima, with its visual probity and stylized uniformity. But the freedom and variety of her new stanzas perfectly match the skittish, inflected voice that projects them. The lines in poems like "Lady Lazarus" and "Fever 103°" can be extended or retracted at will; often they prefer the shortness capable of sustaining a single word or phrase or fragment, giving it the prominence and strangeness of isolation. The thrusting surprise of line lengths is particularly apt for the continually shifting forms of address in, say, "Lady Lazarus," which jumps from invocation to question to command. It is steadied somewhat by the irregular use of rhyme, both internal and external, which establishes an aural "pattern" juxtaposed with the visual one. And Plath's canny use of repeated words and formulas has the same effect —appropriate to a poem that is less about suicide itself than about her obsessive, suicidal hatred of men and marriage, about loathing and self-hatred:

> So, so, Herr Doktor.
> So, Herr Enemy.
>
> I am your opus,
> I am your valuable,
> The pure gold baby
>
> That melts to a shriek.
> I turn and burn.
> Do not think I underestimate your great concern.
>
> Ash, ash—
> You poke and stir.
> Flesh, bone, there is nothing there—
>
> A cake of soap,
> A wedding ring,
> A gold filling.
>
> Herr God, Herr Lucifer,
> Beware
> Beware.
>
> Out of the ash
> I rise with my red hair
> And I eat men like air.

The aural sense of recurrence and the syntactic and visual irregularities together create an unsettling experience, one from which we have no time for distance as the poem, like many of Plath's late poems, rushes forward to exhaust itself. Where her early work was, in every sense, contained, *Ariel* operates at levels altogether more instinctual, uncertain, expelled. In these poems, there is less attention paid to explicit argument or rationale, to conceit or epiphany. To expropriate what her poem "Mystic" asks and answers, "Does the sea // Remember the walker upon it? / Meaning leaks from the molecules." Meaning, that is to say, derives not from the walker but from the water. The poet is not presider but medium, and the poem is not the expression of meaning but its conjuring context. And, for this effect, it is clearly her imagery Plath depended on in this book—the relentless succession of metaphors that seek out equivalence rather than comparison, identity rather than similarity. When such a technique seems unduly compulsive, as it does in "Cut," the result is dully self-indulgent. But a poem like "Edge" demonstrates brilliantly Plath's ability to induce a process—rather than construct a product—by the juxtaposition of paradoxical images rendered with the force of statement:

the smiling corpse, the illusory necessity, the children as serpents (the Greek symbol of Necessity), the rose and the moon's night flower. During the course of this poem, the images meld with and become one another, a series of folding mirrors shifting in value and meaning—from the dead woman to the moon considered as female, an eerily animated dead stone dressed as the corpse is. And which is which?

These are the kinds of nondiscursive "deep images" that Robert Bly and James Wright were also exploring, though in *Ariel* Plath has done so with more conviction. Their programmatic "irrationalism" depends too heavily on accidental correspondences, avoiding as it does both metaphor and argument. Plath's approach was more enlightening, less erratic, and she was more successful than either Bly or Wright in getting beyond the mere physicality and discrete epiphanies of traditional imagism. Then too, poems like "Getting There," "Medusa," or "Little Fugue" make extensive use of the surrealism that poets like Robert Lowell would later turn to as, in Lowell's phrase, the "natural way to write our fictions," or the radical method of capturing the *natural* unreality of experience and of creating a new knowledge of it. Even the source of *Ariel's* subject matter —no longer established themes in the suggested settings, but fragments of the occasional, accidental, domestic, or unconscious—has come to dominate much of the better work now being written. I am suggesting, in short, that Plath prefigured many of the decisive shifts in poetic strategy that occurred in the decade following her death. It is difficult to study her brief career for the kinds of substantial thematic complexities and continuities that one reads in Roethke or Lowell. But, considered from a stylistic viewpoint, Plath was as important an innovator as either of those poets. Her consistency and importance lie in her experiments with voice and the relationships among tone and image and address—axes after whose stroke the wood rings.

Notes

1. From an interview conducted by Lee Anderson, 18 April 1958, now in the Lee Anderson Collection of Recorded Poets at the Yale Collection of Historical Sound Recordings, Yale University Library.

Hugh Kenner

Sincerity kills

Very well, the obligatory note of the theatrical. Let's get on with it. Mr. Butscher can help us oblige: "In the new house, off the kitchen, was a windowless room, fairly large, which disturbed Sylvia. . . . Too dark and airless. . . . She felt uneasy when near that room, and her awareness of its existence plagued her sleep. . . . She would later tell her new-found friend, Elizabeth Compton, that she had 'a very eerie feeling that there was another room behind it' and that the room was always there waiting for her."[1]

Elizabeth Compton, you see, remembered that. Sylvia Plath had a life-long knack for saying things people would remember. It entailed sizing up the person, the occasion, as readily as she sized up the consumer of the magazine fiction she also had a knack for. "I just sat there with the whole summer turning sour in my mouth": that's how readers of *Seventeen* like stories to end, as Sylvia very well knew when she was nineteen and fitted "The Perfect Set-Up" with that ending. "I must study the magazines the way I did *Seventeen*," she wrote her mother not long afterward, disclosing plans to "hit *The New Yorker* in poetry and the *Ladies' Home Journal* in stories," and *Letters Home*, where we find that letter (p. 107), demonstrates, end to end, her thorough mastery of the kind of letter her mother would find gratifying. "Dearest Mother, I am being very naughty and self-pitying in writing you a letter which is very private and which will have no point but the very immediate one of making me feel a little better. Every now and then I feel like being 'babied.'"[2] She had studied *Seventeen*, we may want to reflect, the way she did her mother, for whom she was astute enough to get in there first with jargon like "self-pity," thus becoming the brave funny girl who's sorry for herself and knows it and wants her head patted. Esther and her mother in *The Bell Jar* seem another two people entirely.

If, looking back and forth between Sivvy and Esther, we are so unwise as to wish to choose the "real" Sylvia Plath, Freud seems to guide us toward Esther, as though on the principle that hatred of a parent is more apt to be the authentic emotion. Hatred of "Daddy," too; and hatred of self. But then Sylvia Plath knew quite well what it was that Freud had denominated authentic, and even claimed, with remarkable cool, that in "Daddy" she had merely created a little Freudian monologue. "The poem is spoken by a girl with an Electra complex. Her father died while she thought he was God. Her case is complicated by the fact that her father was also a Nazi and her mother very possibly part Jewish. In the daughter the two strains marry and paralyze each other—she has to act out the awful little allegory once over before she is free of it." Just a fictional exercise, in short; by the same token one might call *Letters Home* an epistolary novel. There's no bottom to this.

Like Aurelia Plath reading Sivvy's letters home, we are continually outflanked by someone who knows what we'll approve and how we'll categorize, and is herself ready with the taxonomic words before we can get them out.

> Daddy, I have had to kill you.
> You died before I had time—

Parlor psychiatry is forestalled; she sketches the complex herself. Lady Lazarus is a bitch? It's not news to *her*; "I eat men like air." (I'm also the only candid person here.) Our fantasies of anarchic candor stir into life and help animate *Ariel*. She persuades us that she's daring to say what we wouldn't, and if we succumb to the spell we're apt to end up believing that *this* is what we've always wished we could say. That experience isn't good for anybody, something else she knows. Fans send up a "brute / Amused shout: / 'A miracle!' / That knocks me out"; and fans need reminding that voyeurism exacts costs:

> There is a charge
>
> For the eyeing of my scars, there is a charge
> For the hearing of my heart—
> It really goes.

Sincerity kills

And there is a charge, a very large charge,
For a word or a touch
Or a bit of blood

Or a piece of my hair or my clothes.

—As who should say, "The price of absorption in pornography is an incremental deadening of the spirit, an attenuation of an already frail belief in the sanctity of personhood. I shall now show you a pornographic film." All her life, a reader had been someone to manipulate.

To facilitate its understanding with its reader, poetry since Homer's time has had formal ceremonies. It is in this connection that Sylvia Plath herself speaks of manipulation:

> I think my poems come immediately out of the sensuous and emotional experiences I have, but I must say I cannot sympathise with these cries from the heart that are informed by nothing except a needle or a knife or whatever it is. I believe that one should be able to control and manipulate experiences, even the most terrifying—like madness, being tortured, this kind of experience—and one should be able to manipulate these experiences with an informed and intelligent mind. I think that personal experience shouldn't be a kind of shut box and mirror-looking narcissistic experience. I believe it should be generally relevant, to such things as Hiroshima and Dachau, and so on.

These unpremeditated words into a microphone will not be confined to a wholly coherent meaning—how a needle or a knife might inform is unclear, nor whether it's to anyone's advantage if the manipulating intellect connects its own fevers with the Hiroshima fireball—but what she started to say is surely that cries from the heart are not poems until subjected to a discipline like that of her own stanzaic and metrical structures. "Study *The Colossus*," said John Frederick Nims in 1970. "Notice all the stanza-forms, all the uses of rhythm and rhyme; notice how the images are chosen and related; how deliberately sound is used. It is no accident, for instance, that there are seven identical drab *a*'s in '. . .salt flats, / Gas tanks, factory stacks—that landscape. . .'. Remember that *The Bell Jar* tells us that she 'wrote page after page of villanelles and sonnets,' and this in one semester of one class. Perhaps for writers this is the gist of the Plath case: without the drudgery of *The Colossus*, the triumph of *Ariel* is unthinkable."[3] So let's notice.

Notice the poem about the lady in the stone coffin, sixteen hundred years dead ("All the Dead Dears"). To abridge the discussion, I'll remark that its six stanzas rhyme *abcacb*, one "*b*" line shorter than the norm, the other longer.

Rigged poker-stiff on her back
With a granite grin

> This antique museum-cased lady
> Lies, companioned by the gimcrack
> Relics of a mouse and a shrew
> That battened for a day on her ankle-bone.

Stanza one, and a single audible rhyme: back/gimcrack. It seems an accident in a rhymeless stanza. Stanza two:

> These three, unmasked now, bear
> Dry witness
> To the gross eating game
> We'd wink at if we didn't hear
> Stars grinding, crumb by crumb,
> Our own grist down to its bony face.

Bear/hear, in the same place, *a/a*, but again as if accidental; it would have been called an eye-rhyme once. Marianne Moore can unsettle in this way, but when Marianne Moore's rhymes fall askew they do so amid a rigorous syllable count. This poem isn't counting syllables. Counting stresses? Perhaps. You can fit the stresses into a 3-2-3-3-3-4 pattern, though with little confidence; "That battened for a day on her ankle-bone" can be read as iambic pentameter, though its partner, "Our own grist down to its bony face," has at most nine syllables, and perhaps five stresses but more likely four. Next stanza:

> How they grip us through thin and thick,
> These barnacle dead!
> This lady here's no kin
> Of mine, yet kin she is: she'll suck
> Blood and whistle my marrow clean
> To prove it. As I think now of her head,

At last an unequivocal rhyme, dead/head, *b/b*; and *a/a* is further off key than before, thick/suck. Which leaves kin/clean; are they *c/c*? In previous stanzas the corresponding words were lady/shrew and game/crumb. The "*c*" rhyme is not proven. And never will be; subsequent stanzas yield in/down, weddings/tang's, go/lie. "*C*" seems a position for—what may we call it?—assonant dissonance.

And in the last stanzas the "*a*" and "*b*" rhymes behave similarly, drifting off into dissonance. In stanza five the "*a*" rhymes are as far apart as "they" and "barbecue"; in stanza four the "*b*" rhymes are "greatgrand-mother" and "hair."

None of which is to assert that poems "ought to" rhyme smartly: simply to notice that between a wholly unfamiliar pattern and a skewing of exemplification, "All the Dead Dears" nearly persuades us that it wasn't rhyming at all, merely striking similar sounds at random. Its mind seems intent on sharp newsmagazine phrases: "Rigged poker-stiff on her back"; "antique museum-cased lady"; "the gross eating game": a smart assurance of diction, O-so-American (she wrote the poem in England; the lady lies "in the Archaeological Museum in Cambridge," where Sylvia Plath was at the time an undergraduate). Stanza one and stanza two articulate with patness one sentence each.

But the sentence in stanza three stops three words into the final line, and when we set out to quote the sentence that offers to fill out the line we find ourselves copying out all the rest of the poem, stanzas four, five, six, unrhymes and all:

> As I think now of her head,
>
> From the mercury-backed glass
> Mother, grandmother, greatgrandmother
> Reach hag hands to haul me in,
> And an image looms under the fishpond surface
> Where the daft father went down
> With orange duck-feet winnowing his hair—
>
> All the long-gone darlings: they
> Get back, though, soon,
> Soon: be it by wakes, weddings,
> Childbirths or a family barbecue:
> Any touch, taste, tang's
> Fit for those outlaws to ride home on,
>
> And to sanctuary: usurping the armchair
> Between tick
> And tack of the clock, until we go,
> Each skulled-and-crossboned Gulliver
> Riddled with ghosts, to lie
> Deadlocked with them, taking root as cradles rock.

—as though the poem had suddenly escaped from a sassy phrase-maker's control and commenced spewing out family secrets. Decorum is jettisoned; the daft father's hair, in a zany glimpse, is winnowed by duck-feet. "Darlings" reaches for the throttle; "they / Get back, though, soon, / Soon" asserts cool sarcasm; American diction is given brief rein as outlaws ride home; the final stanza has sweat on its brow. The armchair is a desperate maneuver, so is "skulled-and-crossboned," so is "Gulliver." The whole thing, once it got loose, has just barely been curbed.

That's what the forms in *The Colossus* are often for, to barely assert themselves and get disrupted. They are not like Yeatsian forms, assurances of "traditional sanctity and loveliness"; nor like Marianne Moore forms, assertions that clickety rigor rides what might be impudence; nor like, say, late-Roethke forms, strumming assurances that the balladeer has all this turbulence under control (sort of).

> The Kitty-Cat Bird, he moped and he cried
> Then a real cat came with a Mouth so Wide,
> That the Kitty-Cat Bird just hopped inside;
> "At last I'm myself!"—and he up and he died
> —Did the Kitty—the Kitty-Cat Bird.

That's pretty dreadful, come to think of it, but the verse won't let you think of it right away. Roethke was cunning in effecting such displacements, and Sylvia Plath was fascinated by his craft but never tried to emulate his confident Dada. She's closer, most of the time, to Robert Lowell, who contrived in his earlier work great rickety pseudo-Pindaric formalisms, the point of which is that they are akin only in geometry to seventeenth-century assurances, and later (e.g., "Skunk Hour") approximated as if casually to formalisms whose teasing near presence serves as gauge for nausea.[4] Ted Hughes calls just one poem—"Point Shirley"—a direct Lowell imitation (she wrote it in 1959, while attending Lowell's Boston University seminar), but the similarities pervade her mature work.

Having said that, I'll talk only about Plath, on the understanding that much adjustment of nuance would be entailed in fitting my statements accurately to Lowell. The formalisms of The Colossus—assonance, rhyme, stanzaic pattern—serve a number of interdependent offices, one of which is to reassure the genteel reader (and notably the one who counts, the one who edits an upper-middlebrow magazine). This reader wants to see the candles lit and the silver laid out (and so do we, so do we), and will half-accept, half-overlook an intrusion of the mortuary, the morbid, or the demonic provided that table-manners are not disrupted. That first level of sheer calculation should not be discounted; it helps explain how The New Yorker came to accept four poems—"Hardcastle Crags," "Man in Black," "Mussel Hunter at Rock Harbor," "Watercolor of Grantchester Meadows"—that scan a scene and come to rest on some deathly emblem capable of disrupting with panic that magazine's normally trite sophistication. "Hardcastle Crags" is especially nightmarish, a journey on foot into fear that keeps inviting us to attend to its compact elegances of phrasing—

> the incessant seethe of grasses
> Riding in the full
>
> Of the moon, manes to the wind,
> Tireless, tied, as a moon-bound sea
> Moves on its root

Sincerity kills

—so that although clues abound, we barely notice the whole world growing steadily more inimical, stark, unassimilable, with one's death the only appropriate resolution:

> Enough to snuff the quick
> Of her small heat out.

Did any editor notice that the poem's walk was into a cosmic grave-yard?

> but before the weight
> Of stones and hills of stones could break
> Her down to mere quartz grit in that stony light
> She turned back.

The wilfully patterned stanzas, the *ababa* off rhymes, effect attention's displacement from perversity to craft.

Perversity? I call it that because, in displacing her own attention too, she indulges herself in reconstructing that walk with lurid specificity, forcing a stated unmeaning into its landscape, transforming a mood into something like an article of belief.

> All the night gave her, in return
> For the paltry gift of her bulk and the beat
> Of her heart was the humped indifferent iron
> Of its hills, and its pastures bordered by black stone set
> On black stone.

Living with the poem, working out its nine stanzas, fifty-four lines, retouching its ingenious assonances (*struck* / street / *black* / ignite / *shake*) and the riding of its sentences over stanza breaks (these coincide only once, at the end of stanza five), she could, telling herself she was solving technical puzzles, pencil taboo combinations into its grid, almost as the rhyme of a limerick gives one license to utter a scatology, and rise from her work perhaps incrementally more convinced than before that Sivvy and the huge physical world were incompatible.

I don't want to melodramatize this; but it's been contrived that the manner of her death cannot but haunt any discussion of her work, and read in that knowledge the poems of *The Colossus* offer us the spectacle of someone accustoming herself to the necessity of a speedy death: the more so the longer, clearly, they took to write (thesaurus on lap, Ted Hughes tells us, for all the world as though nothing of more moment were going forward than the completion of the day's crossword puzzle). Here off rhymes are especially betraying. Since they won't serve as finding devices for one another the way "bright" prompts "light," they entail a search and trial that must linger and brood; that can choose, as if uncoerced, to call the hills "humped indifferent iron," yet justify "iron" by the need of an assonance for "return." So, poem by poem, the universe was fitted with a bleak vocabulary, freely chosen yet seemingly necessary.

By the time her poetic had gone into free fall—Ted Hughes dates this from "The Stones," the last poem in the Knopf *Colossus*—that vocabulary came at call: stones, iron, bleak light, all solid things inimical, all gentle locutions used bitterly ("My swaddled legs and arms smell sweet as rubber" and "There is nothing to do. / I shall be good as new.").

> There is nothing to do.
> I shall be good as new.

That's not an off rhyme nor a dissonant assonance. It's a vibration on target, shrieking its mocking echo of psychiatric reassurance. It's also the rhyme sound of "Daddy."

Here and there, in *The Colossus*, we can detect her working back toward interdicted material: as when "All the Dead Dears" sidles from the innocuous Baedeker note about something you can see in the Archaeological Museum in Cambridge (nothing wrong, is there, with staring at an educational exhibit?) past two stanzas of brisk description to a sudden unmasking of family skeletons: "Mother, grandmother, great-grandmother / Reach hag hands to haul me in" and "daft father" looms "under the fishpond surface" beneath which he has long ago been drawn; and they won't stay dead, and they claim us, keep us "deadlocked." "The Stones," the first free-fall poem, need not sidle; it installs itself at a bound in the madhouse of six years before:

> This is the city where men are mended.
> I lie on a great anvil.

and

> The grafters are cheerful,
>
> Heating the pincers, hoisting the delicate hammers.
> A current agitates the wires
> Volt upon volt. Catgut stitches my fissures.

The unpardonable insult, electroshock therapy. Borrowing a melodramatic image from her, we can say that she has opened the eerie waiting room she told Elizabeth Compton about and stepped into a lurid past. Or we can say that when furies lurk just beyond the rim of consciousness there is paramount danger in improvising. All the formal defenses are down.

For that had been a final use of the intricate formalisms: they detained her mind upon the plane of craft, and so long as it was detained there it did not slip toward what beckoned it. Working on the plane of craft, it made some very good poems indeed, which the vertigo of *Ariel* has since persuaded readers to call contrived, frigid, academic. That seems a doubly erroneous judgment. If we think of *The Colossus* not as the frigid precursor to *Ariel* but as the work of a very intelligent girl in her mid twenties, it is an amazingly good collection. There is no guessing how far in ten more years she might have developed that way of working. It is a plausible guess that the arc of her development might have easily exceeded Lowell's. That rich resourcefulness of diction, that command of craft, that intentness—it is hard to think of a first collection that promises so much. And the other error that adheres in our easy preference for *Ariel* is its overlooking of the fact that as long as she worked in the manner of *The Colossus* she kept safely alive. One prefers one's poets kept alive.

But no, *Ariel* has been made to seem a new and final sincerity. Ted Hughes gives conventional opinion its cue: until "The Stones," at Yaddo, he writes, "she had never in her life improvised. The powers that compelled her to write so slowly had always been stronger than she was. But quite suddenly she found herself free to let herself drop, rather than inch over bridges of concepts." Note the loaded terms: with "The Stones," which I would call her first sick poem, she had overcome the compulsion of inhibiting powers. She is "free" (to drop). And she inches no longer. Inching is an ignoble mode of progress, is it not? Never mind that Milton inched. Hughes goes on: in her final phase she "was able to turn to her advantage all the forces of a highly-disciplined, highly intellectual style of education which had, up to this point, worked mainly against her, but without which she could hardly have gone so coolly into the regions she now entered." What she did now was write "at top speed, as one might write an urgent letter. From then on, all her poems were written in this way."[5]

What had, in Ted Hughes's phrase, "worked mainly against her" was a set of habits that, if I read aright, had kept her producing and alive. I would not blame those habits for the frigidities and immaturities of *The Colossus*: I would guess that she was late to mature, and frigid. The strident insincerities of even the later *Letters Home* may help us gauge how much of her mind was still taken up with role playing; will power and ambition incited, habits of craftsmanship released, extraordinary poems from the part of her talent that could be mobilized nonetheless.

> From Water-Tower Hill to the brick prison
> The shingle booms, bickering under
> The sea's collapse.
> Snowcakes break and welter.

("Point Shirley")

Poets have imitated the sea's sound since Homer, never more authoritatively than in such a detail as this. Alert fidelity to the actual produced the *clou*-word, "bickering," with its aural reminiscence of "brick" and its fine antithetical play against "booms," before "sea's collapse" terminates the wave in a hiss of sibilants. She used less of her talent in better-known lines:

> Dying
> Is an art, like everything else.
> I do it exceptionally well.
>
> I do it so it feels like hell.
> I do it so it feels real.
> I guess you could say I've a call.

I find nothing to alter in the way I described the more lurid parts of *Ariel* the year it was published:

> Sparse rhymes come and go nearly at random, and the number of syllables in a line swings with the vertigo of her thought. Still, these are shaped poems, all but two of them measured out in stanzas, by preference with an odd number of lines (5 or 3). Not that they resemble in the least Villon's ceremonious ballades. Perhaps some of them only play the desperate game of repeating again and again the stanza the opening fell into; there's more of compulsion neurosis than mathematics in those forms; the breaks between stanzas are like cracks in the sidewalk, on which she is careful never to step.
>
> The resulting control, sometimes *look* of control, is a rhetoric, as cunning in its power over our nerves as the stream of repulsions. It in fact enacts its own inability to govern. Naked negation spilling down the sides of improvised vessels, that is the formal drama of poem after poem. Being formal, it saves them from shrillness.
>
> The negation, liquid, labile, repudiates with the gleeful craft of a mad child other persons, the poet's own body, the entire created universe. . . .

> Only let down the veil, the veil, the veil.
> If it were death

I would admire the deep gravity of it, its timeless eyes.
I would know you were serious.

There would be a nobility then, there would be a birthday.
And the knife not carve, but enter

Pure and clean as the cry of a baby,
And the universe slide from my side.

This is insidious nausea; Robert Lowell writes in his Foreword of the serpent he hears whispering from her lines, 'Come, if you only had the courage, you too could have my rightness, audacity and ease of inspiration.' But most of us, he adds, will turn back: 'These poems are playing Russian roulette with six cartridges in the cylinder.'"[6]

Poems like "A Birthday Present," from which that last quotation comes, have a Guignol fascination, like executions. She was somewhere on the far side of sanity, teasing herself with the thrill of courting extinction, as though on a high window ledge. Such spectacles gather crowds and win plaudits for "honesty" from critics who should know better. In those terrible months the habits of craft lasted, a feel for shaping and phrasing gone into her bones. Rhyme, though, was no longer a diffraction grating but a wild heuristic, prompting, encouraging—

You do not do, you do not do
Any more, black shoe.

She could have done without that voodoo encouragement. It's too much to say the poems killed her, but one can't see that they did anything to keep her alive. The death poems—say a third of *Ariel*—are bad for anyone's soul. They give a look of literary respectability to voyeurist passions: no gain for poetry, nor for her.

True Plath fans will detest all of the foregoing. True Plath fans, when articulate, are busy making points about purity and sincerity: in quest (I find I wrote eleven years ago) "of spiritual shortcuts to spiritual virtues, but preferring to see someone else try them out." The true self into which Sylvia Plath's soul merged when her careful habits of composition failed her—the habits Ted Hughes stigmatizes as having "worked mainly against her"—made a virtue of a Manichaean lack of patience with the world's slow turning. The world, its obduracy, respect for the waves and stones of which had once summoned all her craft, came to mean only minatory forms, the yew tree whose message "is blackness—blackness and silence," and the body's "aguey tendon, the sin, the sin." In fever, pulsating at a distance from the world,

I

Am a pure acetylene
Virgin
Attended by roses.

This is bogus spirituality, and it has its admirers, who even seem pleased
that Sylvia Plath did not survive it.

Notes

1. Edward Butscher, *Sylvia Plath: Method and Madness* (New York: Seabury Press, 1976).
2. Sylvia Plath, *Letters Home: Correspondence 1950-1963*, selected and edited with commentary by Aurelia Schober Plath (New York: Harper and Row, 1975), pp. 216-17.
3. Charles Newman, ed., *The Art of Sylvia Plath: A Symposium* (Bloomington: Indiana University Press, 1970).
4. "Skunk Hour," written several years after Plath's "All the Dead Dears," has the same odd *abcacb* rhyme scheme but no other resemblances.
5. Newman, *The Art of Sylvia Plath*, pp. 192-93.
6. Hugh Kenner, "Ariel—Pop Sincerity," *Triumph* 1 (September, 1966): 33.

David Shapiro

Sylvia Plath: drama and melodrama

1

On 15 May 1871 Arthur Rimbaud permitted himself the most discursive of his vatic moods in the by now canonic *lettre du voyant* to Paul Demeny. What is rarely underlined in this letter is the egalitarian modality and the tone of the Commune of the previous year: "When the infinite servitude of woman shall have ended, when she will be able to love by and for herself; then, man—hitherto abominable—having given her her freedom, she too will be a poet. Woman will discover the unknown. Will her world be different from ours? She will discover strange, unfathomable things, repulsive, delicious." Rimbaud, never far from being the expropriator, goes on: "We shall take them, we shall understand them."

Doubtless the *ethos* and *mythos* of Sylvia Plath is part of the history of woman in art as prophesized so melodramatically by Rimbaud. Professor Ann S. Harris has recently demonstrated the impossibility for women from the middle ages on to take an active role in the history of painting; and she has documented in her recent show the peculiar disadvantages women have suffered in relation to the visual arts: lack of proper education, inability to gain access to models or anatomical views, economic boundaries, and so forth. Although literature has seemed to many to be a non-physical door open to all talents, in the last decade competent study has revealed the difficulty for women to progress in the West in this art also, a difficulty made even plainer by the instances of exceptional genius: George Eliot, Emily Dickinson.

In this more than sociological sense, Plath represents an emblematic and problematic triumph, but this is a sense I am not going to pursue. There is no doubt that her poetry is part of the history of sensibility, as it were, rather than centrally involved in the history of our poetry. She had the advantages and disadvantages of a sequestered education at Smith; note the continuous tissue of clichés from the letters of those days to her mother. She had also, of course, as she understood it, the outrageous difficulty of laboring for "women's magazines," and *toward* a largely male literary scene. She had, finally, an embodiment of that scene in her husband; I take it that the peculiar form of the late melodramatic works now so celebrated was largely induced by the all too vivid pseudo-masculine tone of Hughes, a poet notoriously overrated but particularly overrated in relation, as Alvarez never stops telling us, to the bland others of English poetry. Thus, Plath's weaknesses, at least for me, are still part of the history of what Rimbaud calls with precision "the servitude of woman."

This might account for the sense in much of Plath's later poetry that there is less a constructivist bias than a "destructivist" one. The early strenuous attempts to gain money from potboilers lead to a constant melancholy tone of the overwritten and the aspirational in metaphor. She is not one for "the art of sinking." She never properly learned to humiliate her diction, and works constantly in a species of expensive materials. Her mythological tone is what Hughes appropriated from the worst of Lawrence. Her humor, which saves so much of the novel and letters, is a right she largely abrogates in a mode of rigor mortis. One must be necessarily harsh here.

The harshness of my critique is part of the unpleasant task of demystifying (a notion that always involves, as Hartman has said, a slight form of contempt) her critics in their constant enchantments. Alvarez has compared the last year with the marvelous 1819 of Keats; Kroll has contributed a lugubrious study of her mythology, as if moon imagery and rebirth configurations would save the poems; Newman very early contributed a volume decent only in hagiography, whose bibliography of early reviews bristled with vindictive comment by Mary Kinzie against anyone so unfortunate as to have made practical complaints concerning the poetry. It is Sexton who has said somewhere that suicide is the opposite of poetry. Certainly stupidity is the opposite of poetry, and I am going to take to task silently those who have been entranced by the false glamors of biography, glamors Alvarez himself deposes while contributing to them, glamors that unfortunately are part of the weakest poems. As the Russian formalists have pointed out, the diction of the biographies, the life itself, and the poems coincide in much *byronisme* and elsewhere. Here, in the latest of our late romantics, critics and poet have ensnared themselves. Possibly the most interesting work that one might achieve as regards Plath is merely a "deconstruction" of her critics, by now industrialized and more than itching. One doesn't want to become like that don she insults so wittily in the letters, the one who criticizes by comparisons to Donne.

It is not a criticism by comparison alone that operates here, but certainly her work through its notoriety, and her critics by their notorious superlatives, now deserve no less than the severest standards. For example, those who compare her work to that of Georg Trakl should be reminded that Trakl completed his magnificent revision of Rimbaud by the First World War, and it is an expressionism that is controlled and more than controlled in the largest canvasses of his large poems. The small poems brood with a sensuous concreteness and hallucinatory mode that Plath merely parodies in her late poems. If one wants to understand what a real revaluation of Trakl and Rilke might be, one might look at O'Hara's transformations of German expressionism in his most conscious and self-conscious, self-reflexive works of the 1950s. Plath's work is about as jejeune an imitation as her illustrationy drawings and her taste in the visual arts, Baskin, for example, among contemporaries. Trakl proceeds constantly in contrast and balance and his work, adequately meditated upon by Heidegger, needs no mediation here. But I am thrilled negatively by the absence of any criticism that would depose Plath as a parody of German expressionism. The organization of the late poems is so close to Trakl that it seems she may have known them in the Hamburger translations or from the German-English versions extant in the 1960s. I suggest, however, to adopt unwillingly a stern and Leavisite tone, that any practical survey of the specimen texts will show the first intensity in the work of Trakl. Near these texts, Plath is student and imitator.

Alvarez in his study speaks too easily of the "prissy, pausing flourish in the manner of Wallace Stevens." He is constantly searching for depths and deposing the poetry of so-called surface, but one wonders whether he is differentiating at all between the elegances of Stevens and the refinements of a Wilbur or Hecht. He seems unwilling to believe in a methodology that might digest the philosophical kinetics of Stevens rather than diverge to an explicit poetry along the lines of the all too discursive Lawrence (not that Lawrence did not contribute sometimes our finest

Whitmanesque bestiaries and *bateaux ivres*). In other words, Alvarez and so many others see the glory of Plath in early "mastering the craft" and later letting the disturbances rise to a newly opened view. This is the royal lie as concerns Ginsberg, Lowell, Plath, Berryman, and so many others, and I presume that we are beginning to find in the work of Ashbery, for instance, other methodologies that have never involved the empurpled confessionals. All poetry, of course, is a matter of reticence and confession; but it is distasteful to recall a period in which poetry was called upon to deny itself, as it were, in a new form of naturalism. The best of Plath goes beyond this naturalism of occasions. But, as with the novel, it is always an almost Zola- if not Salinger-esque possibility. A whimsical naturalism modulated to a hysterical melodrama was part of her recipe in youth for successful "heartbreaking" potboilers. Like Dickens and Dostoevsky, she of course was involved in sublimating and transforming low genres, but the formula remains and seriously disturbs.

The late work is involved not only with the breakdown of the trope of *reticentia*, but is involved in a desublimation that Lionel Trilling so nobly analyses in his last two studies. One does not want to set too simply *Civilization and Its Discontents* as a "lion in the path" of the bolting horse of Plath. But it is impossible not to sense in her apotheosis and that of the late poems a flight from construction and self-regulating wholes praised by that magnificent structuralist Piaget. Her work is part of an age of the shattered narrative, but what I lament is not the shatter but the lack of any fruitful flatness, of any holding to the picture plane, by analogy here, of composition. In other words, she took to *utterance* and her poetry, which she loved to utter, is exactly deficient in the consciousness of writing itself. This may or may not be attributed to the era of Laing and Brown and Ginsberg. Lowell was always involved in the most devious way with a rapprochement between utterance, anecdote, and the difficulties of writing without mere voice. It does not take a Derrida of negative theology to see what is merely positive in the explicit utterances of the poetry of Plath. It is what now stands revealed in the work of Dylan Thomas as mere performance (called thirteenth rate for good reason by Pound). The flight into performance is like the flight into illness. In an age of Jasper Johns and the rarest forms of self-reflexiveness in American art, Plath's poetry becomes a mere theatre, somewhat akin to the sterile forms of happenings of Kaprow, but even less *dadaist* and *collagiste* than these. Her chants are the insipid corollaries of a notion of poetry as voice and cadence. It infects the Black Mountain School and is part of the detritus of Williams.

Again, let us remember that poetry is not voice or utterance but is structure. Emptiness is not a pretense in poetry anymore than space is in architecture. What is wanted is a well—a *vide*—and not a well-made urn. The works of Plath are overdetermined, largely and with remarkable vengeance jejunely referential. Like her drawings and her sentimental taste for the whimsical in Klee, she uses language as a pencil and does not permit language to speak through her. Thus, one feels in the poems a constant program of the referential in an age of degraded public realisms. While many of her critics have lamented her prose for women's magazines, few have noted the relative ease in which that realism and hyperbolic Grubean prose modulates to the poetry of hyperbole. Alvarez gives us some late poignant scenes in which he remonstrated about the exaggeration in the lines "The nude / Verdigris of the condor." Her response was not even to deal with this as device, but to suggest to her interlocutor that she take him to the zoo, where he might see for himself the factualness of her proposition. Thus, she was twisted upon the poles of a hyperbolic melodramatic masquerading as a realism. Like Bly and Ginsberg, she was quickly attaining the status of prophet for herself and losing the whole delicious sense of the nondiscursive in poetry. Her dream of a perfect language and her hypostasized notion of speech leads inevitably to a horrifying impasse. Poetry as pencil, as voice, and as magic failed her.

2

Practical criticism of Plath's poetry must fasten upon the overwriting and the aspirational quality of her devices. It is not simply in evidence in the late poems, but is part of the very initiation of her career in *The Colossus:* "Incense of death." Here we have neither the incense nor the concreteness of death but a literary abstraction, refusing both. Nor does she refuse the cliché: "Hours of blankness." Repetition is not used as a beautiful persistence, as in Gertrude Stein, but for copiousness and the haunting voice of the Gothic romance: "The small birds converge, converge." I emphasize this, because the shrill repetition in the late poems has been praised, and as a lover of repetition I would point out that she never employs this favorite device of American pragmatics for the sake of difference, but for the sake of copiousness and abundance. She thus uses and abuses the device of repetition, in much the way Bly and Wright abuse certain functions of hallucinatory repetition found in Spanish and French surrealism. Plath is *harping* upon a word here, rather than giving us through repetition the playful poetics of its new position. Her delicacies, learnt explicitly from Auden at times, are all too seldom this *imitatio* of "Museé des Beaux Arts": "Yet desolation, stalled in paint, spares the little country / Foolish, delicate, in the lower right hand corner." Rarely did she permit herself the luxury of spareness. She was always too poetical and lacked the prosiness of Elizabeth Bishop or the constant linguistic research of Laura Riding.

Often the modifiers are dismayingly clotted. This is doubtless part of the heritage of Lawrence and Thomas and of Hughes in his animal poems. In "Sow" the adjectives pile up to inverse effect, as in the ending: "The seven troughed seas and every earthquaking continent." She colors in with her adjectives the way that she colors in in her black and white illustrations. The adjectives have no presence, they are merely stippling for the sake of stippling but always in relation to an object or emotion, never abstract enough to make a fundamental dislocation, as in Rimbaud's floating glimmers. Nor does she control the mock heroic: "Unhorsed and shredded in the grove of combat / By a grisly-bristled / Boar." This is the species of overwriting that is recapitulated in the phylogenies of *Crow*.

The best poem in *Colossus*, it seems to me, succeeds in a Roethke-like vein of accepting smallness for what it is, with a negative capability that does not need the hypostasizing tone. In "Mushrooms," Plath holds herself in, as it were, to present the very quiet voice of the fungus, a parable of *petitesse* and big sensations. She becomes not just an Other, but a nice schizy mass. She ends with the commonplace, "Our foot's in the door," with a Bishop-like smile. As a matter of fact, one thinks of Bishop's "Snail." The little tercets are woven discretely and are concerned with discretions. But there is no mere self-contempt and there is a cry and aggression. While it is still a ghost story of a Gothic forest encroaching, its intimacy is musical and unfaltering.

Everywhere, there is the usual furniture of the Gothic romance and the thriller, for example in the transitional poems, so-called, of *Crossing the Water*. As a matter of fact, speaking of this word "transitional," it is about time to lacerate the Darwinian notion of this young poet. She did not necessarily evolve in her last year to some sudden organic complexity. If anything, as we might see with less dogmatic eyes, the late utterances are simplified and archaic in their explicitness. Yes, they are not drab and academic, but compare the late poems with "Fresh Air" of Kenneth Koch, for instance, a poem also explicitly against the academic strictures of the 1950s, the age of the lean quarterly and the missus and the midterms and myths. Koch has exuberantly given one a whole palette of possibilities, a labyrinth of homages and parodies, an exuberant cadenza with a proper sense of endlessness to its closure. Plath's poems click like boxes in Housman's sense of strict closure. Compared to some of the early and middle work, she sacrificed a great deal to get the histrionic condensations of the late ejaculatory style. It is a pity if this last season is to be judged merely chronologically as the crown. It is as if we called Keats' "To Fanny" the harbinger of a new period and the crown of the balanced odes. Paul de Man comes close to doing this as an homage to consciousness in Keats, but still in both poets we do a disservice by searching for a crown in chronos, which is as we know *not* history.

Many instances of overwriting might be collected; "Finisterre" will be paradigmatic. This is the country of "Black admonitory cliffs, and the sea exploding." The sea in thrilling fashion can do nothing less, one presumes, than explode here, as the surf creamed in earlier poems. All is orgasmic. All is terrifying. Compare this sea, by the way, with the well-excavated grave of Marianne Moore and its terrifyingly prosey acceptances. It is Moore who once said the poet must be as clear as natural reticence permits. The animations amid the pathos of Plath, as with Hughes, permitted no such reticence: "Other rocks hide their grudges under the water." "Souls, rolled in the doom-noise of the sea." One cannot help suspecting that the fashion of the occult, as noticed by Alvarez in Hughes and Plath, infects these lines with the same dreary and lugubrious lack of convincingness that we hear in the worst imitators of Yeats. This is the academic occult, and one mustn't forget that Ginsberg and his continental analogues were as academic as ever in their antiacademic escape into homemade theodicies. Eliot has said that we must get a religion for fear of having unconsciously a bad one; in Plath, we see "Our Lady of the Shipwrecked . . . striding toward the horizon." While Plath speaks of being "in love with the beautiful formlessness of the sea," her much-vaunted forms are mediocre and enclosed in poor thought; they do not uncover new thought, in Heidegger's sense of *aletheia*. Here all is covered in too much speech. Like Eliot's Othello, she is trying to cheer herself up.

"Stillborn" is an almost successful attempt at a more self-reflexive and self-comprehending text. The poem begins with a self-lacerating humor that is reminiscent of the best in *The Bell Jar*: "These poems do not live: it's a sad diagnosis." In too many of her poems, one might say she overvitalizes her texts. Eliot once said the best religious poems are not necessarily those done by mystics celebrating union; too often overpiety mars our religious poetry as overimpiety and the vividly negative mar Plath's and Hughes's work. Here in "Stillborn," she makes her dilemma a type of celebration. The single trope of birth is clumsy but kept up; how congruent with the very *topos* of clumsy death is its style and stylelessness. The poem becomes a criticism in the simplest way, and yet the whole "bulge[s] with concentration." The repetition is bizarrely flat and persistent and concerned with persistence: "They smile and smile and smile and smile at me. . . . They are not pigs, they are not even fish, / Though they have a piggy and fishy air." Here the jauntiness is more successful than the later sacrifice of all gentilities. Here the very tenses of the verbs become alive by contrast. One thinks of Guido's father fainting in Hell because of a change of tense. "It would be better if they were alive, and that's what they were. / But they are dead . . . / And they stupidly stare, and do not speak of me." It is a poem of deletion by a poet elsewhere loading too many rifts with ore. Still, the topic is the uncanny horror of a death before life, an emblem of her father.

Many of her critics assail formalism and speak of Plath's work as the triumph of an antiformal way. But there is no escape from form. Too many critics, like Malkoff on the Projectivists, think of the two roads of American poetry as that of the urn or the tree. But poetry is neither a well-wrought urn nor an esemplasticity of Coleridge's dream. Hölderlin said: To live is to defend a form. The forms of Plath are rarely whole. The letters are as genial as Keats's but marred by constant cliché. She lived indeed in the prisonhouse of language, and one senses the terrible pressure that these clichés—clichés of the college, clichés of education, clichés of the mother, still in her bowdlerizing and her notes—exerted upon her. In *Ariel* and elsewhere she exerted pressure against these clichés, but I sense more pathos and defeat than victory. Thus the expressionsim, which Borges has called the refuge of the young person. Like randomness in a later day, Plath used expressionism and a quasi-allegorical mode to heroize her own attempts. She never lets anything alone. In comparison to the great masters of the colloquial, Gertrude Stein, Riding, and Bishop, and with her great precursor Dickinson in mind, she refused to be domestic but in the end seems falsest in her very flights:

> And I
> Am the arrow,
>
> The dew that flies
> Suicidal, at one with the drive
> Into the red
>
> Eye, the cauldron of morning.

Her best poems, like "Tulips," are relaxations from this Mayakovsky-like bolting toward death.

In "Tulips" she is permitted a wider structure and a tone that is comfortable with still life, even with the insidious, still Gothic sense of *natura morte*. The verbs that were purple and melodramatic have quietly passed to verbs of being, as in the strong beginning that concerns weakness: "The tulips are too excitable, it is winter here." Look, says the poem, and one recalls Heidegger asking us to "Take a look at being." A difficult prescription, but one made even more difficult by the constant unwillingness of Plath to let things alone and, finally, to let language alone. Is this what suicide may also mean, a murder that is unwilling to accept the central lack of explanation? One feels a certain wisdom in Alvarez's confession that he was perplexed to find nothing proposed as explanation by his own suicide. Possibly poetry, as opposed to philosophy of a certain kind, takes pleasure in the unanswerable problem and must not pad itself with too much explanation. Instead of playacting at a constant malevolent drama of self-annihilation, Plath is best when she attempts to give up all theater. Of course, she is always theatrical, and "Tulips," too, is a presentation of the theme: "la vie est un hôpital." It is a constricting topic, it is by now an outworn and *symboliste* convention, and it leads her to a rhetoric never consistently deflated or transformed. Her charm is in certain relaxed poems and in the letters, but her mythical, manic, troubling, late poems charm her critics.

3

> 1902: Daily Chronicle: Melodrama thrives solely upon exaggeration.
>
> 1854: Emerson: My idea of heaven is that there is no melodrama in it at all.

If Aristotle is correct in defining structure as that which dominates diction in tragic drama, then we might define melodrama as that in which diction and spectacle threaten the life of structure. The Oxford English Dictionary's sense of melodrama is that sensational drama in which songs interspersed with incidents gained appeal by violence and sudden happy endings. One also thinks of the orchestral accompaniment of melodramatic action as part of the degradation here. How does this permit us an analogue in poetry? Let us call dramatic those poems whose structure dominates diction; those poems melodramatic in which the whole tendency is to a diction-dominated formlessness punctuated by hyperbole appealing to the emotions. Interestingly, the happy ending in Plath is usually one of revenge in murder or self-murder. My definitions are purposely vague: exactness in some matters, Whitehead said, was a fake. But tragedy is not a snark, nor is melodrama. Too often, in the texts of Plath, we bump into stubborn, irreducible melodrama.

2. Process and influence

Richard Allen Blessing

The shape of the psyche: vision and technique in the late poems of Sylvia Plath

These Songs are not meant to be understood, you understand.
They are only meant to terrify and comfort.

—*John Berryman*

1

As my epigraph suggests, I am not writing to "understand" Sylvia Plath's poems, or not that primarily. Instead I want to try to analyze her power to terrify us and, less often, to comfort. More specifically, I want to discuss a few of her techniques of style, tone, and structure that seem to me responsible for what I think are Plath's most characteristic effects. I want to know what Plath was doing in making the dynamic *Ariel* poems that she was not doing, say, in 1959 when she used to drop in on Robert Lowell's poetry seminar at Boston University. "She was," Lowell remembers, "a brilliant tense presence embarrassed by restraint. Her humility and willingness to accept what was admired seemed at times to give her an air of maddening docility that hid her unfashionable patience and boldness. She showed us poems that later, more or less unchanged, went into her first book, *The Colossus*. They were somber, formidably expert in stanza structure and had a flair for alliteration and Massachusetts low-tide dolor."[1] I don't plan to use *The Colossus* as the "before" picture in a poetic body-building ad. It's too good a book for that. If Plath had written nothing else, she would still have a place in anthologies for a generation or more. But something in the techniques developed after *The Colossus* makes the late poems important to us, important in ways that go beyond formidable expertise or alliterative low-tide dolor.

To begin with, I think Plath changed her notion of what a poem ought to be. In 1961, two years before her death, one of Sylvia Plath's "letters home" to her mother contained the following piece of literary gossip: "Ted and I went to a little party last night to meet the American poet I admire next to Robert Lowell — Ted (for Theodore) Roethke. I've always wanted to meet him, for I find he is my influence.... Roethke said any time Ted wants to teach at Washington State to give him a nod, so in a few years we'll, no doubt, make another American year."[2] It's hard to know how seriously to take any of those odd epistles signed "x x x Sivvy," and I quote this one partly because my recent preoccupation with Roethke's poetry leaves me little choice but to come at Plath by way of some of the affinities I find between the two. I do not believe in Plath's "finding" that Roethke is her influence, as if she had had but one, as if that one had been hidden from her until it burst from its dark closet at a party, scattering sudden illumination. But perhaps her choice of the word "find" is not mere ingenuousness. I think it likely that she really *had* discovered or realized that her vision of what a poem had to be and do was, in fact, very much like that of Theodore Roethke, though it was a vision that she might also have developed for herself or discovered in other poets.

"A poem that is the shape of the psyche itself; in times of great stress, that's what I wanted to write."[3] That's a line from Roethke's notebooks. Here's another. "A poem is an extra — it announces itself by its rhythmical energy: that energy proceeds from the mind, the psyche of the person writing."[4] Sylvia Plath never read those sentences, but she read Roethke's poetry, and his definition of poetry is very close to the one by and with which she lived and wrote during those final brilliant years of creation.

For Roethke, for Plath, the psyche was pure energy, but so was all the universe. To speak of "the shape of the psyche" is to be reminded that it *has* no shape except those momentary ones that are already beginning to change at the moment they come into being. One might as well speak of the shape of the fire (as Roethke does, in fact) or the shape of the wind. "Formidable stanza structure" is quite another thing.

Of Roethke, Stanley Kunitz has written: "He is Proteus and all the forms of Proteus — flower, fish, reptile, amphibian, bird, dog, etc. — and he is the adversary who hides among the rocks to pounce on Proteus, never letting go his hold, while the old man of the sea writhes through his many shapes until, exhausted by the struggle, he consents to prophesy in the claritas of his found identity."[5] Plath, too, has a tenuous grip on herself, but the forms she takes are more horrible than Roethke's: the vampire's daughter, the monster queen of bees, the victim of radiation poisoning, the Nazi artifact, the walking mummy with featureless face, the Medusa, the lamia (in many poems the basic sound is the exaggerated hiss), the paralytic, the zombie, the death camp victim, the Stepford wife. Hers is indeed an ontogeny fearful in its slippery writhings.

Plath's moving universe is animated at times by love but more often by the forces that dominated her emotional life, primarily rage and fear. Her importance as a poet depends upon how successfully she evolves strategies with language to make effective metaphors for the terrific experience of those murderous forces. She is fascinating because the "shape" of her psyche is peculiarly bottomless, a world of infinite plunge. She recalls us to the wisdom of Edgar's observation in *King Lear:* "the worst is not / So long as we can say 'This is the worst'" (IV, i, 29-30). And to Emily Dickinson's terrifying conclusion—the one that refuses to conclude—of the poem beginning "I felt a Funeral, in my Brain":

> And then a Plank in Reason, broke,
> And I dropped down, and down—
> And hit a World, at every plunge,
> And Finished knowing—then—

This is perhaps the darkest form of romanticism—a form darker than Roethke's—the evocation of a series of horrors, each more horrible than the last, and of which no man knows the end. Plath's great and underlying terror is always the nausea of movement itself. Even Plath's pleasures crowd in on her this way, threaten to become too much if she cannot somehow bring them under control, slow their onslaught. It is true, as some have suggested, that the poems may be read as attempts to create a mythical self capable of withstanding the changes in her life, the betrayals and the losses. But it's the kinesthetic sense of pitch and roll, the stomach-tilting sensation of that bottomless series of plunges, that we experience most strongly. And the evocation of that sense is her particular genius.

2

Plath uses many devices, not all of them subtle, to achieve the artistic effect of a world in violent motion. For one thing, many of the late poems make use of the motif of journeying: "Blackberrying," "On Deck," "Crossing the Water," "Ariel," "Getting There," "The Bee Meeting," "Totem," and perhaps "Words" as well. There are also poems like "Black Rook in Rainy Weather" and "Letter in November" that seem to indicate that the shapes of her thoughts, her intuitions, come to her in motion rather than when she is standing still. Another of her devices is the beginning *in medias res*. No one is better than Plath at giving her reader the experience of being swept up in an action that has been gathering momentum for some time. Part of her success stems from a clever use of indefinite pronouns indefinitely used. "I have done it again" or "It happens. Will it go on?" or "How far is it? / How far is it now?" or "What is this, behind this veil, is it ugly, is it beautiful?" "Death & Co." begins with another version of the same device: "Two, of course there are two." And "The Swarm": "Somebody is shooting at something in our town." Used in a first line, the pronoun reaches back to a subject felt but not seen, as if we begin in the realm of the predicate, experience the presence of the prime mover in its absence, piece together a cause from momentum that rushes past as effect. And, to mention just one more of the obvious devices, Plath, to paraphrase Stevens, is of repetition most master. Repetition is one of the techniques listed by Roethke in his teaching notes under the heading "Devices for Heightening Intensity,"[6] a strategy for love-making and name-calling, cursing and praying. Robert Pack calls repetition "an act of love for the word repeated," though in Plath it is often an act of love too difficult to tell from hate, as we see, for example, in the repetition of the word "you" (Ach, du) and its cluster of almost incestuous rhymes in "Daddy." Intensity repeats itself, stutters almost, like Billy Budd before the blow. The effect is that of someone's hovering over the word while searching for a piece of invective strong enough. "Why you, you..." is what the poem is saying, settling finally and inadequately for "you bastard." It is difficult to say *why* repetition hastens the line, though it is a staple of nursery rhyme and nonsense verse, those models of velocity whose cadence, as Roethke once put it, "escape so fast." Perhaps in poetry intensity and velocity are one, emotion the exact equal of motion. At any rate, when Plath closes "Elm" by raising the murdering force of the "isolate slow faults" to the third power or when she urges the applicant to "marry it, marry it, marry it," she has managed to close on a note of pure frenzy. One has the sense that the rest is not so much silence as energy too intense for articulation. As with Dickinson's funeral in the brain, the conclusion seems not to conclude. The urgency of the line seems to extend itself onto the whiteness of the page, much as Plath's trick of beginning in mid act reaches back into whiteness.

I want to devote most of this section of my essay, however, to an examination of two devices—devices hardly Plath's innovations—that seem to me a part of her medium not always sufficiently considered when critics have sought to unravel her message. One of them is the deliberate use of ambiguity, of elaborate puns (another of Roethke's intensifying devices), and the other is a manipulation of images that, in some of her , better poems, makes her the poetic daughter of Wallace Stevens.

One of the best examples of Plath's use of ambiguity and, in my opinion, one of her best poems, is that "exercise" set for her by Hughes and titled "The Moon and the Yew Tree." It is generally read as a poem about the loss of faith in which the yew tree's message of deadly black and tomblike stillness has the final word, in which the bald, wild moon claims Plath as her daughter, replacing forever Mary, that sweeter mother. This, it seems to me, is only half the poem, and thus a distortion. "How I would like to believe in tenderness," Plath says at the crucial point in the poem, and I take her at her word. Like Frost's "Birches," "The Moon and the Yew Tree" is a poem about the power of what the poet would "like to think" or "prefer to think" as it presses against the baldness of reality's "matter of fact."

"This is the light of the mind," the poem begins, "cold and planetary."

> The trees of the mind are black. The light is blue.
> The grasses unload their griefs on my feet as if I were God,
> Prickling my ankles and murmuring of their humility.
> Fumy, spiritous mists inhabit this place
> Separated from my house by a row of headstones.
> I simply cannot see where there is to get to.... (A, 41.)

The battleground is defined, not as the landscape of actual yew, moon, and church, but as the landscape of the mind where "the light" transforms aspects of Plath's world into certain "blue phenomena." The knowledge of death, suggested by the headstones, separates Plath's house—the place where she "lives" emotionally and intellectually—from the church and its spiritous inhabitants. (Similarly, Frost's knowledge of ice storms separates him momentarily from what he would "like to think" about the birches bent to left and to right.) But the line "I simply cannot see where there is to get to" is an ambiguous line, oversimplified if one hears it only as the poet's assertion that, in her opinion, there is no where to "get," no heaven, no door opening beyond those headstones. That meaning is there, but I hear another as well, one that italicizes the word "see" and raises the question of creative seeing, of imaginative vision. In other words, there *is* a place "to get to" but Plath's imagination simply cannot take her there. The first reading is a dismissal of all that she would like to believe—the tenderness of Mary, the holiness of the saints, the resurrection of the dead—and the second is an affirmation of belief in the unseen. (I am not surprised that in the last months of her life Plath seems to have turned mystic, claimed to have "seen God.")

In the next stanza the "moon is no door," presumably to anything transcendent. Cold reflector, it acts as a kind of mirror for Plath, a face "White as a knuckle," "terribly upset," "quiet / With the O-gape of complete despair." This is "here," this is where she lives; but "there" in the world of the church "the bells startle the sky . . . affirming the Resurrection." This affirmation is the triumph of A-gape over O-gape, of the love that passes understanding over complete despair. Small wonder that there is a will to believe.

And what Plath would like to believe she manages to conjure up, at least as a momentary image. She makes her own icon, creates of words "The face of the effigy, gentled by candles, / Bending, on me in particular, its mild eyes." Fallen she may be, yet she moves "Inside the church" as an act of imaginative vision, "seeing" a place she can "get to," "seeing" the saints, "all blue, / Floating on their delicate feet over the cold pews, / Their hands and feet stiff with holiness." At the same time, she is the moon's daughter, heiress of complete despair, and the moon "sees nothing of this."

Plath's ambiguity amounts to more than a single line with two readings, one gaping pun that manages to be simultaneously types *A* and *O*. It relies on such tricks, but goes beyond them to a pervasive double vision in the tradition of Keats or Frost, a vision that tests the fancy's ability to cheat—and with everything resting on the outcome. Sometimes Plath's ambiguity amounts to little more than easy apotheosis, as when her son Nick becomes "the baby in the barn" at the end of "Nick and the Candlestick." But at her best the effect is anything but easy, a kind of verbal illusion modeled on those optical ones in which we see first one thing, then another, then the first again. We can never experience O-gape and A-gape simultaneously in "The Moon and the Yew Tree," but after hearing despair at one time and tenderness at another what we do experience is the restless attraction of each for the other, the motion rocking back and forth between those emotional poles.

Another good example of Plath's uses of ambiguity, "Death & Co.," begins appropriately enough: "Two, of course there are two" (A, 28). As she herself explained it, the poem "is about the double or schizophrenic nature of death—the marmoreal coldness of Blake's death mask, say, hand in glove with the fearful softness of worms, water and the other katabolists. I imagine these two aspects of death as two men, two business friends, who have come to call."[7] Though not mentioned by name, Emily Dickinson is in the poem along with Blake. Blake's death mask has been usurped by a cool salesman, one who never looks up, whose "beak / Claps sidewise" (A, 28). And the seductive courtier of Dickinson's

"Because I could not stop for Death" has suffered a like change, smiling and smoking, a "Bastard / Masturbating a glitter" who "wants to be loved." The strategy of the poem is also Dickinsonian, an action beginning at the point of death or just after, an imaginative excursion into that blank space of possibility that death offers the artist. In fact Dickinson and Blake, it might be argued, are presences in the poem, presences of an order only slightly less substantial than the two businessmen callers; and, since the two poets are part of the long company of Death, they may even be included (along with the narrator?) in the "company" pun of the title.

The poem begins with a revelation. There are *two* deaths; "It seems perfectly natural now." But the revelation is doubly unpleasant, death in its one aspect pushing tawdry perfections, telling the narrator "how sweet / The babies look in their hospital / Icebox"; and in its other, long-haired and lecherous, Dickinson's kindly chauffeur turned seedy exhibitionist. "He wants to be loved," Plath says, but "I do not stir," a line that moves many ways nonetheless. On the other hand, the narrator doesn't stir because she cannot, being dead, or nearly so; and on the other, she is not stirred by the clumsy attempts at seduction that are being made. And behind those meanings I hear another, one that suggests that she will not "stir" the dual aspects of death until they become a single mixture. She is at home with double natures, with ambiguities. (One might also take the line to mean that Plath, like a bit of egg shell in the mayonnaise, will not *be* stirred into the company of death, or not just yet, a reading that could be a variation on her refusal to be "stirred" by the masturbating suitor.)

But the most ambiguous lines—and the most dynamic—are those that follow:

> The frost makes a flower,
> The dew makes a star,
> The dead bell,
> The dead bell.
>
> Somebody's done for. (A, 29.)

The passage turns on the word "makes." One reading, consistent with the obscenity of the onanistic partner who wants to be loved, would be crudely sexual, a destructive "making" smacking of rape at worst, contemptuous sexual exploitation at best. Frost, we remember, kills flowers (perhaps another nod to Dickinson with her blond assassin) and water puts out fire. If dew "makes" a star's fire in this sense, too bad for the star. Another reading, however, would hear artistic or creative "making" in the same passage. In it, ephemeral frost and dew may be artists, makers of metaphor. Frost makes floral patterns upon a winter window, say; and a glint of sun on morning dew might well sparkle *like* a star.

In the end the marmoreal cold, the katabolistic damp, have taken her in, both flower and star. The question that remains is that of the sense in which she has been "made." Has she been—as the main thrust of the poem surely suggests—made victim of the sinister processes of katabolism? Or has she, like Blake and Dickinson, been in some way "perfected," metamorphosed into an artistic self more lasting and more beautiful than the physical one that photographs badly?[8] What is the nature of the "company" of death, the company it "keeps"? In Plath's poem, death seems less a choice than a motion between alternatives. Behind the repulsion one hears joy at the power of quick, bright things to "make" beauty before they are done for.

A more obvious way of imparting motion to a poem is through the manipulation of imagery. Plath is very good at this; at her best, as I have suggested, she is the heiress of Wallace Stevens. "Cut," for example, might be subtitled "Fifteen Ways of Looking at a Thumb Cut," for the thumb stump stands in the center like a blackbird, a glass of water, a pineapple, while the plastic parts of poems crash in the mind. Part of the "meaning" of the poem is the sheer violence from without. In only 10 stanzas, 40 lines, 134 words, the thumb undergoes its myriad metamorphoses before returning to itself, as if at last a balance had been struck between mind and world or as if wit and art had worked their magic so that the thumb stump could finally be accepted in all its blank ugliness. The pace begins slowly, the resemblances casual, expressed as similes, almost not metaphors at all:

> The top quite gone
> Except for a sort of a hinge
>
> Of skin,
> A flap like a hat,
> Dead white. (A, 13.)

Then the similes disappear. Metaphors proliferate, violent both in content and in the associative wrenches they demand, the thumb left behind, a world of pure resemblance. The thumb is the tomahawked pilgrim, source of the million redcoats, homunculus, saboteur, kamikazi man, Ku Klux Klansman, trepanned veteran, dirty girl. This is hitting a world at every plunge, and each world at war. The sense of speed is a revelation in itself, as in those minute-long films that present all of American history as a bombardment of still shots flickering past so rapidly that the viewer must take in many pictures almost subliminally. In fact, Plath's cut thumb becomes a kind of brief history of America if you take, as I suspect Plath did, the Ku Klux Klan to be the emblem of the racial turmoil of the late

1950s and early sixties, rather than an historical organization associated with Reconstruction. The horror, of course, is played off against comic rhymes—fizz / this is, Kamikaze man / Ku Klux Klan, saboteur / your, you jump / Thumb stump—and word play—"I step on it" and "Straight from the heart" and "Whose side are they on?" (an appropriate question for Plath, an Anglo-American, neither colonist nor redcoat). The result is a tone of hysteria contained by fragile wit, the voice of the "thin papery feeling" of shock.

"Ariel" is an even better example, a poem almost as "pure" as Dickinson's "Route of Evanescence." It is a poem about riding a horse in which the word "horse" never appears, a poem in which Plath and her horse become one until at the end both are subsumed into the still larger motion that turns the planets, lifts the red eye of morning. Never mind Isaiah or *The Tempest*. What counts here is acceleration, not allusion. The horse (would we know without biographical materials—would the reference to Godiva, the brown arc of the neck, suffice?) is more rhythm than shape and the images by which it moves are less significant in themselves than for the pace at which they are torn through. One measures motion against resistances, those "Nigger-eye / Berries" with their hooks, the child's cry melting into the wall. And this is a poem of peeling resistances away, "Dead hands, dead stringencies," an unwinding like Roethke's in "Infirmity" "until we are pure in spirit at the end." Except that Plath is less pure spirit than pure act, has become the "dew" that is also "do" (these poems are written to be *heard*, remember), suicidal because the "I" has been given over, made one "with the drive / Into the red / Eye, the cauldron of morning" (A, 27). "Life is Motion" is a title of Stevens's, an aphorism picked up by Faulkner, by other moderns. But this motion that Plath celebrates is almost too intense to be sustained, one that breaks down syntax ("Foam to wheat") and takes in multitudes ("a glitter of seas"). It is a rhythm that strains the pulse rate to its limits and beyond, that finally would do away with all resistances and become pure doing at the end.

3

Tone in Sylvia Plath, like the snows of the Tyrol, the beer of Vienna, is "not very pure or true." In fact, it is that very impurity of tone that makes the late poems so unforgettable. The experience of reading the best of them—"The Applicant," "Lady Lazarus," "Cut," "Death & Co.," "Lesbos," "A Birthday Present," "Daddy," "Kindness"—is exhausting, a round-trip train ride between stations so hideous that it is almost a relief to find that one can never disembark at either of them.

Alvarez has made some shrewd observations about the tone of "Daddy," surely the most anthologized of all Plath's poems:

> the tone of the poem, like its psychological mechanisms, is not single or simple, and she uses a great deal of skill to keep it complex. Basically, her trick is to tell this horror story in verse form as insistently jaunty and ritualistic as a nursery rhyme.... When she first read me the poem a few days after she wrote it, she called it a piece of 'light verse.' It obviously isn't, yet equally obviously it also isn't the racking personal confession that a mere description or precis of it might make it sound.[9]

But isn't it just as obviously both? What but "light verse" is one to call a poem that rhymes "Achoo" with "kill you," "the rack and the screw" with "I'm finally through?" For that matter, how seriously can one take a piece that puns so outrageously on "rack and screw" or the "stake" that the daughter has in the father's fat heart, or the black telephone of the yew tree that's "off at the root" so the voices "just can't worm through"? Even the blasphemy of seeing the father as "a bag full of God, / Ghastly statue with one grey toe / Big as a Frisco seal" is a piece of comic irreverence, one that fits well with the colloquial, slang-ridden speech patterns, the casual phrasing: "a bit of a Jew," "if you want to know," "your gobbledygoo," "So daddy, I'm finally through." Surely the smarmy sweetness of "Daddy" as title, the wonderful campy ending borrowed from a thousand late, late shows, the glued together child (who had come unglued) are jokes played off against that inescapable precis, that "mere" description of Plath's "awful little allegory" that is always what it is—the story of a girl, a woman really, who loves and hates her father in ways so naked as to embarrass the listener. Alvarez calls it "manic defense," this "insistent gaiety to protect you from what, if faced nakedly, would be insufferable."[10] I think of it also as the product of the graduate seminar, a slick, knowing Freudianism capable of daubing witty sophistication over any personal anguish, no matter how deep. It is a tone willing to flirt with tastelessness shamelessly, not caring much about the outcome.

Because finally isn't the light verse more distasteful than the confession? What has the holocaust to do with light verse? On the one hand, if the piece is "light verse," Hitler and Auschwitz and *Mein Kampf* and the rest are being used as comic hyperbole, part of the overstated case that goes together with the superior self-consciousness of a swell Electra complex and the sophisticated, patronizing enjoyment of horror movies. That seems to me dreadful in ways Plath may not have anticipated, a joke so tasteless as to be unforgivable, though something in the hairiest underbelly of the psyche is fascinated. On the other hand, if the poem is confessional, then the Nazi-Jew imagery becomes a metaphor for Plath's deepest emotional life, her way of talking about her love of domination and her hatred of those who dominated her. This is more tolerable, though racking and personal in the extreme. But this reading risks another kind of tastelessness. Finally Plath is only the tiniest bit of a Jew and one feels that she claims too much for her suffering. Otto Plath and Ted Hughes are not Himmler and Hitler; her life is not a train ride to a concentration camp. One hears the sound of madness in this confession, the same self-pitying overreaction that one finds in the letters home about her chemistry difficulties or in the suicide attempt triggered by a rejection from a summer writing program. Thus the poem travels from overstatement to overstatement and back. Life is funny, but to celebrate its atrocities with such jaunty wit reminds us of how terrible such wit really is, of what our gaiety says about us, and of what it masks. And life is horrible, though as Plath tries to create a metaphor for her suffering the result is such hyperbolic self-pity that there is something grimly humorous in the straining, some sense in which the joke is on us all for taking our troubles (and hers) so seriously. This is less the poetry of extremity than of extremities. The pendulum swing between comic hatred and tragic (self-) love enables the poem to build momentum, to swing farther in either direction than it might otherwise go, to feel in the going the building of forces that will carry it back, to feel a bit safer at the edge knowing that the way out is the way back.

Tone in Plath is hard on the readers. Alert as a dog or a saint, we move uneasy among puns as among land-mines. And this is in circumstances —especially in circumstances—that critics have labeled "extreme." In "Lady Lazarus," for example, there is the play on "Comeback," on the "very large charge" for touching the heroine, the "strip tease" itself, the final ambiguity of eating men like air. We have the uneasy feeling that the joke must be on *some*one, but whom? Is she mocking us? herself? her emotional overreactions? life? death? the peanut crunching crowd of her inferiors? and does that crowd include us? In some ways Sylvia Plath seems to be a snob and no denying it. How she despises us for our morbid prying and how she panders to it at the same time. Like all strippers, she is bound to her audience by links of mutual contempt as well as mutual need. A nice girl like Sylvia Plath strips because we watch; we watch because she strips.

I think of Frost's "Neither Out Far Nor In Deep," how underlying the bitterness of the closing lines is a kind of tenderness, grudging admiration for those who keep watch despite their narrow human limits. Plath is bitter, no mistaking that, and we are the enemy. But without us there is no "charge" "For a word or a touch / Or a bit of blood // Or a piece of my hair or my clothes" ("Lady Lazarus"). And if there is no charge, how will she make expenses and what will she use for energy? Either way, her hatred is ambiguous; she needs us. At the end when she rises to eat men as fire eats air (or is it that the men she eats are of airy thinness?) the act is both her revenge for the holocaust we have created and everyman's fantasy climax for the apocalyptic strip tease that ends all teasing.

Poems like "Lady Lazarus" and "The Applicant" are parodies of modern advertising techniques—language that mocks itself while mocking the consumer and the product. At the same time, they are poems advertising themselves, the cleverness with which they exploit their models, and the sensitivity of vision needed to recognize the peanut crunching crowd, the empty-headed bride, and the chauvinistic applicant, for the abominations they are. And such poems presumably require a more intelligent audience, one capable of cracking tougher nuts than peanuts. "No reader of the poem," says A. E. Dyson, "can respond to suffering like the crowd depicted *in* the poem."[11] I am less sanguine about crowds, especially those of which I find myself part. While it is true that no reader of Plath is likely to be so obtuse as to miss the irony in her voice, isn't it also true that most of us are, as readers of this sort of "confessional" poetry with its obsessive subject matter and nakedness of feeling, "shoving in to see" what she will reveal next? It seems to me part of the movement of the poem that we should be watching the crowd so contemptuously, a crowd ourselves, the scent of peanuts wafted by our breaths.

Of all Plath's devices for rendering the dynamic shape of the psyche, tonal ambiguity seems to me the most effective. Plath sets the narrative self, subject, and reader like a triangle of mirrors, each reflecting each in such a way that a change in attitude toward any of them is a change in each of the others and in the whole. The result is a field of flowing energy, an oscillation back and forth among "meanings" that never fully emerge because the onlooker is forever changing what there is to see by his efforts to see it more clearly. If we "crowd in," after all, we play into the hands of one aspect of Plath's narrative self: we make ourselves in part the subject of the poem we read. Small wonder she did not under-estimate our "great concern." It was a necessary part of her poem.

4

Perhaps the most difficult technical problem for the artist who wants to make a poem "that is the shape of the psyche itself" is that of structuring such a thing. After all, if the experience for which the poem is a metaphor is a pure flowing, a "surplus of energy," the poem must have a structure flexible enough to contain that energy and firm enough so that the force is not dissipated by running off in many directions. Perhaps the most common structural device for a twentieth-century writer has been what Eliot called "the mythic method," and indeed many critics have spoken of Plath's use of myth, the "force of her myth" or her "unified mythic vision," as Kroll puts it.[12] Writing of Roethke, I once said some things

I believe almost true for Plath as well:

> The advantage of a "mythic structure" is that, in a sense, it is no structure at all. A myth is itself pure action, the motion of a hero through time and space, usually toward more abundant life. What counts is not the sequence of particular events falling into a chronological order, but the urge, wrestle, and resurrection, the thrust toward the light, which drives the hero onward. The power of the myth is not a matter of plot, but of tropism, not a function of structure, but of energy and direction. The "structure" of the myth, like the "structure" of the atom, is a kind of artificial construct, a graspable metaphor created to stand for the unstructured flowing that is life itself.[13]

Kroll's version of Plath's myth, surely the most extensive, is a variation of the archetypal patterns of death and rebirth. The heroine has a true self and a false self; the false self is frequently called forth by an eminently powerful male. The false self (and sometimes the male) must die so that the true self can live. "Life lived by the false self is death-in-life," Kroll writes, "while the rebirth of the true self promises life-in-death, expressed in the poetry in images of purgation, purification, and transcendence."[14]

Death and rebirth again. There's no denying the general accuracy of Kroll's description, but somehow it falls short. The pattern of Plath's energies feels more uniquely her own than that, more violent, more sexual, more perversely exciting. "Daddy," after all, is a long way from "Lycidas," or, for that matter, from "The Lost Son." Richard Howard has a casual remark that seems to me to be a provocative way into a better understanding of Plath's "mythic" structure, a remark that may be all the more useful because it is about her tone rather than about her methods of ordering material. "There is no pathos in the accents of these final poems," he writes, "only a certain pride, the pride of an utter and ultimate surrender (like the pride of O, naked and chained in her owl mask, as she asks Sir Stephen for death)."[15]

"Every woman adores a Fascist," she wrote, and in whose flesh does that barb fail to stick? Is the irony directed at fascists? women? the reader naive enough to take the line straight? the sophisticate patronizing enough to hear *nothing* but irony in it? The fact seems to be that Plath did adore a fascist and hated him for it, that after his rack and screw other forms of relationship were of little interest. Shortly before Hughes entered her life, writing of the temporary loss of a young man friend, she told her mother,

> It would be a good thing if someone from this world could overcome his image and win me, but I seriously doubt that, however I seek, I will find someone that strong. And I will settle for nothing less than a great soul; it would be sinful to compromise when I have known this. I feel like the princess on the glass hill; what possible knight could overcome this image? This dynamic holy soul which we share?[16]

Well, Plath was not yet twenty-four years old and we all write silly things to mother. But the point is that she regarded herself as "too strong" for most of the young men around her, and that "strength" became the quality she most admired (or at least most commented upon) in Hughes.[17] He was finally someone strong enough for her, by which she meant too strong: "I can't for a minute think of him as someone 'other' than the male counterpart of myself, always just that many steps ahead of me intellectually and creatively so that I feel very feminine and admiring."[18] Or again, "I could never get to be such a good person without his help. He is educating me daily."[19] One could multiply painful examples.

It is my hypothesis that the energies of Plath's poems flowed along channels gouged by her own sexual myth, that dominance and submission are as important in her poetry as are imagination and reality (summer and winter) in the poetry of Wallace Stevens. In a down-the-rabbit-hole world of infinite plunges, dominance and submission are complementary strategies for survival, ways of exercising power despite intimations of powerlessness. To dominate some one or some thing, however small, is to play "sweet God" as Plath has it in "The Arrival of the Bee Box" (A, 60). It is to forget the larger context in which one has little control. And, on the other hand, to give over to some other all of our powers, all control, is to become pure in one's adoration and thereby take on the special powers of the devotee, the worshipper. "I could never be such a good person. . . ." She needed such power, that transference of energy between victim and victimizer that enables each to become the other, at least in the imagination. For Plath the cycle of dominance and submission was a way of attaining that sense of special election that she always sought, another way of saying she wished to be immortal, free of limits. It was a darker version of her dabbling in spiritualism, ouija boards, and tarot packs — in magic that might enable her to make for herself a high destiny by controlling an otherwise uncontrollable universe.[20]

The paradigmatic poem for all this, too long and not good enough to quote fully, is "In Plaster," one of the *Crossing the Water* pieces. The tone is that of an extended joke, perhaps because the piece would otherwise be too revealing. In it the narrator is in a plaster cast that she imagines to be "certainly the superior one" because the white "person" needs no food, has no faults. She is "unbreakable," in contrast to the narrator, and binds the narrator closely. When the poet realizes that the cast wants to be loved, that without the human being inside the cast would not exist, the poet "patronized her a little." "You could tell almost at once," she says, "she had a slave mentality." The plaster form is allowed to "wait on" the narrator and, the narrator gloats, "she [the cast] adored it." Then the tables turn again. The cast grows apart from the body, seems "offish." Now the narrator begins to worry, realizes that the plaster has been "resentful" and had been hoping the narrator would die. Like all masters, the narrator feels guilt. Besides,

> I wasn't in any position to get rid of her.
> She'd supported me for so long I was quite limp—
> I had even forgotten how to walk or sit,
> So I was careful not to upset her in any way
> Or brag ahead of time how I'd avenge myself.

In the end it is the human being who is resentful, plotting revenge. "I'm collecting my strength; one day I shall manage without her, / And she'll perish with emptiness then."

In poem after poem we see this pattern, or a part of it. Love is Plath's season, but it becomes adoration, then submission, absolute helplessness. There is a certain fatal attractiveness in this process, and the one who holds her captive is sometimes a male, sometimes her father, sometimes nature, disease, or death itself. Probably no other poet relies so heavily on images of bondage. Plath is gagged by wind, by mist ("Finisterre" and "Parliament Hill Fields"); racked and screwed; more than once wrapped like a mummy; has her tongue stuck in a barbed wire snare; is buttoned in, made one with the bee people by a black veil that moulds to her face; is "roped in" by Death; identifies imaginatively with Gulliver ("The spidermen have caught you, / Winding and twining their petty fetters") and with the paralytic ("The still waters / Wrap my lips, / Eyes, nose and ears, / A clear / Cellophane I cannot crack"). And beyond bondage there is the being laid out, artistically arranged, the "perfected woman" like the sweet babies in their hospital icebox. "I do not stir," she says in "Death & Co.," and it is not clear whether the tone of that observation is one of pride or horror.

This is the point at which a poem like "Lady Lazarus" begins. Bound hand and foot, the Jew as victim, she has suffered so intensely at the hands of the enemy—the audience, the nazi, God, the devil, men most specifically—that she has devised and justified revenge so terrible as to be all but unspeakable. It is as if she has drained the controlling force from her oppressor and turned it on him. This is the turning point of the myth. Submission turns to resentment, to rage, to hate (we began, remember, with love). The energies gather in confinement, as if bondage were a necessary stage for the release of emotions of such intensity as those of "Lady Lazarus" or "The Applicant" or "Daddy." And when the energies break out, the tables are turned. The slave becomes the master, a master more cruel than the original because all revenge is appropriate after the humiliations and torments suffered.

And this is the point at which the bee-keeping poems have their place.

In them, Plath is the master, the dominant figure playing "sweet God" to the tiny "Roman mob" of the bees. She tries to deny her "ambition": "I am not a Caesar. / I have simply ordered a box of maniacs. They can be sent back. / They can die, I need feed them nothing, I am the owner" (A, 59). Nonetheless, she is afraid. "It is they who own me. / Neither cruel nor indifferent, / Only ignorant" (A, 67). In a sense, they have reversed the roles. Now it is she who is the vampire in the castle, facing the villagers who—terrified and tormented too long—are coming at last with pitchforks and torches, more terrible in their desire for revenge than the monsters and scientists they hunt. Small wonder that at other moments she identifies herself with the queen bee, leader of the swarm of tiny slaves, mindlessly of one mind, who are not kindly disposed toward their keeper and who, incidentally, "have got rid of the men, / The blunt, clumsy stumblers, the boors" (A, 68). Dominance, mastery, is destroyed by its own guilt, pity, sympathy, by the exhaustion of its creative rage, an almost sexual release of a passion that cannot be long sustained. And the slave mentality is worn away by resentment, a demand for revenge, a surfeit of humiliation and pain, the sense that one's suffering has absolved one of whatever sins might once have made punishment appropriate. And so it goes on, like the circular pursuits on Peter Pan's island "so long as children are gay and innocent and heartless." Except that on Plath's island things escalate, each nazi becoming more cruel than his predecessor because he is gaining revenge for his suffering during his turn as a Jew. Thus, "Daddy" begins with the father as God, turns him by metaphor into the devil and the nazi, but ends with him as buffoon and victim, tormented even beyond death by villagers who never liked him. If Plath herself is "a bit of a Jew," she is also the nazi's proper daughter, his love child for whom even the bones would do; and she is his wife through marriage to his surrogate, his model. Is it nazi or Jew who kills two men, who drives the stake in the fat black heart, who dances at last on the grave of a son of a bitch? Finally it is both and neither. The longing of each for the other validates the other and the whole as, in Stevens, winter devises summer in its bosom. This is the shape of Plath's darker myth, a circular flow of energies from dominance to submission and back, less a matter of rebirth than of escape and mastery and bondage and escape again.

Perhaps the act of writing poetry might be seen as an act of freeing the self, of affirming that one is not gagged or bound. Looked at in that way, Sylvia Plath's poems become the poetry of an escape artist, the only strategy she had for releasing the energy of her psyche from the mortal wrapping against which she had struggled until the end.

Notes

1. Robert Lowell, Foreword to *Ariel: Poems by Sylvia Plath* (New York: Harper and Row, 1966), p. ix. References to Plath's poems from this edition have been given parenthetically and signified by the letter "A." Poems from *Crossing the Water* (New York: Harper and Row, 1971) have been abbreviated "CW."
2. Sylvia Plath, *Letters Home: Correspondence, 1950-1963*, selected and edited with commentary by Aurelia Schober Plath (New York: Bantam, 1977), p. 476 (paperback).
3. Theodore Roethke, *Straw for the Fire: From the Notebooks of Theodore Roethke, 1943-63*, selected and arranged by David Wagoner (Garden City, N.Y.: Doubleday, 1972), p. 178.
4. From the Theodore Roethke Collection at the University of Washington's Suzzallo Library, box 28, folder 11. I am grateful to Beatrice Roethke Lushington for permission to use this material.
5. Stanley Kunitz, "Roethke: Poet of Transformations," *New Republic* 141 (23 January 1965): 24.
6. Roethke Collection, box 65, folder 2. I give the complete list of devices on page 159 of *Theodore Roethke's Dynamic Vision* (Bloomington: Indiana University Press, 1974).
7. M. L. Rosenthal, "Sylvia Plath and Confessional Poetry," in *The Art of Sylvia Plath: A Symposium*, ed. Charles Newman (Bloomington: Indiana University Press, 1970).
8. Judith Kroll argues that "Perhaps the speaker will also take a more permanent form and 'make' something new, achieving the finality and perfection of a work of art, her death the magical third in the series of transformations." *Chapters in a Mythology: The Poetry of Sylvia Plath* (New York: Harper and Row, 1976), p. 143.
9. A. Alvarez, "Sylvia Plath," in Newman, ed., *The Art of Sylvia Plath*, p. 66.
10. Ibid.
11. A. E. Dyson, "On Sylvia Plath," in Newman, ed., *The Art of Sylvia Plath*, p. 210.
12. Kroll, *Chapters in a Mythology*, p. 4. The entire book develops this theme quite compellingly.
13. Richard Allen Blessing, *Theodore Roethke's Dynamic Vision*, pp. 87-89.
14. Kroll, *Chapters in a Mythology*, p. 13.
15. Richard Howard, "Sylvia Plath: 'And I Have No Face, I Have Wanted to Efface Myself . . . ,'" in Newman, ed., *The Art of Sylvia Plath*, p. 87.
16. Sylvia Plath, *Letters Home*, pp. 249-50.
17. Ibid., p. 263. "I have met the strongest man in the world."
18. Ibid., p. 307-8.
19. Ibid., p. 303.
20. See Ernest Becker's *The Denial of Death* (New York: Free Press, 1973), especially "The Naturalness of Sado-Masochism," pp. 244-48. The entire book seems to me useful for an understanding of Sylvia Plath.

J. D. O'Hara

Plath's comedy

Discussions of general and abstract ideas, such as comedy, can stay afloat only so long as they too remain general and abstract; when they sink to examples and specific instances they soon founder. The squirming facts exceed the squamous definition, if one may say so. To speak of Plath's comedy, then, is to introduce an awkwardly rocky specific into the calm sea of comedy. Or, to notice yet another snag, one does not wish to commit synecdoche: Plath's comedy is by no means contiguous with comedy as a misty whole. Let us nevertheless begin with some remarks about comedy that do not pretend to define that subject but that may help us to think about Plath's particular kinds of comedy. These are assertions, not facts, and they may permissibly be rickety if only they will allow us to ascend to our subject.

Comedy is not necessarily funny, witty, humorous, enjoyable, or laugh-provoking. Murphy's favorite joke—"Why did the barmaid champagne? . . .Because the stout porter bitter"—is unlikely to amuse anyone else so much.[1] Indeed, as we may see, bad jokes may make the best kind of comedy; but not because they are enjoyable.

Comedy is sometimes a matter of character: because of their mannerisms, their philosophical or psychological cast of mind, or some other oddity, some characters impose upon almost anything serious that they say or do a sense of impropriety or imbalance that may suggest comedy. Perhaps this is why the topic of the clown who wishes to play Hamlet remains perennially amusing.

Comedy may sometimes be profitably opposed to tragedy, of the Greek sort, in that tragedy suggests inevitable trains of cause and effect in life and morals, while comedy deals often in the unexpected, the inconsequential, and the peripheral. The tragedy of *Hamlet* is made complex, or, if you will, is confused, by its comic elements: not merely the clowns and Osric and Hamlet's own one-liners but the apparently irrelevant or incongruous structural elements—a play within a play; a farcical murder through a tapestry on a false assumption; a hero sent not merely offstage but out of the country in midplay; a plot that climaxes in what seems a flurry of accidental slaughters; and of course the central incongruity between the uncommon hero and his obligatory role. Yet what troubles the spectator at a tragedy may function quite differently elsewhere: Wallace Stevens's title "The Revolutionists Stop for Lemonade" suggests how immediately functional incongruity may be.

The subject of incongruity demands more discussion than this, though. There are many types and effects, some of them far from comic. We might twist Johnson's definition of wit (from "Abraham Cowley," in *Lives of the English Poets*) to serve our purpose here; "a kind of *discordia concors*: a combination of dissimilar images, or discovery of occult resemblances in things apparently unlike.... The most heterogeneous ideas are yoked by violence together." But such incongruity may be used for purposes other than comedy: "in the midst of life we are in death," for instance.

In verse, the effects of incongruity are usually complex. In Robert Lowell's "The Charles River" two lovers lie sleepless in a motel next to highways. Two sentence fragments end the poem: "morning's breathing traffic...its unbroken snore." Here the basic incongruity probably issues from the personification of traffic; but to comprehend that personification the reader must imagine the traffic as not only alive but as paradoxically moving to produce the relevant sounds and simultaneously sleeping and snoring; and then the reader must deal with the strange contrast between the sleepless lovers who wish not to be alive and the living, sleeping traffic. (Plath's "Insomniac" is interestingly similar.) In "These Winds" Lowell addresses this passage to his daughter: "Since you first began to bawl and crawl / from the unbreakable lawn to this sheltered room." The attributes "unbreakable" and "sheltered" make little sense in their context until the reader deduces Harriet's age from "bawl and crawl." Then one can infer parental concern: the lawn offers no shelter but the room is full of breakables. These examples are quite different in tone, but they are both essentially comic; and they allow us to note that one quality of comedy is that it obliges the reader to think rather busily and therefore to forgo simple emotional responses while resolving apparent incongruities.

Sometimes this resolution of incongruities is not attainable, or only partially so. When Donne compares the parting of two lovers to various uses of a drawing compass and also to gold beaten to airy thinness, the reader understands easily enough the application of each image to the central situation, but the appropriateness of the compass to that situation remains questionable (though it may suggest navigation, charts, the measurement of distances, etc.). The gold leaf is still more incongruous, both with the parting lovers and with the compass. In order to lessen the incongruities, we are probably obliged to sketch some conception of the poem's speaker—to imagine a mind so unusually wired that it might think these thoughts and find these expressions for them.

A generalization may be hazarded about poems that deal to a large extent with incongruities of this sort: the materials are far from being inevitable; the relationships are questionable; the unusualness of the expression may imply an individualized and untypical speaker; and by the difficulties and limitations of understanding, the reader is prevented from saying "how true" and drawing general conclusions from the poem. Indeed, the use of incongruities seems always to retard or render impossible the expression of general truths: Lowell suggests no general truths about lovers, lawns, or life in the passages above, and Donne's reader, however anxious to hear that absence makes the heart grow fonder, will surely be kept by the disparities among lovers, compasses, and gold leaf from finding any reliable and comforting evidence in that poem's imagistic arguments. Indeed, the assertion of connections between incongruous things may be a device precisely for weakening the imaged truth. Polonius, for instance, giving his apparently fine advice to Laertes, assures him that "it must follow, as the night the day, / Thou canst not then be false to any man." But day does not *cause* night; we sense the false analogy. What is more, we know that while day is honorific, night is pejorative; if night is the consequence of this advice, then it might not be good advice. And sure enough . . .

Comedy, then, has among its qualities an emphasis on the unexpected and incongruous, a willingness not to amuse, a tendency to develop out of individualized characters, an insistence on the reader's thought rather than his emotion, and an unwillingness to state general truths. With this handful of assertions let us turn to Sylvia Plath.

Two of Plath's most likeable minor poems, "You're" and "Cut" (both from *Ariel*), reveal immediately how like Donne she can be. Like Donne's

"Valediction" (and like Stevens's "Sea Surface Full of Clouds," "Thirteen Ways of Looking at a Blackbird," and "Someone Puts a Pineapple Together") these consist mainly of images threaded on the simplest of grammatical strings. "Cut" follows a chronological sequence from the cutting almost off of the top of the thumb to its bandaged ageing. "You're" ignores even that structure: there are only the vaguest of suggestions in the sequence of the images to imply that they follow the course of fetal development, and in fact the suggestive nine-line stanza is repeated, which naturally vitiates any "symbolic" significance. (Compare the earlier "Metaphors.")

In neither poem do the images establish among themselves any coherence. In "Cut," there is a game-playing sequence from pilgrim to Indian to turkey to Redcoats, but that is undermined by the pun that mixes "turkey wattle" with "turkey carpet," and of course the other images of the poem are irrelevant to this sequence. In "You're," one can sometimes justify the fancy's progress—"Bent-backed Atlas" intelligibly generates "prawn," and the prawn may suggest "sprat" and "eels," with "Gilled like a fish" as their remote ancestor—but it would be as absurd as impossible to attempt to link all the images. In both poems they are connected neither to each other nor to the poem's structure; their link is only to the poem's theme or topic. But they are generated so exuberantly and randomly that we cannot consider either poem to be a complete statement of truth about its theme—if indeed the idea of truth or completion can even be relevant to metaphorical statements.

But there is at least one sense in which we can understand these poems as complete and as justifiable image by image and tone by tone. We must emphasize their very obvious subjective element, signaled to us by the irrationality and incongruity of the images and by such heretofore unmentioned matters as the colloquial diction and the direct address of the grammatical structures. These poems are whole and structured when imagined as *speeches*, soliloquies, if you will, or monologs. It was after all misleading to say that one poem is about a cut thumb, the other about an unborn baby, since neither poem achieved direct statements on those subjects. They are rather about someone's ideas as occasioned by a cut thumb and a pregnancy. (*Ideas* in the root sense.) Or, even further, each poem creates a someone who on this subject has these ideas. And in each case the speaker is comic in her energetic unpredictability of image and of response to the topic.

This emphasis—through comic incongruities of thought, feeling, and image—on the speaker of the poem, by way of the poem as speech, may be clarified if we move for a moment to a more serious poem. Consider "Daddy": again, a poem composed largely of imagery, though there are other elements that emphasize speech and narrative. But no sensible reader attempts to discover by reading the poem closely what the speaker's father was really like or what he really did to the speaker, nor does anyone read the last lines with some sense that an objective discussion is reaching its conclusion. The poem's rhetoric is its primary quality, and we respond primarily to its creation of a persona in an excited psychological state. This response requires no discovery of structural, symbolic, or thematic connections among fascists, vampires, statues, and black shoes (the images related to the father). Rather, we intuit a consciousness that might use these disparate images, and the others of the poem, to construct a diatribe against a daddy—with all of that term's incongruous connotations of childhood and affectionate dependence.

We will return to "Daddy." But now let us test these heaped-up assertions about the significance of the speaker against a poem that may scatter them: "Berck-Plage." The setting is put together from a beach, a hospital or sanitarium near it, and the countryside behind it, including a graveyard. (Here as throughout the essay, biography is eschewed when possible.) The poem therefore possesses an external occasion, as it were, that is lacking in "Daddy," and setting this scene requires the voice of the poem to do more than soliloquize. In fact the poem tells a story: after parts one and two have described the ominous approach of a black-garbed priest walking down the beach ("Here he comes now"), part three turns to "the hotel," with its "tubular steel wheelchairs, aluminium crutches," nurses, and an old man dying as his wife weeps. In part four the man has died and is prepared for and placed in the coffin; in part five he is laid out in "the stone house," from which there is a view of the countryside; in part six the coffin reaches the cemetery; and in part seven the speaker, "a member of the party," arrives behind the coffin-carrying cart and watches the burial. Surely these scenic and narrative elements overwhelm the creation of any rhetorical persona; surely the function of metaphor and attribute here is primarily the evocation of these scenes and events, or perhaps even the creation of the old man and his wife.

But in fact the status of this "hotel," as it is perceived, is never clarified; we learn nothing individualizing about the old man and almost nothing about his wife; we cannot even tell whether the priest of parts one and two is the same as the priest of parts six and seven; and in short the narrator might better be termed the obscurer or distorter of the scenes and events of the poem. Indeed, he or she suggests this potentiality for distortion from the very beginning: "How the sun's poultice draws on my inflammation," the second line exclaims.

The first two sections of the poem describe a beach scene. To the extent that it can be reconstructed objectively, this scene is cheerful enough: people eating sherbet, distant voices on a long beach, fishermen with a catch of mackerel, women in bikinis up in the dunes, two lovers embracing, and a priest walking and reading a book. But the persona turns everything into nightmare: "Obscene bikinis hide in the dunes," the lovers "unstick themselves," and a weed is "hairy as privates"; the priest "affects a black cassock," his "black boot" is "the hearse of a dead foot," and he causes the fishermen to "wall up their backs against him," the lovers to unstick themselves, and the bikinis to hide. Obviously the priest is bad, and yet the speaker sympathizes with him at least in part, agreeing that the scene is so painful that one is right to shield oneself from it ("Is it any wonder he puts on dark glasses?"), stigmatizing the bikinis as "obscene," and describing the fishermen as handling their nets "like the parts of a body" near the "many-snaked" and hissing sea.

At the end, in the cemetery, the speaker's perceptions are still askew. The widow's earlier practical thoughts by the coffin, "Full of dresses and hats and china and married daughters," now lead the speaker to see her lined face as a domestic article ("The widow . . . Enfolds her face like fine linen, / Not to be spread again"), and the funeral flowers lead the speaker to turn the burial into a comic wedding of the dead man's soul with a "red and forgetful" groom. Meanwhile the children who on the beach were "after something, with hooks and cries," now stare silently at the unintelligible ceremony, and an earlier aspect of the beach—

> Obscene bikinis . . .
>
> Breasts and hips a confectioner's sugar
> Of little crystals, titillating the light,
>
> While a green pool opens its eye,
> Sick with what it has swallowed—
>
> Limbs, images, shrieks

—reappears grotesquely here as "the coffin on its flowery cart like a beautiful woman, / A crest of breasts, eyelids and lips / Storming the hilltop," to land not in a swallowing pool-eye but in the gaping grave. Even more grotesque, however, is the image resulting from the speaker's description of the sky over the cemetery as an animal infected with worms, excreting: "a sky, wormy with put-by smiles, / Passes cloud after cloud." Obviously we have come a long way from the metaphysical poem, where the images, however startling (lovers like compasses and gold leaf?), justify themselves to the amused reason, which recognizes their unexpected accuracy and the speaker's wit. Few readers, one hopes, will recognize in the persona's description of the bathers and the clouds any objective accuracy; none, one hopes, will consider the poem as expressing any objective truth.

This might be said more generally: as an objective description of a death and its consequences the poem is uninteresting; it tells us nothing new about these subjects, it shapes its narrative in no clear fashion (the most striking images have no necessary connection with the events and characters), and it reaches no conclusion except that of narrative chronology. But surely the poem has quite other fish to fry, and it is as a dramatic monolog in the Browning tradition—all the way back to "Madhouse Cells"—that we should read it. (Those poems, too, are likely to cause uneasy laughter when read aloud.) The scenes and events of the poem then become intelligible as plastic materials for the poet to shape or misshape in such a way as to evoke most startlingly the persona of the narrator. Not that any other scenes and stories would have served equally well: the topics of religion, death, and physicality seem central to the narrator's concerns, and these events are particularly evocative of them. But we are not informed directly about seaside vacation life, death in old age, and funerals. Indeed, it would be more persuasive to suggest that the poet relies on our own previous knowledge of such things, playing off the narrator's abnormal sensibility against our own normality. (Robert Lowell has less confidence in his readers, often, and signals more specifically the presence of an abnormal sensibility: "My mind's not right," says the narrator of "Skunk Hour.")

What is one to say about this narrator, this abnormal sensibility? Obviously the question is not irrelevant or even tangential; to read the poem with the desire of turning incongruities into understanding involves attempting to understand the sensibility here presented, not merely recognizing that the narrator's imagination distorts this and that but evaluating and connecting the various details as they testify to the sensibility that generates them. What kind of person perceives on a summer beach these flamboyantly sexual bathers, these furtive fishermen out of an Edward Gorey illustration, and this black death of a priest glooming down the beach like an obsessed parch from one of Dylan Thomas's Welsh tales? What kind of person sees the tree-edged beach as a sick man's ribs and nerves, and the flat round sea as the surgeon's "one mirrory eye"? Who imagines the shaking hands of the dying man as busy with farewell handshakes, pauses in middescription to ask "What is the name of that colour?" and imagines a wormy sky shitting clouds? And what kind of poet will report all this without emendation or comment?

Conventional responses involve the assumption of a near identity between the speaker and the poet, after which one takes down the old Freudian or Jungian or eclectic handbook of symptoms and terms. But let us look at the matter from a literary viewpoint. There are kinds of comedy that deal not with shallow, trivial, basically cheering material, but with serious and unsettling subjects—such as mental illness. Comic treatment of such a subject can be as unsettling as the subject itself (consider the songs that Shakespeare has Ophelia sing when mad); in literature, we expect that mentally disturbed people will comport themselves in certain ways and will be presented by an author who implies certain attitudes toward those people. Comedy disturbs these expectations. A persona who is troubled, frightened, insecure, mentally unstable can be understood and pitied by good-hearted readers who see that the persona is unhappy, seeking help, and consciously vulnerable. A persona who is one or more of these things and is still self-assured, perhaps even sufficiently in control to be deliberately amusing about them, throws off the reader's kindly responses. We cannot easily pity people who make us smile or who are capable of the pose and detachment needed to perceive and phrase the comic elements in their own serious predicaments, especially if their comedy is "sick," "black," or otherwise tasteless, unfeeling, and undignified, as is so much of the comedy in "Berck-Plage." (The curtain "flickering from the open window" of the stone house, for instance, becomes decently a "pitiful candle" and then absurdly "the tongue of the dead man" blabbing "remember, remember," and then there is the dead man's "wedding-cake face" and that wormy sky.)

If one quality of this persona's comic self-characterization is a total indifference to ingratiating herself with her audience, another is a lack of decorum. One useful sense of decorum was offered by John Locke, who inaugurated word-association tests by differentiating between those decorous associations that all socialized humans have in common (up/down, cup/saucer) and those undisciplined associations that are improper or idiosyncratic (up/yours, cup/D). Almost any poet will attempt to extend our sense of relevant associations through image and metaphor, but in the monologs of Plath's comic personae the idiosyncratic and improper nature of the associations is characteristically emphasized, while conventional associations are suppressed or minimized; and the results are so thoroughly unconventional or even anticonventional that one can hardly doubt her deliberate intentions. (In her cheerful poems about babies, on the other hand, the verbal texture is thick with idiomatic expressions, folksy phrasing and imagery, and all the signs of conventional attitudes and associations happily expressed and reinforced.)

Most authors are careful to counter the assertions of their improper personae, or at least to dissociate themselves from them. In her later poems, Plath does not. In such comic monologs as "Berck-Plage" she intended (of course this is only an educated guess) to immerse her reader in dramatic situations, sequences of thought, or perceived events, uninterpreted except by the excited and abnormal consciousness reporting them. This consciousness does not attempt to explain to an audience precisely what events are actually taking place; even the poems about handling bees make this evident, as does the poem about riding the horse Ariel. Neither does the voice seek to clarify or even to acknowledge the distinction between what seems to be happening and what really is happening. Yet the poems are not puzzles to be solved: readers are not expected to realize that she is riding a horse and assume that they now understand the poem. Instead, they are primarily dramatic immersions in these excited and abnormal consciousnesses, in which the persona and poet alike are unconcerned with the reader's irritable reaching after fact and reason, and in which the techniques of writing are employed primarily to communicate the experience of being in the intense mind of a comically unconventional character.

The experience of reading these monologs is sometimes taken by readers to be valuable not simply because they are curious or exciting, but because they are revelatory of essential truths about life, the world, the nature of existence, and so on. It would be both pointless and tactless to deny such readers their truth; a truth, however encountered, is still a truth. Yet if our speculations so far have been fairly accurate, the occasions of characteristic Plath poems are not the primary concerns of these poems. Whether the topic is suicide attempts or daddy or death at Berck-Plage or a cut thumb or whatever, the poem does not set out to state truths on the subject, neither general truths about fathers nor specific truths about the persona's father. The poems' central concerns are the personae themselves. But it is precisely the abnormality, idiosyncrasy, or downright wrongness of these personae that the poems display. Therefore, to think of them as revealing general truths is to ignore—rather willfully, in some cases—the care with which Plath implies a norm by distancing a persona from it. (Kafka is often misread in a similar way, despite his similar care.) Nor can we think of Plath as setting out to illustrate typical psychological problems, embodying in them the truths of this or that psychosis.

Of course, all of her personae are not mentally unstable or trapped in extraordinary circumstances. Equally, all disparities are not humorous, and certainly not in the sense of characterizing and individualizing a speaker's mental set. From its beginnings, Plath's poetry specialized in yoking together incongruous materials. "The Manor Garden" offers us "The pears fatten like little buddhas." If the images were reversed, they might have something of the comic surprise of Butler's "Then like a lobster boil'd, the morn / From black to red began to turn"; as it is, the conjunction is merely and isolatedly amusing. The next poem in *Colossus*, "Two Views of a Cadaver Room," juxtaposes a dissecting room and a painting; the painting juxtaposes life and death. But one gets no particular sense of a special viewpoint adding to these materials meaning that they do not have in themselves. When the young Plath tries to characterize an uncommon speaker, she does so by common means. In "The

Eye-Mote," for instance, she creates a persona whose view of the world is now distorted and who imagines herself Oedipus wishing to have back "what I was" before his "blameless" state ended. But the speaker's distortions of reality are not disturbingly humorous or indicative of character; they are just odd—"Horses warped on the altering green, / Outlandish as double-humped camels or unicorns." The later Plath personae will imply the nature of their uncommonness in their perceptions, and they will almost never identify their distortions as "outlandish" or unusual; this is left to us.

The early Plath has difficulty, in fact, imagining comic distortions. The Electra figure of "The Colossus," for instance, who takes the earth to be her father, describes it in such terms as "the weedy acres of your brow," "the bald, white tumuli of your eyes," "your fluted bones"—terms that convey little sense of her uniqueness and certainly no difficult abnormality. In fact the one really strange image in the poem—"The sun rises under the pillar of your tongue"—remains baffling because neither the father nor the daughter has been portrayed as capable of acting out or perceiving this strangeness. Similarly, nothing in "Full Fathom Five" justifies the sudden death wish of its last stanza.

The early Plath is usually linked firmly to the conventional, even when dealing with unusual material, and there is a relevant interest in watching her attempts to disconnect her viewpoint and those of her personae from this convention. "Spinster"—a curious companion poem to Frost's even odder "The Subverted Flower"—comes almost as close as any of the early poems to an acceptance and vivid development of the central figure's odd world; yet there is a bit of hedging. We are told, for instance, not that the petals were in disarray and the season sloven, but that "she judged" them to be so. We are therefore welcome to keep our distance and make our own judgments, and the last line's mention of "love" makes us glad we did; we have not given it up. The one closer early poem is the "Poem for a Birthday." To be sure, the speaker of this seven-part poem admits on occasion to being abnormal—"Once I was ordinary"; "I shall be good as new"—but for the most part we are drawn complexly into the strange and extraordinary worlds that she creates. But there is little humor. Images abound, as usual, and many are strange, certainly; but the voice still shows little interest in the unsettlingly peripheral. "This shed's fusty as a mummy's stomach," for instance; "boneless as noses"; "I am a dartboard for witches"—at these moments one senses not simply that the speaker inhabits a very strange world but that he or she is unsettlingly at home there, able to make casually odd observations about it, somehow domesticated. This is not the way conventional people speak of their suffering; one doubts that Saint Sebastian ever joked about his own role as dartboard.[2]

Readers who admire Plath's poems on more than technical grounds must feel by now that they have been led down a dark alley where things seem to be getting worse. Persuaded that the central subject of Plath's most characteristic poetry is the persona, usually evoked in a dramatic situation, they have submitted to hearing that persona described as abnormal, wrongheaded, and indecorous, and as unable to perceive and report general truths because of this extreme idiosyncrasy, an idiosyncrasy often tacitly posed against those very truths—about love, death, fathers, husbands, and social relationships, for instance—with which the persona cannot come to terms. And all this has been asserted to be comic.

But these personae and all their errors and incapacities need not be abjured; nor need these poems be written off as mere exercises in the grotesque. Only the highminded search for truths, decorum, and moral values need be dismissed for a while. Instead of hoping for them, let us listen to Plath's voices again, irresponsibly, and consider what sources of enjoyment might be found in the attempt, while reading, to keep up with, and to speak in proper voices, those flows of helter-skelter images, excited tones, and rapidly shifting subjects. Let us begin by considering a few poems from *Winter Trees:* "The Detective," "For a Fatherless Son," "Purdah," and "The Tour."

The last of these, in which a "maiden aunt" is conducted through the persona's grimly nightmarish house (a frost box, an exploded furnace, a blue-starch people-eating pool, and a bald and eyeless nurse) is too obvious an instance of Plath's grim comedy to require much comment. The aunt's conventionality is lightly satirized, as is her shock at the way the speaker lives; but the maiden aunt is a stock figure of comedy and Plath does nothing to complicate or individualize her here. Instead, she plays with our own stock responses. Amused at the aunt, we begin reading by siding with the speaker. We too are unconventional, we think; we too could shock this aunt. But the speaker's life turns out not to be adventurous or avant-garde or intellectually precocious or any of the acceptable lives with which one shocks maiden aunts. It turns out, in fact, to be a shocking life, although the speaker's viewpoint and her consequent comic descriptions turn the dreadful facts into cartoon dangers and her painful situation into a parody of the conventional housewife's nightmare: "And I in slippers and housedress with no lipstick! // And you want to be shown about!" Withdrawing from our expected easy identification with the persona, we intuit a cold life and a woman "bitter" and "averse"—the only epithets with which the poem admits conventional value judgments for a moment. But we intuit this without finding any way to understand or pity the speaker. Indeed, we may feel that she dismisses us along with the maiden aunt, to whom finally we are superior only because we have stayed sufficiently detached to be amused at the speaker's heaping up of these absurdities of desolation and fear. Yet at the same time we are the speaker, since reading the poem (as differentiated from reacting to it, studying it, etc.) obliges us to take on her voice, her tones, her situation, and her point of view, so far as we can imagine them. We are, then, simultaneously the shocked and the shocker—a comic situation in itself.

"Purdah" is more complex. The speaker (and again we are she, though very different from her) describes herself as a carved jade ("at this facet the bridegroom arrives") but also as a cross-legged woman who for most of the poem displays herself in various poses and ritual acts. This would seem rather silly and pretentiously stylized, the poem as well as the poses, if the reader were not troubled and involved—tentatively—by the early mentions of the "agonized / Side of a green Adam" from which the jade came (the "agonized" seems too strong for the precious conceit) and the disconcerting moon "with her cancerous pallors" and the trees that become polyps and then nets. When the bridegroom arrives, the still shallow speaker preciously summons the "attendants of the eyelash," her parakeets and macaws, and announces to them that "I shall unloose / One feather, like the peacock," and the reader winces and longs to skim. Her next act is to "unloose / One note," which startlingly and rather absurdly will shatter "The chandelier / Of air"; and then—after the comic suspense of a repeated "I shall unloose"—the poem's tone suddenly deepens, the speaker's identity is revealed, and the jarring clashes of imagery and ideas come to a climax as the speaker unlooses that moony net, "the cloak of holes" wielded by "the lioness" Clytaemnestra and producing Agamemnon's "shriek in the bath." Upon which the reader realizes, among other things, the joke of the title "Purdah": this is not a mere piece of oriental decoration but a reference to those veils of glamorous docility behind which the real persona lies dangerously waiting, the lioness disguised as a bird of paradise. But the reader's realization can only operate retroactively. He has not been asked to comprehend the persona's position sympathetically, to react against it, to participate in any act of judgment. The monolog has simply stopped, leaving the reader to return to that quite different voice with which one usually speaks.

The comedy of "Purdah," which is unlikely to provoke even such brief laughter as "The Tour" might generate, is based as we might expect on the varieties of incongruity and surprise offered us. The obvious disparity between the cliché elegance of the phrases and actions and their murderous conclusion is compounded by others. For instance, the description of jade as "Stone of the side, / The agonized / Side of a green Adam," which fancily describes the jade as taken from the earth (Plath is fond of the etymology that makes *Adam* mean *red clay*), turns out at the end of the poem to have as its primary allusion that in which Eve, Adam's rib, causes him agony of another kind. Similarly, the apparent meaning of

85

"purdah" turns out to veil another kind of concealment. But the ending primarily requires a reenactment of the voice of the poem, hearing and speaking now not simpering clichés but murderous irony; and of course the reader's sense of the speaker has been revised, giving her now the respect that might be given to Lady Macbeth and recognizing in her something of Clytaemnestra's ability to stay cool under stress and to play with her sense of the situation. Yet the poem is not simply a redramatization of Aeschylus; although the personal application cannot and should not be specified, few readers will doubt that the poet is playing with a situation much closer to home.

Plath does the same thing in "For a Fatherless Son," a painful mixture of the cheery Plath baby poem and the grim Plath poem about adult situations. Here again disparities are exploited repeatedly for comic effect as the poem runs its course and creates its uncommon voice. The title and most of the first line are serious, but "an absence, presently," plays an unexpected verbal game. Already our pious and sad earnestness about divorce, father, child, and wife is flouted and our reading voice is obliged to alter. Then, soberly again, that present absence is evoked as a bleak but rather arbitrary landscape of tree and sky, a landscape then turned into a cartoon by the metaphors heaped on it: the tree has been gelded by lightning and is balding (these events, with a bit of feminine wit, are treated as of the same order), while the indifference of the sky is expressed by the ridiculous image of "a sky like a pig's backside." One might think that the mother is trying to amuse the son, but the next stanza makes it clear that he's not listening; he's grabbing at her nose. This act leads the poem to a dual ending: harshly the mother imagines what he would touch if he could reach inside her head ("The small skulls, the smashed blue hills, the godawful hush"), but happily the child smiles at his play, and these smiles are like "found money," as the painful monolog ends with a homely simile in a tone characteristic of Plath's baby poems.

All three poems deal with unusually grim subjects, literally close to home, and yet any potential pity or sentimentally offered empathy is deflected by each speaker's self-sufficiency, a quality suggested primarily by the deliberate use of humor. One can hardly say that they have the situation under control, even in "Purdah," and yet some such impression is produced. Bitter they surely are, but they will not break up their lines to weep. The killing of Agamemnon, as we know, solved nothing for Clytaemnestra; the dismissal of the maiden aunt leaves the persona where she was, in her house of horrors; and in whatever quantity, found money will not improve the small skulls, the smashed blue hills, the godawful hush. These speakers postulate no way out and discover none, yet the speakers are capable of amusing themselves even as they report their situations—or, if one wishes to be conventional, one might say that they are so insensitive and imperceptive that they cannot separate what is central and grim in their situations from what is peripheral to them, an inability especially evident in their prolific and irrelevant metaphors; what has a husbandless mother to do with gum trees and pigs? But, as "The Tour" makes clear, such situations remove one from the conventional world, invalidate the ordinary laws by which ideas are associated, and open up mental, linguistic, and imagistic possibilities that are certainly absurd but are not therefore unthinkable.

As far back as Edmund Burke's eighteenth-century study, *On the Origins of Our Ideas of the Sublime and Beautiful*, a notion was introduced into aesthetics that made dubious any connections between aesthetic effect and moral and veridical propriety (Plato had had his doubts too, of course)—the idea that we are primarily affected by intensity and not particularly interested in the propriety of its source. Keats, echoing Hazlitt, agreed; gusto is what is wanted. This idea has faded out of literary considerations recently, perhaps because there is so little gusto in mid-century poetry, but it deserves to be resuscitated here. Plath shares many of her tones and techniques with Lowell, John Berryman, Ted Hughes, and others, but none of them (not even Berryman) is so consistently and wittily intense as she.

Let us listen to that intensity again, this time displayed rather paradoxically in "The Detective." Despite the title, the reader is not likely to identify the speaking voice as the detective's until well into the poem (he is identified only three lines before the end), and in the context of *Winter Trees* and of Plath's other works, readers almost inevitably recognize early on the theme of the crumbling marriage as presented from the woman's viewpoint. In any case, whether identified as that of a bitter woman or a professionally energetic detective, the voice is quick, busy, intense.

It begins by taking us on a tour of the house, characterizing in the process both itself and two occupants: the woman, who is a simple homemaker—she arranges cups, polishes, and has two children—and the man, who smiles, has evasive eyes, and tamps a wall and a pipe. We learn this as line after line throws out a complication of normal actions and places incongruously coupled with unpleasant images: a valley where lilies and cows thrive is also "the valley of death" where "the train shrieks echo like souls on hooks"; the homely action of tamping a pipe turns into the concealing of a body; and sunlight in a well-kept room becomes a "Bored hoodlum" playing with a knife. Meanwhile the reader is searching for the "it" of the first line ("What was she doing when it blew in"), but though much is ominous, nothing positive is offered: "No one is dead. / There is no body in the house at all." Yet the fifth stanza rattles off a swift list of weapons before the investigation picks up the pun on "no body" and concludes that "it is a case of vaporization," which the speaker then busies himself with detailing. Then, in a comically conventional scene in which the detective sums up the baffling situation for his assistant, the poem plays the game of anticipating the discovery of the murderer (which of course may never be made, at least by the detective):

> There is only the moon, embalmed in phosphorous.
> There is only a crow in a tree. Make notes.

If the reader himself notes these images correctly, he will solve the crime. There is a body after all, as "embalmed" reveals; and—the murderer returned to the scene—there is the criminal, the crow, the central image of so many poems by Ted Hughes.

A fierce accusation in a bitterly personal poem...and yet look not only at the inventive energies already displayed but at the incidental comedy along the way: the first image of the crime, eyes like slugs sliding toward lilies; then the crime as pipe-tamping; then, after the creepy image of the sun as a hoodlum with a knife, the cheerfully witty image of the wireless talking to itself like an elderly relative. And the identity of the speaker, withheld until almost the end, is revealed in a casual remark after the business of turning the vaporized woman into natural images is itself made comic: after itemizing a mouth like brown fruit and breasts like stones, the speaker hurries to sum the whole thing up, like a busy poet:

> Then the dry wood, the gates,
> The brown motherly furrows, the whole estate.

That estate finishes off the dead woman; she has turned to earth. But since she has also been vaporized, there is a complicated joke in the speaker's puzzled remark, "We walk on air, Watson"—a joke complicated still further by the remark's casual revelation that the detective is, absurdly, none other than Sherlock Holmes. And all this is happening to the reader pell-mell as the poem hurries toward its slyly revealing conclusion!

If we ask what has released this untrammeled exuberance of image, allusion, phrasing, and tone—in the poems that have just been examined and in many others—"The Detective" offers a useful metaphoric clue. The crime has already occurred; it is too late to evade or to seek help; the situation is beyond relief. These voices so self-possessed amid chaos; that poet heaping up indecorous disparities, sillinesses, games, tasteless images, irrelevant tones; those poems so energetic in their speeches about despair, death, loss, and madness—it is precisely the despair that enlivens them.

To be sure, speakers in poetry may be intense in other ways—pleading with a God to spare them or to reverse fate, begging someone to love them, denouncing someone and calling for vengeance, but under such circumstances, when there is still hope or fear, no rational person would risk a joke or any other lapse of taste: Kafka's pitiful petitioners make that quite clear; if they are comic, it is quite inadvertent.

Not that the poet is obliged to share the sense of hopelessness with the persona. Let us consider briefly the character of Hamlet. Witty himself, he is also the cause of wit in another—Shakespeare himself. On hearing of his father's murder, what does Hamlet do? He whips out his notebook, crosses out "all saws of books, all forms...that youth and observation copied there," and replaces them with another youthful observation—that one may smile and smile and be a villain (adding the cautious limitation, at least in Denmark). This is sadly unheroic behavior—he might better have reached for his sword—and it was anticipated a few minutes earlier. When the ghost began to reveal its shocking news, Hamlet interrupted to accept heroically the part for which the ghost had just cast him:

> Haste me to know't, that I, with wings as swift
> As meditation or the thoughts of love,
> May sweep to my revenge.

Now either this is bad poetry—a tedious and irrelevant comparison (neither meditation nor thoughts of love are swift) when we are anxious to hear the news—or it is good art, and of course it is good art. Hamlet has known little of life but rhetoric, meditation, and thoughts of love; to what else could he refer? Ironically, his malapropos images reveal his unfitness for the revenger's role. Ironically and comically: when to his speech the ghost replies, "I find thee apt," that response seems as comically inappropriate as when at the end of the play Horatio hears Hamlet's last words, "the rest is silence," misunderstands *rest*, cannot believe *silence*, and responds: "flights of angels sing thee to thy rest."

These moments are indecorous, and they are so because they shatter precisely the decorum of the genre into which they are introduced and the mood created by the events depicted. Yet their result is not the inadvertent comedy of incompetent writing ("O Sophonisba! Sophonisba, O!") but a heightened intensity to which the reader or spectator must respond by holding simultaneous and disparate ideas and images in his mind. Plath is not Shakespeare, but they share at times this bleak and comic vision. Sometimes they share it with their characters, as Plath does in the poems just discussed; sometimes they impose it upon their characters, as we have just seen Shakespeare do in making Hamlet earnestly reveal his unfitness. (The last instance is much more complex than a simple undercutting of Horatio, of course.) To see Plath behaving in a similar way, let us return to the very popular poem "Daddy." Perhaps the most frequently anthologized of Plath's poems and therefore the most frequently discussed and annotated, this poem has caused a considerable amount of trouble for its analysts.

The five-line pseudostanzas are written in the long, run-on sentences, full of colloquial and slang elements, that justify Ted Hughes's description of her poetic language as "direct, and even plain, speech."[3] Here this plainness is intensified by elements that are familiar to us. There is much insistent, blatant, and unilluminating rhyme, overemphasizing the sound *oo*, and sometimes obviously forced: "Achoo," "gobbledygoo," "They always *knew* it was you." The emotionality of the poem is also conveyed through insistent name-calling (but the names are sometimes unevocative or merely absurd: "black shoe," "a bag full of God," "one grey toe / Big as a Frisco seal," "The black telephone's off at the root")[4] and equally insistent repetition (but often of raucous sounds or rather obvious ideas: "Ich, ich, ich, ich," "the brute / Brute heart of a brute like you," "get back, back, back to you").

The speaker characterizes herself as a victim, in opposition to her bullying father, but here too there are weakening elements: she lived absurdly in her father the shoe like a foot afraid to breathe or achoo ("There was an old woman who lived in a shoe"); she asserts in odd terms that he "bit my pretty red heart in two"; she describes her marriage in a pop-song phrase, "I said I do, I do"; and in climactically announcing that her vampire father now has a stake through his heart and that the villagers "are dancing and stamping on you," she adds an absurdly childish attempt to hurt him: "The villagers never liked you." Such elements are familiar, not because we have necessarily seen any one phrase or image before, but because they compose a characteristic comic monolog of the sort that we have been considering and because in life such tones and such verbal music have been heard in childish tantrums. In the poem, these elements evoke comically a hopeless and painful situation as experienced by a speaker indifferent to our pity who exposes her feelings without any attempt at maturity or disguise, her speech that of someone "in slippers and housedress with no lipstick."

Serious readers will object that the serious elements of the poem have been suppressed, thereby distorting its sense badly. They will point to at least three subjects that give weight and significance to what has been disparaged, apparently, as a comic monolog: the painful relationship of father and daughter; the suicide attempts; and the allusions to Nazi soldiers, concentration camps, Hitler, and the mistreatment of Jews. The first two topics must be held in abeyance until the third has been considered, since similar topics in other Plath poems have been used as motifs of comic monologs.

It would be stupid to deny the seriousness of the third subject. If, in addition, we admit biography and recognize that Plath spoke of her concerns about politics, torture, and mass inhumanity in several interviews, then one is easily persuaded to take the high moral line and to follow the lead given by Plath herself: " . . .my concern with concentration camps and so on is particularly intense. And then, again, I'm rather a political person as well, so I suppose that's part of what it comes from."[5]

If we take these facts as relevant, we must reach such a conclusion as that offered by the Plath scholar Eileen Aird, who links "Daddy" with "Lady Lazarus" (quite appropriately), points out that "in 'Lady Lazarus' the poet again equates her sufferings with the experiences of the tortured Jews," and concludes that "if we categorize a poem such as 'Lady Lazarus' as 'confessional' or 'extremist' then we highlight only one of its elements. It is also a poem of social criticism with a strong didactic intent."[6] Unfortunately, if we attempt to take "Daddy" seriously and to find in it any valuable didactic social criticism, we must conclude that Plath is sadly incompetent and not much of a "political person." But can we believe that she thought of fascist tyranny in terms of such clichés as the Luftwaffe, the Panzer divisions, *Mein Kampf*, and Hitler's "neat moustache" and "Aryan eye, bright blue"? (An incongruous list, surely.) That she imagined the persecutions of the Jews as similar to parental abandonment of a daughter, and that "every woman adores a Fascist, / The boot in the face"? And that the "obscene" German language was causally connected to the concentration camps? Surely not; nor did she think that Tyrolese snow and Viennese beer were impure and untrue. What is more, the images of torture and tyranny and violence hardly constitute social criticism; social critics do not waste their time pointing out such blatant evils, nor do they immerse their criticism in overwhelming personal contexts. In short, "Daddy" (and "Lady Lazarus") can be seriously taken as social criticism only if Sylvia Plath is not taken seriously.[7]

But suppose we try to justify the inclusion of these elements in another way. Let us go back to Aird's comment and quote it at greater length: "In 'Lady Lazarus' the poet again equates her suffering with the experiences of the tortured Jews, she becomes, as a result of the suicide she inflicts on herself, a Jew." This time let us imagine that we are to take this deeply serious topic, the torturing of the Jews, and understand it as clarifying the suffering of the daughter at the hands of the father. Again we encounter difficulties. At the present time Jews are still debating the old question, what constitutes Jewishness; but no faction speaks in favor of this simpleminded definition:

With my gypsy ancestress and my weird luck
And my Taroc pack and my Taroc pack
I may be a bit of a Jew.

Anyone who seriously claims Jewishness on such grounds alienates us, whether we are Jews or *goyim*. Similarly, anyone who claims an equality in suffering with concentration-camp victims must offer us something more than "the suicide she inflicts on herself" and the image of the father at the blackboard; but his biting of the persona's pretty red heart is not demonstrated to us in the poem. Even crucifixion is not necessarily serious: John Lennon was not serious in singing "they're gonna crucify me"; he was making black comedy out of the fuss that had developed over his misunderstood remark—itself comic— that the Beatles were more popular than Jesus Christ. Plath cannot be serious in making her persona claim an equality with those Jews. (The persona is surely serious; that is quite a different matter. Hamlet was serious about his comparisons and his notebook.)

As Aird recognizes, Plath herself described "Daddy" in quite different terms, and very usefully for our purposes. Aird quotes A. Alvarez: "When she first read me this poem a few days after she wrote it, she called it a piece of 'light verse.' It obviously isn't." But perhaps it is; an author should know, and occasionally does. She may have meant the remark disparagingly—"Daddy" is not a very good poem—but she is also accurate generically; our acceptance of her term requires only that we understand humor in perhaps a broader sense than that in fashion.

"Daddy" is primarily about its persona, not about Daddy or the Jews or suicide (just as Browning's "My Last Duchess" is about the Duke more than marriage or aristocracy or the Renaissance), and it is about the persona especially in the sense that the reader, urged on by sounds, rhythms, phrases, images, reported events, and consequent tones of voice, is obliged to *become* that persona as he or she reads or rather enacts her monolog. The poem does not seek to judge, explain, or merely stare at this persona. Rather, the monolog's jumble of light and serious elements, upsetting our sense of decorum and rebuffing our easy sympathetic understanding (much as neurotics do in real life, incidentally) communicates on the pulse, as Keats might say, rather than rationally or clinically. And what it communicates, beyond mere symptoms (and they belong to the persona, not to the poem), includes these odd and oddly mixed elements that we have been calling comedy.

Seeing it coming at last, the sensitive reader winces. Discussions of comedy are always disaster areas, especially when they attempt to define and categorize its elements and effects. They are especially bleak when they grapple with such gallows humor as Plath's personae specialize in, when the arbitrariness of literary terms becomes especially evident. One of the finest practitioners of this grim comedy is Samuel Beckett. Like Plath, he specializes in end-game humor, the comedy of the psychological lost cause. The persona of his *How It Is* speaks appropriately of the laughs that "convulse an instant resurrect an instant then leave for deader than before";[8] properly understood, Plath's humor at its ultimate is of this sort. Occasionally a grace but never a saving grace, it awakens us—especially if, as a monolog demands, we enact the part sympathetically and become humorist and audience at once—to the psychological realities of a subjective situation, clarifies them in that sudden enlightenment that humor can provide, and then goes out again, leaving us more knowledgeably where we were, trapped.

Beckett's most extensive analysis of humor is offered by the departing servant Arsene in *Watt*. Its totality, which deserves the praise of every reader of Plath, is beyond quotation and application now, but some approximation of it will be useful. Here it is, then, shortened:

> Of all the laughs that strictly speaking are not laughs, but modes of ululation, only three I think need detain us, I mean the bitter, the hollow and the mirthless. They correspond to . . . successive excoriations of the understanding, and the passage from one to the other is the passage from the lesser to the greater, . . . from the outer to the inner, . . . from the matter to the form. The laugh that now is mirthless once was hollow, the laugh that once was hollow once was bitter. And the laugh that once was bitter? Eyewater, Mr Watt, eyewater. . . . The bitter laugh laughs at that which is not good, it is the ethical laugh. The hollow laugh laughs at that which is not true, it is the intellectual laugh. . . . But the mirthless laugh is the dianoetic laugh . . . , the laugh laughing at the laugh, . . . in a word the laugh that laughs—silence please—at that which is unhappy.[9]

It is fair to suspect that Plath felt the longings of most civilized Westerners for those twin props of human morale, God and the idea of tragedy.[10] God's existence connected us to a reliable source of ultimate value. Tragedy explained why, in a universe created by God, suffering still occurred; and it allowed us to imagine ourselves as antagonists worthy to grapple with fate. In either case, tragically or religiously, we were responsible to God and could hold his interest; we had marvelous connections and importance, no matter how lowly we were or unhappy. (See Kafka's "In the Penal Colony.")

But the contemporary sense of existence, as shaped by the Higher Criticism, astronomy, geology, history, ethics, statistics, aesthetics, etc., denies humankind any role in existence and an individual specimen any very impressive significance or value, while it also questions the validity of any system of values by which people might measure themselves.

To be sure, each person still suffers as intensely as when that suffering had meaning, value, and perhaps even dignity. Bereft of those roles and systems, however, the sufferer is left with nothing but a recognition of disparities. The pain is disproportionate to its use, the internal awareness exceeds any external manifestations, the mental reality eludes verbal expression, suffering has no connection with justice. All are incongruous with each other; in an existence without a center, all is paradoxically peripheral; and the result, God and tragedy being absent, is comic, absurd, grotesque.

Add to this situation a modern human's trained ability to exist subjectively and painfully and at the same time to see his existence from a detached viewpoint, and in Plath's poetry the result is the comic exploitation of disparity, imaged for instance as a maiden aunt's shocked visit to a dreadful life, a woman's irrationally inflated obsession with her dead father acted out mockingly in the strident fishwifery of "Daddy," and a desperate attempt to say what has gone wrong with a marriage presented in the comic search structure of a Sherlock Holmes story. Perhaps existence does have a center after all, though not an objective one. Given the exquisite pain of a psychological situation, however, what is *not* peripheral?

The disparity between the control of art and the absence of control in its materials—that is, their disparity, disconnection, uselessness, peripheral irrelevance—is one of the most easily misunderstood qualities of humor. Perhaps most people who customarily read literature seek in it some revelation of the coherence, significance, and value of life. Perhaps the formal qualities of art imply—as Beckett fears—some equivalent and valid form in existence. In any case, Plath's readers are reluctant to hear the accents of comedy, especially of that comedy that implies that it is too late to evade the crime or to seek help. In a valuable study of Plath's poetry, Judith Kroll has found that "there is one overriding concern: the problem of rebirth or transcendence; and nearly everything in her poetry contributes either to the statement or to the envisioned resolution of this problem."[11] But such hoping for hopefulness may mislead. For instance, Kroll says that in "Purdah" "the threat to destroy the oppressive bridegroom prefigures relinquishing the false self and liberating the true one."[12] She recognizes the allusion to Clytaemnestra, but she will not accept its full, pessimistic relevance.

But Plath's speakers and poems are not comic because they can afford to be, because they see a loophole, an escape, a rebirth in the offing. Rather, they recognize a cul-de-sac, a fixed situation, in which words cannot successfully conjure, supplicate, transform, or otherwise improve upon the status quo. Conventional verbal responses to such end-game situations range from tragedy to lamentation, but a few authors—as disparate as Knut Hamsun, Laforgue, Firbank, Beckett, Céline, Kafka, and Donald Barthelme—have responded by exploiting despair for comic ends. That a well-shaped, knowledgeable, witty cry of despair is no better than any other only adds to its comedy, for such authors. Though Plath cannot save or improve upon her life, she is able sometimes to improvise such shaped and comic expressions of this helplessness, and to give to these improvisations the detached control of the artist no longer believing that poetry can make something happen. To be "an obstinate independency / Insolvent among the mountains" ("The Courage of Shutting Up") one must do without hope. "Once one has seen God, what is the remedy?" ("Mystic").

In a simpler time—he thought—Hemingway was able to define courage as grace under pressure. But grace implies the reestablishment or continuation of balance, harmony, control, and therefore wholeness. Let us suppose that the world, or at least human life, is *not* harmonious itself or in its relations with the rest of existence, and that we have only partial and unreliable control even over ourselves. Then we must replace this graceful hero with a truer ideal image—for example the clown, teetering and tottering but diligent about the impossible as he sweeps up the spilled spotlight, absurd even in his suffering, especially in his suffering, which he refuses either to be noble about or to collapse under, however undignified his cries. The bitter laugh was once tears, Arsene tells us, but the mirthless laugh has left tears far behind, and with them that last infirmity of noble minds, the attempt to lose gracefully. From time to time Sylvia Plath evokes this painful terminal guffaw. Now *that's* comedy.

And the poems that evoke that response do so by comic means. They communicate many things, piece by piece. When we attempt to put the pieces together we find that the poem has admitted so much that seems peripheral or irrelevant that we can no longer find any reliable basis for distinguishing relevance from irrelevance; disparity is the order of the day.[13] We are in a sensibility in which great and small, dignified and foolish, brave and paranoid elements coexist, jangling; and the poet —aesthetically in control of this experience, though refusing to misrepresent it as coherent—has handed us a script that we must perform even as we attempt to understand it. We may never reach that understanding: "you'd hafta been there," people say, and who would wish to go? But certainly Plath has held back nothing that might have aided our understanding the part—nothing, at least, except the terrible absence of control that her poetic skills keep at bay so successfully.

Notes

1. Samuel Beckett, *Murphy* (New York: Grove, 1957), p. 139.
2. Ted Hughes comments relevantly about one of the "Birthday" poems: "The sudden enrichment of the texture of her verse, and the nimble shifting of focus, were something new and surprised her. At this time she was concentratedly trying to break down the tyranny, the fixed focus and public persona which descriptive or discoursive [*sic*] poems take as a norm." "Notes on the Chronological Order of Sylvia Plath's Poems," *Tri-Quarterly*, no. 7 (Fall, 1966), p. 85.
3. Ibid., p. 88.
4. Ingrid Melander, in *The Poetry of Sylvia Plath: A Study of Themes*, Gothenburg Studies in English no. 25 (Stockholm: Almqvist and Wiksell, 1972), p. 42, remarks in connecting "Daddy" with "The Colossus" that "it is true that the statue is still 'ghastly,' but the sense of humour with which the imagery is employed ('a bag full of God'; 'Big as a Frisco seal') makes it at first appear less impressive and frightening."
5. "Sylvia Plath," in *The Poet Speaks: Interviews With Contemporary Poets*, ed. Peter Orr (London: Routledge and Kegan Paul, 1966), p. 169.
6. Passages from Aird are taken from *Sylvia Plath: Her Life and Work* (New York: Harper and Row, 1975), p. 84.
7. For Plath's sensitive, straightforward treatment of this difficult material see "The Thin People." Notice that there she avoids the egocentric overtones of the first-person singular.
8. Samuel Beckett, *How It Is* (New York: Grove, 1964), p. 110.
9. Samuel Beckett, *Watt* (New York: Grove, 1959), p. 48.
10. "I admit, I desire, / Occasionally, some backtalk / From the mute sky" ("Black Rook in Rainy Weather"); "How I would like to believe in tenderness— / The face of the effigy, gentled by candles, / Bending, on me in particular, its mild eyes" ("The Moon and the Yew Tree"). Even this longing does not escape the commentary of Plath's wit.
11. Judith Kroll, *Chapters in a Mythology: The Poetry of Sylvia Plath* (New York: Harper and Row, 1976), p. 3.
12. Ibid., p. 19.
13. Kroll (ibid., p. 180) complains that in "Fever 103°" the experience grows "out of a reverie in which the mind is flooded with ingenuous and, in a sense, extraneous images . . . which distract the reader's attention from the experience they signify."

Sister Bernetta Quinn

Medusan imagery in Sylvia Plath

Medusa, though we do not immediately recognize the fact, presides as Muse over Sylvia Plath's poetry; between the Stone Goddess and the often bewildering, finally bewildered genius there extended vital ties of kinship. Plath's lyric "Medusa," composed a few months before her death, is the starting point for the present exploration. The primary analogate is the invertebrate named medusa by Linnaeus because of its resemblance to a head with snaky locks. Just as Dante's Jerusalem is first of all the city in Palestine, then the just soul, next the Church, and lastly the Heavenly Kingdom, so tropology in the Plath poem moves from (1) jellyfish to (2) Gorgon to (3) the lunar Muse over art conceived of as "sculpted form" to (4) the "false heaven" of drugs as counteractive to the emotional disorders that led to her suicide and to the petrifaction she finally achieved on that grey London morning in 1963.

George Starbuck, friend of Sylvia from the days when they, together with Anne Sexton, were coauditors of Robert Lowell's workshop, has described this poem as "a strong out-and-out Medusa poem if ever there was one, though it constructs its own myth, its own imaginative connection, directly from the pelagic animal to the projection of archetypal harridan."[1] The medusa is a free-swimming coelenterate, distinguished from its polyp (or larva) form in that it is the "adult" or sexually reproductive phase of the organism. This marine creature forms the subject of one of Louis Agassiz's finest treatises, about which Guy Davenport writes: "Our culture can be gauged as exultantly in Agassiz's long study of the naked-eyed Medusa as in Marianne Moore's dilation upon the edge-hog."[2] Ezra Pound, who urged on literary critics Agassiz's tools of observation and comparison, would I think have approved the following vertical examination as one means of arriving at an understanding of Sylvia Plath's metaphorical use of the creature, since "Plath's metaphors, terrible as they can be, form new, agonizingly exact identities."[3]

The poem begins:

> Off that landspit of stony mouth-plugs,
> Eyes rolled by white sticks,
> Ears cupping the sea's incoherences,
> You house your unnerving head—God-ball,
> Lens of mercies.

This stanza is a tissue of metaphors: "landspit"—a spit is an instrument for impaling, in this case the sea, as in "this battered, obstinate spit / Of gravel" near Plath's grandmother's home ("Point Shirley")—"Eyes," "sticks," "Ears," "cupping," "head," "God-ball," "Lens," "house." Though jellyfish have neither eyes nor ears—their tentacles do the work of these—they resemble in shape these organs, just as their rods or stalks resemble "white sticks." "Ears" here recalls Wallace Stevens's "Idea of Order at Key West," with its implication that only humanity, and in particular the artist, can give meaning to the sound of the waves; Plath had earlier ascribed incoherence to the ocean in "The Moon and the Yew Tree," where the moon is "in love with the formlessness of the sea."

Several scholars have called attention to another name for the common medusa, *Aurelia aulita*—moon jellyfish—the first element suggesting Sylvia's mother, Aurelia Schober Plath, and the second lunar symbolism. In accordance with "white sticks," the *Aurelia* is described in science texts as white, clear, even milky. "Unnerving" means "depriving of courage or steadiness, as by calamity or shock," appropriate if applied to Mrs. Plath's presence that last summer in England, face to face with Sylvia's suffering over her husband's infidelity. In "The Stones," the word "house," as here, is employed as a verb: "The vase, reconstructed, houses / The elusive rose"; in "Medusa" the sea is the house of the unwelcome acaleph.

One of the most persistent images in Plath is that of the eye; sight/blindness passages are as pervasive as in *Oedipus*. In "Medusa" an optical conceit begins with that startling kenning "God-ball," which the rest of the poem will develop in terms of the lens. The obvious reason is the shape of the jellyfish; etymologically "lens" involves a sphere, for it derives from the seed of the lentil. "God-ball," resembling "eyeball," prepares for the last line of the stanza, "Lens of mercies," not necessarily ironic in that if mercy is compassion toward the condemned, the medusa's effect upon the speaker can be seen as a blessing. A lens, like the *Aurelia*, is transparent. It magnifies or diminishes objects—"blows up" the intolerable circumstances of Plath's struggle to surmount the crushing melancholy deepened by abandonment in London with two children to care for, or reduces her to the nonfeeling "I'm a stone, a stick" of "Parliament Hill Fields." "Epitaph for Fire and Flower" stresses the gorgonizing action of the camera-lens:

> Seek no stony camera-eye to fix
> The passing dazzle of each face   [the pelagic animal is called
> In black and white, or put on ice   "dazzling" in "Medusa"]
> Mouth's instant fare for future looks

Although in her prosody Plath is far from the school of Donne, conceits like this of the lens often relate her to the metaphysicals.

That this same conceit of the lens occurs in James Merrill's "Medusa" may indicate that Plath was influenced by him; his Yale Series of Younger Poets book *First Poems* containing that lyric appeared in 1951 and specializes in the sophisticated metrics and imagery of her own *The Colossus*. Merrill pictures two lovers as autumn begins, sitting in a garden, disconsolate that their summer romance is at an end. The genius of this garden is a stone Gorgon, possibly a figure in a fountain. The poet describes her deadly eye as "that slight crystal lens / Whose scope allows perfection to be conceived" and goes on to equate the lens with "godhead in a world of sense," true in that it is the eye, tied by nerve filaments to the brain, which allows man entrance into an external Eden, returned to him through perception as an interior landscape of joy.

Still another stratum of the lens symbol, since "medusiform" means "bell-shaped," is visible in Aurelia Plath's letter to Sylvia's Harper and Row editor, reporting words her daughter once used about the title of her single novel: "I've tried to picture my world and the people in it as seen through the distorting lens of a bell jar."

The second stanza modifies through participles the subject-predicate "You house" of line four:

> Your stooges
> Plying their wild cells in my keel's shadow,
> Pushing by like hearts,
> Red stigmata at the very centre,
> Riding the rip tide to the nearest point of departure,

"Stooges" refers to the small commensal animals called medusafish that look like tiny heart-shaped muscles and swim near the larger medusa, unharmed by its tentacles. As an Americanism, the word "stooge" means "one who serves or cooperates with another in a subservient manner." Anthony Libby considers the metaphorical significance of these to be Sylvia's children described in foetal terms,[4] but such an interpretation seems unlikely. More apposite are those people whom Aurelia enlisted as she tried to rescue her daughter from the grip of depression, women like the midwife Winifred Davies or friends of the family who were abroad and could write her back reassurances.[5]

One meaning of "plying" is "offering service," which is what Mrs. Plath was begging of persons like Winifred Davies as Sylvia's psychological crisis grew more frightening. As for the "wild cells," the expression seems well glossed by a book on invertebrates:

> Playing the role of host, on the other hand, are the many jellyfishes and large tropical anemones that shelter fishes, all the large attached coelenterates that provide a place for myriads of tiny invertebrates to hang onto in a restless ocean, the coral crevices that shelter hundreds of kinds of fishes and crabs and worms, and—*most important of all*—the widespread mutualistic ties of coelenterates with green or yellowish brown algae cells.[6]

The simile of hearts recalls "Apprehensions" in the posthumous *Winter Trees*, where Plath speaks of her own: "This red wall winces continually; / A fist, opening and closing." Red for her, like white, has negative connotations; as Butscher remarks, "Red would be the color of life itself, vibrant but forever tinged with blood, the agony of an existence poised on the painful edge of extreme sensibilities."[7]

The "red stigmata" is consonant with the religious vocabulary set up in "God-ball" and "Lens of mercies." The phrase, in a tonal fury that conveys both verbal irony and denotative literalness, suggests the martyrdom of a too-devoted mother; linked with it is "pushing," an excellent choice to convey the solicitude that so annoyed its object. There are other levels as well. In "stigmata" Plath returns to the lens conceit, since optically it designates the convergence of rays of light at a point in a lens (this lens surrounded by the "jelly" of the eyeball); too, "stigmata" can mean "signs of disease or defect, as in leprosy." For Sylvia Plath, who knew the Nietzschean theory of the manipulative strength of weakness and knew its practice from having grown up an American girl, such defects are telling. They extend to the metaphor "jellyfish," "a person without stamina, weak and indecisive." This meaning coincides with the fate of the medusae, their swimming power so feeble that the tides pile them up in great numbers along the seashore, where they perish helplessly as soon as they are out of water. Plath intensifies their difficulty in swimming by the expression "rip tide," a clash of opposing currents.

With the third stanza the eleven-line sentence introducing the addressee concludes and the religious imagery is resumed:

> Dragging their Jesus hair.
> Did I escape, I wonder?
> My mind winds to you
> Old barnacled umbilicus, Atlantic cable,
> Keeping itself, it seems, in a state of miraculous repair.

In the uncollected "Thoughts," Plath speaks of weeds in the sea as "a maze of mermaid hair," but why "*Jesus* hair" in "Medusa"? She might have intended the long hair with which Jesus Christ is painted, but a more pertinent interpretation would be the *Aurelia* as savior, a role Mrs. Plath consistently tried to play. The resemblance of the moon jellyfish's tentacles to hair is heightened by a secondary, botanical definition of "tentacles": sticky hairs whereby certain bog plants trap insects.

With an ocean between herself and her mother, the poet should be free, yet she remains connected by what Sidney Howard called "the silver cord" to her first home, the womb, if only (in "Medusa") through metonomy: the umbilicus is not the cord itself but the scar on the abdomen where it had been attached, the navel. In "Maenad" Plath seems to mean the latter in the verse wherein the same verb, "wind," appears: "Time / Unwinds from the great umbilicus of the sun / Its endless glitter." Its title referring to "madwoman" as well as "bacchante," that lyric seems a flashback to the author's childhood—"The mother of mouths did not love me"—as the adult reflects upon this childhood.

The noun "umbilicus" in "Medusa" stands in apposition to "Atlantic cable," the latter though "old" and "barnacled" "in a state of miraculous repair." A barnacle is "a thing or person who clings tenaciously," as in "All the Dead Dears," a poem about the mummified corpse that Plath once saw in a Cambridge museum, one of those corpses who grip the living "through thin and thick, / These barnacle dead!" In physics, "umbilicus" means a conduit through which power is transformed, such as an electrical cable used in operating a rocket or missile and disconnected after launching; or again, a strong life-line linking an astronaut working in space outside his vehicle to that vehicle. On the autobiographical level, "cable" stands for both the telephone calls and cablegrams mentioned in *Letters Home*.

Sylvia knew she had not really escaped, nor would she, as long as telephone or cablegram permitted her mind to wind back to Wellesley, or her mother's anxiety to project itself to London, where, husbandless and poor, she was trying to fit together the pieces of her life. In a review of *Letters Home* with a Medusan title, Gene Ballif comments thus on her query in line twelve: "The emotions of the poem turn decidedly ugly as the sense of being paralyzed and engulfed by the bell-jar medusa pushes the question of the third stanza ('Did I escape, I wonder?') towards its negative answer."[8] On the very day that she composed "Medusa" —16 October 1962—Sylvia wrote two desperate letters to her mother, one of them including this sentence: "I'm getting an unlisted phone put in as soon as possible so I can call out; you shall have the number."[9] These so alarmed Aurelia that she cable Winifred Davies, her daughter's midwife and friend: "Please see Sylvia now and get woman for her. Salary paid here. Writing" (*LH*, 470). But the response to this kindness came back in an angry letter of 21 October: "Will you please, for goodness sake, stop bothering poor Winifred Davies! . . . She is busier than either you or I and is helping me as much as she can and knows and sees my situation much better than you can" (*LH*, 473). This outburst was followed two days later by a remorseful: "*Please* forgive my grumpy, sick letters of last week" (LH, 474).

The telephone metaphor continues:

> In any case, you are always there,
> Tremulous breath at the end of my line,
> Curve of water upleaping
> To my water rod, dazzling and grateful,
> Touching and sucking.

In the letters and here also, the tenderness that Sylvia entertained for her mother, incompatible as they were, comes through poignantly. As a little girl, she had been in the habit of slipping verses under her mother's napkin at the dinner table, and during college years the degree to which she shared her experiences indicates the strength of her attachment, one that the McLean Hospital psychiatrist later taught her to suspect as a major cause of her illness. Even though the correspondence was winnowed for publishing by Mrs. Plath, eager to correct what she felt a cruel public caricature of her daughter, there can be no doubt from the extravagantly affectionate greetings ("Dearest, darling mother") that the poet depended emotionally on her surviving parent. She knew, as "Medusa" affirms, that her mother would be "always there," at the end of the line.

In the fourth stanza, the concluding three lines seem like a fishing metaphor, though that is not the way Robert Phillips views them;

comparing the lyric to "Elm," he says: "The guilt there is developed more completely in the poem titled simply 'Medusa.' Here Plath communicates with her unconscious, becoming the poetess with a Divining rod who summons the image of the Father-God who is 'Always there, tremulous breath at the end of my line' [sic]. If Plath is at the end of her rope, it is, she still feels, her father's fault."[10] Yet none of the connotations of "tremulous" suggests in the least the autocratic Otto Plath; nor would he rise, except in the most extreme fantasizing, "dazzling and grateful, / Touching and sucking." Moreover, a divining rod, used for locating underground water, is out of place in the context of the speaker's traveling over the sea. On the level of the primary analogate, the water content of the *Aurelia* is so high that "Curve of water" seems to describe it; as for "upleaping," Martin Wells writes that "Many of the smaller medusae have a shelf, the velum, projecting inwards from the rim of the bell, restricting the water flow into a jet."[11] "Sucking"—drawing water as if by suction—fits in with the medusa's locomotion as jet propelled by contracting muscles that force water from the subumbrellar space. Earlier in the essay quoted from, Phillips says: "In the world of her private mythology, the sea and her father and herself become one."[12] This introduces a second referent, the ocean itself, for "Curve of water upleaping," one reinforced in "Contusion": "The sea sucks obsessively." It is fairly safe to conclude that this laminated figure, though difficult to unravel, is not a mixed metaphor, so unerring is Plath's logic even in the constructions of Freudian dream-work.

If the poet-as-fisherman is taken as vehicle here, the next stanza's opening would refer to an unwanted catch:

> I didn't call you.
> I didn't call you at all.
> Nevertheless, nevertheless
> You steamed to me over the sea,
> Fat and red, a placenta.

This echo device, as characteristic of Plath as it is of Williams and Jarrell, is a way of underlining the thought as if to convince both herself and the hearer. The repetition finds elucidation in a letter she wrote her mother on the very day of the genesis of "Medusa." Years before that, she had begged her brother, Warren, to protect both of them from Aurelia and Aurelia from the stigmata of her own excessive maternalism: "You know, as I do, and it is a frightening thing, that mother would actually kill herself for us if we calmly accepted all she wanted to do for us. She is an abnormally altruistic person, and I have realized lately that we have to fight against her selflessness as we would fight against a deadly disease."[13]

On 16 October 1962, her mind saturated with Medusan symbolism, she pours into her letter home a blank desperate appeal: "it would be psychologically the worst thing to see you now.... I must not go back to the womb" (*LH*, 466-69). The poem uses more moderate language. "I didn't call you at all" may allude to Mrs. Plath's trip to England the previous July, when she had witnessed the humiliating ravages of jealousy. Whether Plath's mother came to Europe by ship or air is not clear, but if the former, "steamed" fits, just as it does with what Muriel Lewin Guberlet remarks about medusae in *The Seashore Parade*: "The motion of the jellyfish is regular and continuous like the beating of the human heart and he really keeps moving all his life." ("To steam" means "to move rapidly and evenly.")

Plath must have felt that her mother would not be likely to decipher in the intricate symbolism of "Medusa" the agonized plea and frustration that underlay the poem; like the jongleur whose singing wooed the wife of the medieval French Lord under his very nose, she counted on a certain impenetrability of metaphor. Certainly this lyric appears less autobiographical than "A Birthday Present," with its direct "Is it impossible for you to let something go and have it go whole?" In the earlier piece, the speaker is asking for death as a birthday present, and she is asking it of the most famous victim of decapitation in antiquity:

> I know why you will not give it to me
> You are terrified
>
> The world will go up in a shriek, and your head with it,
> Bossed, brazen, an antique shield,
>
> A marvel to your great-grandchildren. [i.e., Minerva's buckler]

"Fat and red, a placenta" agrees with the etymology of "placenta" as "something with a circular form," which is equally descriptive of the medusa. Though certain jellyfish *are* red, the color may refer to phosphorescence. Guberlet relates: "I recall the last time we went boat riding at night a jellyfish stuck to the paddle where it looked like a ball of fire, and each stroke of the oar left a path of light behind it."

If this next stanza is a figurative account of Mrs. Plath's summer visit, it reflects great pain:

> Paralyzing the kicking lovers.
> Cobra light
> Squeezing the breath from the blood bells
> Of the fuchsia. I could draw no breath,
> Dead and moneyless.

Medusan imagery in Sylvia Plath

If stung by the most deadly of all jellyfish, the sea wasp (analogue of the queen bee in the Plath bee sequence), bathers die in seconds, but even though here the medusa is paralleled with that snake that yearly kills five thousand people in India, the comparison is hyperbolic. Jellyfish are armed with stinging capsules that discharge a narcotizing poison into prey, stunning it (*meduser* in French means "to stun"). The prey is then carried to the mouth and ingested and digested by a stomach, as is the way with spiders, which are not insects at all but belong to the same invertebrate tree as medusae.

Freud, whose works Sylvia purchased as a college student, interprets a dreamed spider thus: "According to Abraham [1922] a spider in dreams is a symbol of the mother, but of the *phallic* mother of whom we are afraid."[14] "Totem" might as well be describing the jellyfish tentacles when it says: "I am mad, calls the spider, waving its many arms." Perhaps even more apposite than the spider as analogue to the medusa is the scorpion, with its venom-inflicting tail, under whose zodiacal sign Sylvia (a confirmed believer in astrology) was born. As a child she was probably familiar with Scorpio as a constellation, as well as with Perseus, wherein Medusa's Head forms a cluster of stars, the largest being Algol, a name derived from "demon." Thus in her early years by the Atlantic she could read her life story written across the New England skies.

With "Cobra light" the symbolism goes back to the shape of the pelagic analogate, since this venomous snake has the ability to flatten its neck into a hood; it is, in addition, in India called a blood snake, recalling "Fat and red, a placenta." A passage from "Totem" associates blood imagery with the eye, presented above as a medusa metaphor:

Shall the hood of the cobra appal me—
The loneliness of its eye, the eye of the mountains

Through which the sky eternally threads itself?
The world is blood-hot and personal

Dawn says, with its blood-flush.

A third employment of "cobra" appears in "Edge," making of the moon itself a hooded snake, at least in the similarity of their shapes: "The moon has nothing to be sad about, / Staring from her hood of bone."

The speaker at this point identifies herself with the fuchsia, or evening primrose, a bell-like flower that if cultivated must be protected from strong sunlight; the invertebrate, compared by "Cobra light" to the intense glare of the sun, "poisons" it. From "paralyzing" and "unnerving" it is a short step to petrifying. Though unable to breathe, the "I" in the poem is describing an acute emotional petrifaction that stops only a little short of death, something comparable to a catatonic state. The words "I could draw no breath" recall the technician's warning as an X-ray is in progress: "Hold your breath!" "I cannot face you again until I have a new life," Sylvia tells her mother in a letter written just a week before "Medusa" (*LH*, 465); a few days later, even though "moneyless," she vehemently resists her "saviour": "I want no monthly dole, especially not from you" (*LH*, 473). She feels stripped to the skeleton by Aurelia's knowledge of the misery and humiliation she has experienced through her husband's desertion; and the memory of this violation of her interior landscape explodes into aggression:

> Over-exposed, like an X-ray.
> Who do you think you are?
> A Communion wafer? Blubbery Mary?
> I shall take no bite of your body,
> Bottle in which I live.

To the sarcastic question posed in this stanza, Plath offers two alternatives, the first a Eucharistic allusion such as occurs in others of her poems. Although Judith Kroll is misleading in identifying Aurelia as a Roman Catholic—actually, she was a Unitarian Sunday school teacher—Sylvia's maternal grandparents were Catholics, and Communion is a sacrament with which she was familiar. In "Mystic" she speaks of the "pill of the Communion tablet"; in "Tulips," she imagines the dead shutting their mouths on peace "like a Communion tablet"; in the puzzling "Totem," she urges the consumption of a sacrificed hare: "Let us eat it like Christ"; and in "Nick and the Candlestick," she suffers "A piranha / Religion, drinking // Its first communion out of my live toes." Here in "Medusa," the image "Jesus hair" finds its complement in "Communion wafer" as metaphor for the medusa.

"Blubbery Mary" has been variously explicated. Ballif explains it thus:

> The comic rage registered in the next two lines abusively ridicules the (implied) mother for offering herself eucharistically, as it were, as if being blood of her blood, flesh of her flesh, promised the consolations of holy sacrament; or again, for seeming to be a super-compassionate Blessed Virgin Mother, shedding tears unctuous as blubber—the epithets "Communion wafer" and "Blubbery Mary" together intimating a sort of parody of extreme unction.[15]

While it might be tempting to use blubber as Ballif has, particularly because of the adjective "fat" a few lines earlier, the sense of "blubbery" as "weeping so as to disfigure the face" seems to accord better with Mary as Sorrowful Mother (though it might also refer to Mary Magdalen, who washed the feet of Jesus with her tears and dried them with her hair[16]). It does not follow, as Kroll believes, that line four of this stanza is a rejection of Mary; in fact, in what they say about Mary, Sylvia's poems reveal her longing for a truly understanding mother—and in images usually associated with the most affirmative of her color words, blue. On the level of the primary analogate, in French dictionaries "blubber" in its nautical usage is synonymous with the medusa.

As microcosm/macrocosm, the "womb" of the medusa is juxtaposed to the gigantic womb of the sea, foreshadowing the grave. "Bottle in which I live" recalls Sylvia's final sentence in the autobiographical "Ocean 1212-W": "Whereon those first nine years of my life sealed themselves off like a ship in a bottle—beautiful, inaccessible, obsolete, a fine, white flying myth."[17] What Plath does reject as this stanza closes, imprisoned as she feels herself, is further nourishment from her earthly mother.

As the lyric ends, she almost screams at what Ballif calls "the transparent medusa of conscience she feels bottled up in,"[18] termed here a "Vatican":

> Ghastly Vatican.
> I am sick to death of hot salt.
> Green as eunuchs, your wishes
> Hiss at my sins.
> Off, off, eely tentacle!

Overtones of unwelcome authority are undeniable in this introduction of "the Pope's house," uncancelled by the etymology ("spiritual") of the modifier "ghastly." The poet's own tears are the "hot salt" she is tired of, though the expression could also go back to "Blubbery Mary." In Matthew 19: 10-13, Christ divides eunuchs into three categories, their condition based on voluntary or involuntary impotence; they are all "green" or inexperienced in regard to sexual consummation, just as Aurelia's wishes, here the snakelike tentacles, are impotent through her inability to enter into her daughter's pain. As applicable to the moon jellyfish, "green" has the significance "pale," "wan." If the autobiographical answer is yes to the question asked in Plath's B.B.C. radio play, "Three Women"—"Is this the one sin then, this old dead love of death?"—"Medusa" becomes a suicide note written three months before the fact.

Judith Kroll applies the word "exorcism" to the fifth line of this stanza. If by this noun is meant "a ceremony by which someone is freed from a malignant influence," the ritual did not work. The troubled, affectionate letters continued to arrive at Wellesley during that winter. On December 14 Sylvia writes that she plans to dedicate her third book of poems to her mother (*LH*, 491), an intention her publishers did not honor after her death.

What is one to make of "There is nothing between us," the single line coda? George Steiner, without specifying, writes: "The ambiguity and dual flash of insight in this final line are of a richness and obviousness that only a very great poem can carry off";[19] but it is hard to see how something can be obvious and ambiguous at the same time. Gary Lane is more helpful. He reads the conclusion as summarizing the two-edged thrust of the poem. There is "the desired exorcism of the mother, and beneath it the recognition of an unalterable similarity with her. The line thus means that (a) we've nothing in common, and (b) we, two separate images, are merged."[20] The rest of this essay will develop the ways in which the latter idea pervades Plath's image.

To concentrate on the medusa only in a reading of "Medusa," ignoring the Gorgon, is like trying to divorce the narcissus from Narcissism. Her story told by Hesiod and Ovid, and affecting all Western literature through Homer and Dante, this daughter of the sea-god Phorcys symbolizes the worst horror the human imagination can create. Although the Augustans preferred out-and-out abstractions and the early Romantics found their inspiration in Nature, with Keats ("Endymion") and Shelley the classical gods and goddesses returned. If today neo-Romantics like James Wright avoid them, myriads of other poets see in Medusa a way of "incarnating" their insights. Among them are Robert Lowell, Randall Jarrell, Ezra Pound, Allen Tate, Archibald MacLeish, W. S. Merwin, Ben Belitt, Louis MacNeice, John Nerber, Daryl Hine, Robert Conquest, James Merrill, Basil Bunting, R. P. Blackmur, Howard Nemerov, Edgar Lee Masters, Louise Bogan, William Alexander Percy, Samuel French Morse, and any number of others.

That Sylvia Plath, while an instructor at Smith, was fascinated by the myth of Medusa is clear from a letter she wrote to her mother on 22 March 1958:

> Just a note to say that I have at last burst into a spell of writing. I was rather stunned Thursday morning, my first real day off after a week of correcting 70 papers, averaging midterm grades and writing a report on another senior thesis, but I had about seven or eight paintings and etchings I wanted to write on as poem-subjects, and bang! After the first one, "Virgin in a Tree," after an early etching by Paul Klee, I ripped into another, *probably the biggest and best poem I've ever written*, "Triumph of Wit over Suffering." A total of about 90 lines written in one day. (*LH*, 336; emphasis added).

Art News, for which she intended these poems, did not use them, but the Perseus one in transcript was given by her mother to the Lilly Library at Indiana University.

Medusa as Stone Mother belongs not only to the mythic transformations traced by Erich Neumann in *The Great Mother* but is also involved in one of Sylvia's great literary enthusiasms, Robert Graves's *The White Goddess*. In the first, the following deities are interchangeable: Hecate, Artemis, Demeter, Selene, Medusa, Aphrodite, and even Ishtar (the derivation of the name "Esther," which Sylvia chose for the heroine of *The Bell Jar*). Several of these are lunar, as Neumann notes: "In Greece, the Gorgon as Artemis-Hecate is also the mistress of the night road, of fate, and of the world of the dead . . . . as Hecate she is the snake-entwined moon-goddess of ghosts and the dead, surrounded, like Artemis, the wild goddess of the hunt, by a swarm of female demons."[21] Judith Kroll comments on how "The Moon-muse of the late poems is a kind of witch, resembling the witch-goddess Hecate" and quotes a conversation with Ted Hughes in which he described the astrological poster that decorated their wall, showing among personae of the Moon Goddess Diana, Luna, Hecate, and Proserpina.[22] Another obvious Stone Mother figure in Plath is "Lucina, bony mother, laboring / Among the socketed white stars, [whose] face / Of candor pares white flesh to the white bone" ("Moonrise").

A protean sorceress, Medusa has wandered through the centuries as Circe,[23] as Geraldine, as Lamia. She is *"la belle dame sans merci"* who destroys where she would love. Frederick Thomas Elworthy labels her a witch: "The story of the Medusa is but an incident in the evil eye and should be carefully studied by all interested in the subject."[24] Though little known because uncollected, Plath's "The Lady and the Earthenware Head" develops the evil eye theme. An amateur artist makes an unflattering head of the "I," which she lodges in the crotch of a willow tree to prevent any injury to what she superstitiously regards as an effigy. It glares down at her: "An antique hag-head, too tough for knife to finish / Refusing to diminish / By one jot its basilisk-look of love."[25] The use of "basilisk" makes of the head a Medusan figure, as Goldsmith notes: "The glance of its eye would kill. It could only be destroyed by holding a mirror up so that it must see itself, when it would burst asunder with horror at its own appearance. . . . In sacred art the basilisk used to represent the spirit of evil."[26]

Of all Gorgon figures, the one to be developed most fully in a lyric, apart from "Medusa," is the Lorelei, based on the legend of the siren who haunted a rock on the Rhine and by her loveliness led sailors to destruction. It is strange that Judith Kroll does not even mention "Lorelei" in her investigation of Plath's mythology. On the stratum of the primary analogate, the lorelei is a genus of amphibian also called a mud eel, suggesting the "eely tentacle" of "Medusa." Plath in "Lesbos" pictures herself as a lorelei: "I should sit on a rock off Cornwall and comb my hair." Richard Howard, who finds "Lorelei" and "The Stones" the most moving poems in *The Colossus*, regards Plath in the former as begging for death from "the Rock Maidens—the Mothers, the Sisters, the Fates, the Muses, the Lorelei: her names are many for the Medusa figure that will release her from the bonds of life."[27] It may well be the Lorelei that "Crossing the Water" refers to in "A snag is lifting a valedictory, pale hand; // Stars open among the lilies. / Are you not blinded by such expressionless sirens?" In "Lorelei," these sirens made of stone rise ponderously from the depths until they "Lodge / On the pitched reefs of nightmare," where their heroic forms are mirrored in the silver flux of the river (possibly, time). Like a dark bell, the poem tolls out this prayer: "Stone, stone, ferry me down there."

Throughout the ages, Medusa has been a symbol of duality, depicting the contradictions within that creature man, the supreme paradox. Leo Frobenius has called her a fusion of opposites: lion and eagle, bird and serpent, mobility and immobility, beauty and horror. Other mythic representations of a double nature—Janus, centaur, Sphinx, satyr—drop into insignificance beside her. When Allen Tate encounters a stone Medusa while exploring a Southern cemetery, he refers to her as brute and angel, the first suggesting the Libyan beast claimed as her origin by folklorists and the second that extraordinary beauty that led to her love affair consummated within the very temple of Athena and punished by what amounted to a life sentence of solitary confinement. It was not fortuitously that Sylvia Plath chose for her Smith dissertation *The Magic Mirror*, a study of the double in two Dostoevsky novels.

To select as muses three Medusae minus their snake-hair—that persistent nightmare of her childhood found later in the metaphysical paintings of De Chirico—is as fantastic as anything in Bosch. In the Milan canvas, mostly done in the color of blood, one Muse has a stitched leather head on a column, another has taken off her head and leaned it against her knee, and the third bald muse stands back in the shadows at the painting's right. These lunar "divinities" inspired the artifacts that on 11 February 1963 entered into that ideal order described by Eliot in "Tradition and the Individual Talent," and it is on their action that this third level of Medusan symbolism will focus.

The moon as Gorgon comes through most clearly in "Elm":

> What is this, this face
> So murderous in its strangle of branches [cf. "breathless" in "Medusa"]
>
> It petrifies the will. These are the isolate slow faults
> That kill, that kill, that kill.

Tree branches also appear as "snake hair" in "The Munich Mannequins" (which may, like "The Disquieting Muses," refer to De Chirico mannequin paintings): they "blow like hydras." In "Elm," the triple repetition is as if Sylvia is beating her fists against a surface, an effect similar to that achieved in "The Moon and the Yew Tree": "The moon is no door. It is a face in its own right, / White as a knuckle and terribly upset." Knuckles are not white unless the hand is clenched in anger or grief. This grief is over and over again associated with the shape of the moon as an O. It comes through in "The Disquieting Muses" as fist-beating again: "I learned, I learned, I learned elsewhere, / From muses unhired by you, dear mother." Had she accepted a Muse hired by her mother she would have been satisfied with the *Ladies' Home Journal*, or would have written only happy poems, only stories about "decent, courageous people" such as she begs her mother to stop asking her for (see *LH*, 477).

To know what the Moon Muse is like, the reader can consult her double in "The Rival," written near the beginning of Plath's final phase of development:

> If the moon smiled, she would resemble you.
> You leave the same impression
> Of something beautiful, but annihilating. [like Medusa]
> Both of you are great light borrowers.
> Her O-mouth grieves at the world; yours is unaffected,
>
> And your first gift is making stone out of everything.

The expressionless face had occurred earlier in "Small Hours"—"The moon lays a hand on my forehead / Blank-faced and mum as a nurse" —where it is suggestive of a gorgoneion, such as the Rondanini mask in Munich.

To see the artistic process as stasis—"a state of equilibrium caused by opposing equal forces"—is not quite the same as seeing it as petrifaction, but the two are related. At Smith, where Leonard Baskin was artist in residence while Sylvia was there, the poet felt his work to be "life livelier than ours, / A solider repose than death's." And what she says about Baskin in this lyric, "Sculptor," Charles Newman applies to her own practice of poetry.[28] An attempt to arrest motion (petrifaction) shows up on almost every page of Sylvia Plath. Like the moon that makes stone of everything, she strives for a lapidarian imagery. Oberg puts her technique thus: "As the images turn to stone there is the reduction of words to fixed objects that neither the poetry of Pound nor Williams ever aspired toward, but that the decadent poetry of number and nightmare curiously did."[29] Richard Howard has brilliantly discussed how she exercises the "lithic impulse" in regard to her portrayal of parts of her body; a few examples are "Lazy Lazarus," "Tulips," "Two Campers in Cloud Country," "Paralytic," and "The Bee Meeting."[30] Just as Actaeon is both hunter and hunted, so Plath is petrifier and petrified.

111

Art as arrested life is not a new concept—Keats's urn, Yeats's golden nightingale—and Plath expresses it in "Two Views of a Cadaver Room," where a skeleton fiddler in a Breughel canvas dances behind Flemish lovers: "Yet desolation, stalled in paint, spares the little country / Foolish, delicate, in the lower right-hand corner." "Stall" here means "to bring to a standstill," in this case time, the stoppage of which Medusa has repeatedly symbolized (see, for example, Louise Bogan's "Medusa"). In "Night Shift" Plath uses "stalled" as "stabled" for the Chrysaor-like monsters tended by workers in the factories that all night long turn out silver under the silver light of the moon. John Nerber's poem "The Factory" employs the same word for the triple Gorgon personality (invention-inventor-Time) whose head will never, like the Baptizer's, be "stalled upon a platter" since no Perseus is possible in the modern world.[31]

On one anagogical level, Medusan symbolism in Sylvia Plath has as the tenor for its vehicle a "false heaven" of drugs. The prescribed drugs she had taken since her adolescence were at least an apprenticeship to death; there can be no rehearsals, since death is a unique event. Robert Bly has commented on what he wrote about drugs in *Sleepers Joining Hands*: "I said I thought the Medusa, or Stone Mother, was connected with all alcoholism among males, and heroin use. So Sonia Sanchez's poems on heroin in *For We are a Baddd People* would be to the point and Berryman's liquor-poems."[32] The common slang term "stoned" for intoxication with either drug bears out Bly's suggestion. In that last dreadful winter, Sylvia's nights were so dispirited that only music and brandy and water got her through them; like an infant, she turned to the breasts of Medusa: "Drunk as a foetus / I suck at the paps of darkness" ("The Stones").

In Plath's case, sedatives, antidepressants, and tranquillizers were a sort of salvation, as in "Cut," "Face Life," and the uncollected "The Jailer," where she calls sleeping capsules her "red and blue zeppelin," though the trip they provide ends in a crash "from a terrible altitude"; in "Tulips" the nurses "bring numbness in their bright needles, they bring sleep." "The Surgeon at 2 A.M." compares the operating room to heaven —"The white light is artificial, and hygienic as heaven"—and its speaker thinks of how the patient he has just operated on "has shut its mouth on the stone pill of repose"; about another patient he reflects, "The angels of morphia have borne him up. / He floats an inch from the ceiling, / Smelling the dawn drafts." Behind all of these drug references lay the initial real experience of 1953, when Sylvia lay for days in a coma induced by the quantities of sleeping pills taken from the bottle in her mother's medicine cabinet.

Her longing for death intensified as illness, poverty, and isolation made an inferno of that last January and early February. Rising at four, unable to sleep, as is the case in severe depression, she poured out her psychic energies into poetry in those quiet hours before Frieda and Nicholas awoke. For her, at this low point, art seemed to be the only accessible and effective therapy. It served her as the mirror-shield served the ghost Plotinus in Pound's "Canto XV": it hardened the oozy slime of hell into ground firm enough for a human foothold. Medusa as prototype of "the outsider" in contemporary poetry is often obsessed with a death wish. What Marya Zaturenska says of Medusa in her poem so named could have been applied to Sylvia in her final days:

> How long she waited for her executioner!
> She who froze life to stone, whose hissing hair
> Once grew as waved and flowing as the sun.
> . . . .
> But now her Perseus comes, foe or deliverer?
> Bringing her welcome end.[33]

On a more affirmative anagogical level, another, more mystical side of Plath appears, coinciding with Yeats's horseman as a type of the artist and as his own choice for epitaph. In the poem that gives the title to her best collection, she and her horse Ariel become one creature; interestingly, it is as partly equine that Medusa herself is often pictured. One meaning of Ariel is "lioness"; Robert Phillips in the essay earlier referred to considers Sylvia "God's lioness," and in this connection we may note that "The Lioness, in Egypt, like the cat and the vulture, typified maternity, and was given to the primitive mother goddesses who frequently had the head of a lioness."[34]

Several critics deny to Sylvia Plath meaningful religious experience, but William V. Davis convincingly sees in both "Ariel" and "Years" (also about riding) accounts of transcendental experience. Davis argues that Plath often used ordinary experience to translate the privateness of what she felt; and that what she felt was "almost like a revelation."[35] In both poems the reader senses "stasis in darkness," the appearance of "stasis" in each being scarcely accidental. It is this stasis that Davis identifies as "a religious mystery." Ariel has two further transcendental senses; it is Jerusalem, fourfold in symbolism, and the spirit of light in The Tempest versus that of Caliban or darkness. One definition of faith is belief in what has already been experienced; in this sense, Sylvia Plath, flying along in the ecstasy of her oneness with Ariel/Pegasus, has every right to be termed an apocalyptic figure.

In the blackness of the moods that immediately preceded her death, as she emptied herself in a cataract of verse, a manic extravagance so different from the thesaurus-centered method of earlier years, Sylvia came to see as the only solution stepping over "the edge." "Freud believed that the aim of all life is death, and for Plath life was poetry. So by extension, poetry for her now becomes death, both conditions inseparable."[36] No one was there to pluck her back, as on that childhood day when she had run into breakers. Alone, she entered that "sea" that even as a child she had imagined to be "*the* mother, mother of the universe that transformed the ordinary processes of existence into the stuff of myth and poetry."[37]

Notes

1. Personal correspondence, 26 February 1974.
2. Introduction to *The Intelligence of Louis Agassiz*, ed. Guy Davenport (Boston: Beacon Press, 1963), p. 12.
3. Pamela Smith, "The Unitive Urge in the Poetry of Sylvia Plath," *New England Quarterly* 45 (September, 1972): 325.
4. Anthony Libby, "God's Lioness and the Priest of Sycorax: Plath and Hughes," *Contemporary Literature* 15 (Fall, 1974): 397.
5. It might be well to introduce a defense of Mrs. Plath. On 9 January 1909, Ezra Pound wrote back from London to his father: "Being family to a wild poet ain't no bed of roses but you stand the strain just fine" (Beinecke Rare Book and Manuscript Library, American Literature Collection, Yale University). Anyone who reads Edward Butscher's *Sylvia Plath: Method and Madness* must realize the difficulties Aurelia Plath was up against in trying to promote her daughter's physical, mental, and spiritual welfare. That Mrs. Plath's role was no bed of roses is clear, and she probably stood the strain as well as most mothers.
6. Ralph Bucksbaum and Loras J. Milne, *The Lower Animals: Living Invertebrates of the World* (New York: Doubleday, 1967), p. 62. Emphasis added.
7. Edward Butscher, *Sylvia Plath: Method and Madness* (New York: Seabury Press, 1976), p. 10.
8. Gene Ballif, "Facing the Worst: A View from Minerva's Buckler," *Parnassus: Poetry in Review* 5 (Fall/Winter, 1976): 244.
9. Sylvia Plath, *Letters Home: Correspondence 1950-1963*, selected and edited with commentary by Aurelia Schober Plath (New York: Harper and Row, 1975), p. 469. Further references to this book are identified within the body of the text as *LH*.
10. Robert Phillips, "The Dark Funnel: A Reading of Sylvia Plath," *Modern Poetry Studies* 3 (Summer, 1972): 68-69.
11. Bucksbaum and Milne, *The Lower Animals*, p. 65.
12. Phillips, "The Dark Funnel," p. 58.
13. Quoted in Judith Kroll, *Chapters in a Mythology* (New York: Harper and Row, 1976), p. 253.
14. Sigmund Freud, *The Standard Edition of The Complete Psychological Words of Freud*, ed. James Strachey (London: Hogarth Press, 1964), vols. 21, 22.
15. Ballif, "Facing the Worst," p. 245.
16. That Plath both acknowledges and rejects this figure for herself—"I am no drudge / Though for years I have eaten dust / And dried plates with my dense hair" ("Stings") —makes it the more likely identification for her mother.
17. In *The Art of Sylvia Plath: A Symposium*, ed. Charles Newman (Bloomington: Indiana University Press, 1970), p. 272.
18. Ballif, "Facing the Worst," p. 245.

19. "Dying Is an Art," in *The Art of Sylvia Plath*, p. 216.
20. Personal correspondence, 22 August 1977.
21. Erich Neumann, *The Great Mother* (Princeton: Princeton University Press, 1974), p. 70.
22. Kroll, *Chapters in a Mythology*, pp. 39-40.
23. See Rober Graves, *The White Goddess* (New York: Farrar, Strauss, and Giroux, 1966), p. 230.
24. Frederick Thomas Elworthy, *The Evil Eye* (New York: Julian Press, 1958), p. 66.
25. Cited in *Letters Home* (Harper and Row, 1975), p. 296.
26. Elizabeth A. Goldsmith, *Ancient Pagan Symbols* (New York: AMS Press, 1929), p. 164.
27. Richard Howard, "Sylvia Plath: 'And I Have No Face, I Have Wanted to Efface Myself . . . ,'" in *The Art of Sylvia Plath*, p. 85.
28. See Charles Newman, "Candor is the Only Wile," in *The Art of Sylvia Plath*.
29. Arthur K. Oberg, "Sylvia Plath and the New Decadence," *Chicago Review* 20 (Spring, 1968): 67.
30. See Howard, "Sylvia Plath."
31. In *The Spectre Image* (New York: Simon and Schuster, 1946), pp. 27-28.
32. Personal correspondence, March, 1974.
33. Marya Zaturenska, *Collected Poems* (New York: Viking, 1965), p. 63.
34. Goldsmith, *Ancient Pagan Symbols*, p. 69.
35. William V. Davis, "Sylvia Plath's 'Ariel,'" *Modern Poetry Studies* 3 (Winter, 1972): 183.
36. Phillips, "The Dark Funnel," p. 71.
37. Butscher, *Sylvia Plath*, p. 9.

Gary Lane

Influence and originality in Plath's poems

The early burden of most poets is the search for voice, a search that involves, as Harold Bloom and others have shown, the anxious digesting and reconstituting of a meaty precursor, the struggle with a father poet. Theodore Roethke's work, with its early, formal embrace of Yeats and its subsequent, meditative disengagement, is a model of the process; Sylvia Plath's search is more complicated, less paradigmatic. It begins with a scurry among many voices—Plath's gift for poetic mimicry was always exceptional—quickly narrows to four major influences, and at last, as the first poem in her first volume prematurely announces, "Come[s] clear of the shadow,"[1] etching a wholly original voice deep into the landscape of contemporary poetry. My concern here is two-fold: to track the early, imitative phase, marking borrowings as they appear in the poems and suggesting a logic to their appropriation, and to characterize the originality of the voice Plath finally made her own.

This division admits both preference and value judgment. I can remember hearing John Ciardi speak strongly for the absence of a vocal signature—the materials of the poem, not the stance or presence of the poet, he urged, should shape its voice—but I am not of his party. Much as I admire some of the early, variously influenced poems of Plath, it is for me the later ones, in which influence has been largely subsumed, that count most. There she found her special and terrible voice, her intensity; and that, if anything, is what constitutes the force of her individual talent on poetic tradition. I examine influence, then, with an ear to the realized poet who succeeded or digested or disengaged from it, and with adherence to the critical piety, now unpopular, that without *The Colossus*, the utterances of *Ariel* would have been unthinkable. My justification, however, diverges from Peter Davison and John Frederick Nims, who argued that only the deliberate technical training of the first book made possible the internalized discipline of the second. Rather than a process of technical assimilation, the influenced phase was for Plath primarily a shield and a permission: it defended her from the nakedness of her pain and her ferocity, and yet it allowed her to begin struggling with the materials from which those feelings arose. Thus, though her early scurry among voices seems to imply indiscrimination, we are misled to suppose so; though Plath may appear merely to be dragging the lake of poetic voice, her catch corresponds precisely to the creatures of her own psychic depths. From "under the fishpond surface" that is both accumulated literature and individual psyche, mirrors "Reach hag hands to haul [her] in." And she winds up fishing particularly the work of Dylan Thomas, Theodore Roethke, Wallace Stevens, and W. B. Yeats, because in each of them she hears formulated a crucial aspect of herself.

This is by no means to dismiss the presence in her work of other borrowings, nor to set up the writers I have mentioned as a sacred quartet. Other poets were important to Plath, and we hear some both early and late. Emily Dickinson, for example, lies behind both the structural reversal of "Lorelei" (1957-58) and a crucial image in "Contusion" (February, 1963). In the former, Plath adopts Dickinson's trick of beginning with a firm, one line declaration—"I know that He exists." "This World is not Conclusion."—and undermining it as the poem develops "—Narcotics cannot still the Tooth / That nibbles at the Soul." The speaker of "Lorelei" begins by asserting that "It is no night to drown in," but the seductive muses beneath the river lay siege to that intention, and in the end she asks, "Stone, stone, ferry me down there." In the last week of her life Plath would return to Dickinson, whose permanently fixed heart, closing "the Valves of her attention— / Like Stone," is the mechanical weight behind "Contusion": "The heart shuts." Auden, an early enthusiasm, sustained dozens of unpublished imitations and such published ones as "Ballade Banale" and "Notes on Zarathustra's Prologue":

Today bright jetplanes cry abroad
their whirlwind message: God is dead!

Look to lightning for tongues of pain:
steep are the stairs to the Superman.

His fine rendering of Breughel's *The Fall of Icarus*—"the expensive, delicate ship that must have seen / Something amazing, a boy falling out of the sky"—finds its way into Plath's recreation of another Breughel painting, *The Triumph of Death*: "Yet desolation, stalled in paint, spares the little country / Foolish, delicate, in the lower right hand corner." There is even an occasional bit of Eliot, whose strongly cadenced drawing room sirens—"In the room the women come and go"—are transformed, with an extra metrical foot, into pickled sybils by Plath: "In their jars the snail-nosed babies moon and glow."

I want to distinguish, however, between influences—poets to whose cadences or strategies Plath turned so often that we induce emotional terrain from vocal signature—and acquaintances. Hopkins chants from behind these lines of "Strumpet Song"—

Walks there not some such one man
As can spare breath
To patch with brand of love this rank grimace

—and the Frost of "An Old Man's Winter Night" can be heard behind this section of "Hardcastle Crags":

All the night gave her, in return
For the paltry gift of her bulk and the beat
Of her heart was the humped indifferent iron
Of its hills.

But these echoes are not central to Plath's search for voice. Like similar mimicries—of Shakespeare and Cummings, Lawrence and Hart Crane, Lowell and Ted Hughes—they are nods of acquaintance, hats tried and returned to the shelf: they do not quite become her.

We might develop the Frost example as a means of clarifying the distinction between influence and acquaintance. I attach two conditions to the status of influence and argue for their coincidence: the influential poet is heard frequently in the receiving writer's work; and the rhetorical strategies that define the influential poet generate an emotion that is crucial to the receiving poet. A reading of Plath will easily verify the absence of the first condition, frequency, with respect to Frost. For the second, we must look more closely. In "An Old Man's Winter Night,"

Frost articulates the diminution of identity in his poem's aging subject; more precisely, he dramatizes that diminution by animating the old man's surroundings and making him inanimate:

> All out-of-doors looked darkly in at him
> Through the thin frost, almost in separate stars,
> That gathers on the pane in empty rooms.
> What kept his eyes from giving back the gaze
> Was the lamp tilted near them in his hand.

As the threatening and encompassing night "looked darkly in" at an old man whose eyes were "kept . . .from giving back the gaze," the reversal of expected roles and power begins. The genitive in the poem's title prefigures it: he who "can't keep a house, / A farm, a countryside," can scarcely own a winter night. Instead, the title ironically breeds its obverse, a winter night's old man.

In the passage quoted earlier from "Hardcastle Crags," Plath relies on these lines from Frost. Her poem, however, does not share an emotion with his. Nature and the loss of identity are subjects common to the two, but there is fullness and recognition and acceptance in Frost's poem, while Plath's is the barely soothed record of a scare. Frost's old man is a fallen warrior, age his Achilles heel; Plath's nervous heroine, withdrawing from the massive threat to her consciousness, remains intact. The relationship between the poets is external, casual; and because it is, because Plath's material cannot draw usefully on the emotional resonances of Frost's voice, her mind's ear led her away from that cadence.

Examples like this might be multiplied almost at will—in Plath's early poems we hear an irregular babel of other poets' voices—but only coerced industry would catalogue them all. I can find no poem in *The Colossus* that does not utter vocal indebtedness, though the debt ranges from a dim, purely reflexive echo of Frost at the close of "The Manor Garden" to the wholesale vocal theft of "Maudlin," all Dylan Thomas's;[2] ranges, that is, from the just perceivable link between two sets of closing lines that resemble each other in key word repetition and archaism—

> The small birds converge, converge,
> With their gifts to a difficult borning.
>
> (Plath)

> Better to go down dignified
> With boughten friendship at your side
> Than none at all. Provide, provide!
>
> (Frost)

—to the appropriation of another's idiom, cadence, and opacity. We are interested, however, in a logic of borrowing, not in the overwhelming richness of a catalogue's detail. To see that logic, we must turn to major voices.

Dylan Thomas is the vocal colossus of *The Colossus*, the father poet whose virtual suicide corresponds in a curious way to the needless death of Otto Plath. It is Thomas's rhetorical surf of assonance, of clicking consonants, of syntactic swells, that we hear throughout the early poems. Plath knew it, and we may suppose that she heard behind the putative subject of "Hardcastle Crags" its deeper one, the struggle to escape the "Loom[ing]. . . antique world" of poetic inheritance. Certainly she must have been thinking of her immersion in that self-confessedly "windy boy," Dylan Thomas, when she wrote, perfectly mimicking him:

> The long wind, paring her person down
> To a pinch of flame, blew its burdened whistle
> In the whorl of her ear, and like a scooped-out
>   pumpkin crown
> Her head cupped the babel.

The threat of an alien nature in "Hardcastle Crags" is as much a veil as is its borrowed voice. Both conceal, though to different degrees, the danger that would not there be voiced: individuation undone, the absent, omnipresent father. For Plath, the gigantism of Thomas, always Ann's bard on a raised hearth and erecting skyward statues, is a scale commensurate to the greatness of her need. Later, maturing as a poet, she would mold her own mask and through its mouth-hole pour like plasma the intensities of her feelings. Wearing Thomas's voice, however, in its size and character, she might encode yet be protected from these feelings.

Size and character—these determine Plath's investiture of Thomas. She is drawn to his grandness, never to his modesties (which *are* modest for Thomas, though they might be other men's brags); romantic overreacher, she embraces "After the Funeral" rather than "Poem in October." But grandness, though it points to performance rather than poetry, makes sense for Plath. She would evoke, confront, ultimately exorcize a colossus; woman and stickless, she could not speak softly. Thomas's borrowed style meets the colossus on his own terms—though of course they are not yet *her* terms—defiant in volume and language and cadence whatever the avowed stance of a poem.

"Maudlin" is a demonstration of this, a gesture of defense in Thomas's grandest and densest manner. The poem mixes "If I were tickled by the rub of love" and "Altarwise by owl-light," shakes them, but does not stir:

> Mud-mattressed under the sign of the hag
> In a clench of blood, the sleep-talking virgin
> Gibbets with her curse the moon's man,
> Faggot-bearing Jack in his crackless egg:
>
> Hatched with a claret hogshead to swig
> He kings it, navel-knit to no groan,
> But at the price of a pin-stitched skin
> Fish-tailed girls purchase each white leg.

Here lifelessness is less interesting than strategy. In undercutting the spiritually invulnerable Christ—"Faggot-bearing Jack in his crackless egg" —and humanizing both his physically distressed mother and the "Fish-tailed girls" hopeful of phylogenesis, Plath defies a colossus. Using Thomas's grandness, she could do so without facing her true king, without risking her own fish-tail.

Thomas's voice has also the advantage for Plath of its character. He is at heart an elegist, in poignant mourning for the lost Eden of Fern Hill, presexuality, deathlessness. Plath, too, is an adult whose grieving child cries within, and Thomas's sensuous cadence echoes her longing for "A place, a time gone out of mind." We have but to hold "The Eye-mote" or "Ocean 1212-W" against "Fern Hill" or "Poem in October" to feel how Plath's anxious nostalgia merges with Thomas's: adults who know they can't go home, both beat nonetheless upon the door. Yet for Thomas the expulsion is general, natural, inevitable; for Plath it is narrowly specified, a personal injustice. Thus Thomas's elegiac swell draws us with him and somehow extends what he would mourn, while Plath's appropriation of him, like the past that she envisions, is at last a dead end: "My father died, we moved inland. Whereon those nine first years of my life sealed themselves off like a ship in a bottle—beautiful, inaccessible, obsolete, a fine, white flying myth."

Thomas never died in Plath's poetry—an influence absorbed becomes an aspect of the realized new poet—but her poems did move inland, away from the crashing periodicities of rhetoric. I am not arguing purely from chronology here; development is a different though related matter and must be left for another place. But Thomas as father poet, even during the period of his sway—between the earliest published poems and somewhere around 1959—might have days off. Inland, Plath encountered Theodore Roethke and Wallace Stevens, and for a time their voices, too, propped up her poems.

Roethke's is the more acknowledged influence, and the more susceptible of delineation. Ted Hughes tells us that when they stayed at Yaddo in the fall of 1959 she was reading Roethke "closely and sympathetically for the first time," and certainly his voice overwhelms the major composition of that stay, "Poem for a Birthday."[3] But Plath had known Roethke long before. She was lost daughter to his lost son, both of them discovering a bewildering precision behind the easy euphemism, "to lose" one's father; in their long and painful searches for a dead Papa Otto —searches whose Oedipal tug might be reflected in the very process of vocal influence—they were nearly siblings.

No surprise, then, that as early as 1956 Plath was echoing Roethke, though the Roethke of *Open House;* she was not to find a use for the rooty, dissociated language of *The Lost Son* and *Praise to the End* until "Poem for a Birthday." "All the Dead Dears" amalgamates for its Freudean gothic several of Roethke's first poems, "The Premonition," "Prognosis," and "Feud." In Plath's poem, a sixteen-hundred-year-old museum skeleton suggests the grinding of "Our own grist down to its bony face"; like the devouring mother in Roethke's "Prognosis" and her own later "Medusa," the skeleton will "suck / Blood and whistle my marrow clean" in claiming kinship. Roethke had grappled with a similarly ferocious past and found, in "Feud," that "The spirit starves / Until the dead have been subdued." An adjacent poem, "The Premonition," suggests the origin of his spiritual haunting. Walking an Edenic field with "my father," the poet forsees death and paradise lost:

> He dipped his hand in the shallow:
> Water ran over and under
> Hair on a narrow wrist bone.

The discovery of the skull beneath the skin is of course no patent of Roethke's—in the passage just quoted he borrows Donne's "bracelet of bright haire about the bone"—but it is Roethke's treatment of this mortality theme that gives strategic direction to "All the Dead Dears." Moving, like him, from the amorphous, kin-claiming dead to the event that animated them, Plath echoes his enactment of first loss. In Roethke's poem, the father's

> . . .image kept following after,—
> Flashed with the sun in the ripple.
> But when he stood up, that face
> Was lost in a maze of water.

In Plath's, behind "Mother, grandmother, greatgrandmother / . . .an image looms under the fishpond surface / Where the daft father went down."

Sharing father-loss as a crucial event, Plath and Roethke shared its fragmentation; and both longed for a return to coherence, a coherence associated with the absent father and one that might be regained by a process of psychic reconciliation with him. Among Roethke's most important poetic leaps was to find for himself a language that might *enact* rather than *convey* this process, the language of speech-gifted tendrils, of rocks and roots, ids, kids, and madmen: a language simple, dissociative, unindividuated, uncensored. Using it he might recapture the feelings that a carefully defended adult had not permitted himself; and recapturing them, he might at last make peace with his loss and reintegrate his present. Out of that new language came poems like "The Lost Son," "The Shape of the Fire," "I Need, I Need," psychological process poems, as if Thomas's "The force that through the green fuse drives the flower" had gone underground:

> Stop the larks. Can I have my heart back?
> Today I saw a beard in a cloud.
> The ground cried my name:
> Good-bye for being wrong.
> Love helps the sun.
> But not enough.

It was this new kind of poetry that overwhelmed Plath's birthday sequence. She had been in the habit of composing laboriously, a thesaurus on one knee; now the confluence of Roethke, her first pregnancy, and Paul Radin (whose collection of African folk tales she was reading at Yaddo) brought her to a turning point. She would discard the academic baggage from her poems, free herself, as Roethke had, to go native; she would hear the archetypal language of the subconscious, the universal child within her.

Yet the birthday sequence does nothing of the kind. Even in Roethke's voice Plath stays too narrative, too plot conscious; she had not his gift for surrender, and everything died too hard with her. In the most child-spoken parts of the sequence—"Dark House," "Maenad," and "The Beast," poems whose language and cadence is wholly Roethke's—we miss the child's surprising flights, imagination's leap: "Stop the larks. Can I have my heart back?" Instead, Plath's imagining remains linear, disciplined, an adult trying baby-talk:

> He won't be got rid of:
> Mumblepaws, teary and sorry,
> Fido Littlesoul, the bowel's familiar.
> A dustbin's enough for him.
> The dark's his bone.
> Call him any name, he'll come to it.

There is considerable difference between this passage and "The Colossus" or "All the Dead Dears," but it is less different than meets the eye. In "All the Dead Dears," the ankle-bone of a skeleton or "Any touch, taste, tang's / Fit for those outlaws to ride home on"; in "The Beast," "The dark's his bone. / Call him any name, he'll come to it." Major changes will not come until Plath controls her own voice, however discursive: "The police love you, you confess everything." With the birthday sequence Plath announces the search for a door to her material. Roethke's voice would not open for her, but its adoption in these poems was a crucial gesture, a recognition that the carefully modulated chamber of *The Colossus* could not contain her.

Most careful of the modulations in that chamber is the voice of Wallace Stevens, elegant, gaudy, aesthetically cool. Stevens's is the vocal consciousness of distance, of the mind's analytic play and freedom. Plath borrows his diction because its dandified, portly resonances suggest a mind that is taking calm stock of itself, an idea of order; she pursues his philosophical subject matter for the same reason. Stevens, as has become clear from recent writings, was a man deeply threatened by emotional fragmentation; in the gorgeous play of the mind in poetry, in his rage to order existential chaos by "ghostlier demarcations, keener sounds," he protected himself from the domination of black. Plath's poems face the same fear—the domination of black is for her embodied in "the black man who / Bit my pretty red heart in two"—and her early adoptive poetics found in Stevens a useful weapon.

"Night Shift" exemplifies both the fear and the defense. Indebted to Stevens's "Not Ideas about the Thing but the Thing Itself," whose plot and language it echoes, the poem presents an escape from solipsism, a shaky but apparently salubrious recognition that there is a reality external to the self. The movement—the title's pun on "shift" prefigures it—is from the speaker's initially solipsistic frame of mind to her awareness of "blunt / Indefatigable fact." Like Frost's white wave, however, the poem runs counter to itself. Beyond its conscious surface, Plath images self-containment as vibrant and interesting, the world as coarse and sterile. At a level she may not have been aware of, reality has become Stevens's fixed, infertile Tennessee jar, solipsism, an internalized, fecund wilderness.

The poem begins with an assertion, yet one so structured into repetition and insistence that we hear in it the counter-assertion's terror:

> It was not a heart, beating,
> That muted boom, that clangor
> Far off, not blood in the ears
> Drumming up any fever
>
> To impose on the evening.
> The noise came from the outside.

The telltale rhetoric here shades toward Poe's italics—his guilt-crazed murderer declares: "the noise was *not* within my ears," though of course it was—and betrays the speaker's fear of self-enclosure. It suggests as well the difficulty of identification, and by extension, self-identification: we learn first what the noise is *not*. As the poem develops, the sound is verified as external. It is the speech of civilization, the mechanical drum of "Main Street's / Silver factory"; it is otherness, the Johnsonian rock upon which a Berkleyan consciousness can kick its own refutation. And though the sound lacks the color of imagination—men in "white // Under-shirts" tend it, the analogues of Stevens's disillusioning white nightgowns—it is *there*, "blunt / Indefatigable fact."

Plath's debt to "Not Ideas about the Thing but the Thing Itself" is considerable. In that poem, the external noise seemed at first "like a sound in his mind." But "It was not from the vast ventriloquism / Of sleep's faded papier-maché"; instead, it "was coming from outside. / . . .It was like / A new knowledge of reality." Plath has seized Stevens's poem of the mind and ordered her own chaos from its strategies. If her material remains under wraps—the deeper subject of "Night Shift" is the exacer-bated sensibility of its first five lines, something the poem does not explore—Plath manages nevertheless to suggest both its force and its danger. In the process of denying it, she touches on the isolation that would ultimately overwhelm a lost daughter in a fatherless land; without specifying them, she brushes past the rich terrors of internal experience and counterpoises them only to the hellish round of the world, ceaselessly "hoisted, . . . / Stalled, [and] let fall."

A second aspect of Stevens's influence lies in his endless exploration of poetry as subject, in his devotion to the relationship between creative imagination and the world. Plath, too, thought constantly about that relationship—it is the subject of "Mad Girl's Love Song," one of her first published poems, and "Words," her last—and she found in Stevens a model whose strategies she could usefully appropriate. "Black Rook in Rainy Weather" is a case in point. In her concern for the poet in a dry spell, Plath echoes "The Man Whose Pharynx Was Bad." There,

> The time of year has grown indifferent.
> Mildew of summer and the deepening snow
> Are both alike in the routine I know.

In Plath's poem, we hear a similar "fear / Of total neutrality." Plath's metaphor for the epiphany that suspends this neutral condition also echoes Stevens. In "Angel Surrounded by Paysans" he writes of "the necessary angel" in whose imaginative sight we "see the earth again"; she awaits "the angel" in whose presence "A certain minor light may still / Leap incandescent // Out of kitchen table or chair."

125

A final and less obvious example of Stevens's influence is "A Winter Ship," one of those curious still lifes that suggest the importance of painting to the *Colossus* poems. Unlike "Watercolor of Grantchester Meadows," where the still life is a deliberately deceptive surface, foil for the predatory drama enacted when the nursery plate darkens, "A Winter Ship" seems largely static. Read, however, in the context of its precursor, Stevens's "The Man on the Dump," Plath's poem has movement. Its deeper subject is style, Plath's picturesque, academic poetry of the fifties. Composed at Yaddo in 1959, during her first pregnancy and just before the final move to England, the poem is a farewell to what has been and an indication of what's coming.

Stevens's poem yearns for the renewal of imagination by an exposure to unmediated reality, by an abandonment of metaphor. The man on the dump is the poet perched upon the rubbish heap of stale images:

> Day creeps down. The moon is creeping up.
> The sun is a corbeil of flowers the moon Blanche
> Places there, a bouquet. Ho-ho . . . The dump is full
> Of images.

The poet's renewal is a purification:

> Everything is shed; and the moon comes up as the moon
> (All its images are in the dump) and you see
> As a man (not like the image of a man),
> You see the moon rise in an empty sky.

Achieving this, he would be reunited with the naked earth, the raw specificity of the phenomena, "The the." Plath's poem turns on a similar desire. Amid the metaphors that had become easy and stale for her—"The sea pulses under a skin of oil," "A gull holds his pose . . . / . . .in a jacket of ashes," "A blimp swims up like a day-moon or tin / Cigar over his rink of fishes" (this last wholly derived from Stevens)—the speaker misses the primacy of things, of self. The poem has proceeded through twenty-odd lines of glossy metaphor when, for the first and only time, the speaker talks of herself: "We wanted to see the sun come up / And are met, instead, by this iceribbed ship." Here is the poem's tension. Poising the unmodified sun against the iceribbed ship, Plath encodes—I cannot think she does so consciously—her disappointment with the masked, rigid thesaurus poems she had been writing, her desire for a direct and vulnerable poetry. The ship becomes Dickinson's soul-bearing frigate, a craft in two senses; it is the poem as vehicle, here becalmed and magnified in its own bell jar, "every winch and stay / Encased in a glassy pellicle."

As the sun rises in an empty sky, we await the dissolution of the frozen ship *Colossus*, the blood jet of the new poetry: "The sun will diminish it soon enough: / Each wave-tip glitters like a knife."

The influence of Yeats on Plath, extending more broadly than the poetic fatherhoods of Thomas, Roethke, or Stevens, is such as to legitimize him grand- or god-father. Barnett Guttenberg has admirably set out the dialectical aspects of the relationship. Plath, he argues, "builds a complete system, with a Yeatsian antithetical vision and consistent clusters of Yeatsian imagery. In addition, she seems to offer a series of rejoinders on various points of disagreement."[4] It will be well to confine discussion here to the way Plath uses Yeats's voice.

An early example is the essentially hermetic impulse of "Spinster," a poem in the thrall of Yeats's glimmering nineties. His Maud/Helen figure in "The Sorrow of Love" disrupts

> The brawling of a sparrow in the eaves,
> The brilliant moon and all the milky sky,
> And all that famous harmony of leaves.

She plays havoc with natural order. Plath's spinster fears a similar disruption. "During a ceremonious April walk / With her latest suitor" —the formal adjective carries Yeats's sense of tradition, of ritual as a defense against chaos—she is "intolerably struck / By the birds' irregular babel / And the leaves' litter." It is the subjectivity of passionate involvement that apprehends Yeats's sparrows and Plath's birds as discrepant polyglots, that makes litter of harmonious leaves. Plath's heroine longs instead for winter, "Scrupulously austere in its order[,] / . . .each sentiment within border"; like Yeats's Sligo hermit,

> She withdrew neatly.
>
> And round her house she set
> Such a barricade of barb and check
> Against mutinous weather
> As no mere insurgent man could hope to break
> With curse, fist, threat
> Or love, either.

She will fence off an Innisfree, have her regular "Nine bean-rows. . . / And live alone." Both poets show an early fear of freckled life, a fear that poses as aristocratic disdain. Yeats, who imperiously scorned the casual, comic Ireland he misunderstood before the Easter Uprising, thought he lived "where motley is worn"; Plath's spinster scorns April love, "a burgeoning / Unruly enough to pitch her five queenly wits / Into vulgar motley."

A somewhat later example, "Heavy Women," echoes the more mature Yeats; the glimmer is gone, replaced by the ominous shadow of historic inevitability. Plath's pregnant women, "Irrefutable, beautifully smug / As Venus," are

> calm as a moon or a cloud.
>
> Smiling to themselves, they meditate
> Devoutly as the Dutch bulb
> Forming its twenty petals.

Both within and without, however, "The dark still nurses its secret." "Looping wool" on the bobbin of self, the women are unwittingly bound by the skein of history. Though, hooded in "Mary-blue," they "listen for the millennium, / The knock of the small, new heart," the twenty-petaled Christ children within them can accomplish "nothing in particular": "On the green hill" waits "the thorn tree." Against the warmth of a desired future, the historic "axle of winter / Grinds round, bearing down with the straw, / The star, the wise grey men."

All is diminished here, mechanical, threatening. The straw was once grass, the life-governing star is, as we will later learn in "Words," "fixed," and the wise grey men are Yeats's pale, rigid magi, unsatisfied by Calvary's turbulence. Plath's concern for Hiroshima surfaces, as she said, obliquely —in "a child forming itself finger by finger in the dark." Behind "Heavy Women" is Yeats's "The Second Coming," a specter of savagery and recurrence:

> but now I know
> That twenty centuries of stony sleep
> Were vexed to nightmare by a rocking cradle,
> And what rough beast, its hour come round at last,
> Slouches towards Bethlehem to be born?

In Yeats's poem, "The darkness drops again," a falcon is "Turning and turning" in the widening gyre, and the troubling image comes "out of Spiritus Mundi." In "Heavy Women" we hear a similar language: "The dark still nurses its secret," the women are "Looping" wool, and they step "among the archetypes." In both poems, history is an iron wheel, a juggernaut crushing petty men beneath it. Yeats's rough historical beast is an ancestor of Plath's colossus—his is "A shape with lion body and the head of a man, / A gaze blank and pitiless as the sun," while hers has "Mule-bray, pig-grunt and bawdy cackles," "Immense skull plates," and "bald, white tumuli" for eyes — but Yeats's beast is public, Plath's colossus quite personal. And though in "Heavy Women" that colossal father is abstracted, made "pithy and historical," he remains traceable. At bottom, Plath's historical voice is another mask, an investment in public system against the terrible risk of private confrontation. Yeats, whose personal anguishes lived intimately with his political ones, might make great poetry in such a voice; from the lofty slope of his vision he truly surveyed the human scene. Plath's vision was far narrower. It never compassed much more than the arc of herself, and its poetic fulfillment required that she speak from a less elevated vantage, the valley of the shadow of death.

Intensity is what that valley had to offer. In the late poems, travelling light and unshepherded there, Plath cast aside what had by then become academic baggage — "Dead hands, dead stringencies" — and was able to weld, at great heat and under great pressure, a uniquely intense voice. The acetylene burning of image, the fury of tone, the headlong acceleration — these were compressed, dark ink on light paper, like her wintering bees:

> Now they ball in a mass,
> Black
> Mind against all that white.

She became "The pure gold baby // That melts to a shriek," at once the immolated innocent, orgasmic siren, and self-destroying poet; but always wringing intensity from the lines, always "turning the burners up."

The change is a function of simultaneous castings off, and though Plath had been working toward them for some time, a biographical event almost symbolically coincides with their first full realization. The later voice begins in March of 1961 with "Tulips," written while Plath recovered from an appendectomy. It is as if the operation, removing something unnecessary, completed her freedom. Ted Hughes tells us that "She wrote this poem without her usual studies over the Thesaurus, and at top speed, as one might write an urgent letter. From then on, all her poems were written in this way." Appendix and thesaurus are analogues here, two vestigial storehouses now discarded. Internally, Plath would no longer hold to the polished evasions of her previous work; externally, she would cease depending on the voices of the past that had formed and informed that work. A quartet of fathers had made possible the collective defense against personal terror, a compelling fear of disintegration. Yet for Plath their embrace was curiously self-contradictory. More suitable and fruitful would be a process of simultaneous struggle, of symbolic correspondence. In the early poems she had adopted new fathers to fight against what Roethke ambiguously called "Father Fear." In the later ones, perhaps consciously realizing the significance of the act, she would free herself from the voices of others as she fought to free herself from public and private history.

Plath's originality lies in the uniqueness of the voice that emerged. Alternately self-enlarging and self-appalled, wild at its hurts and wild to avenge them, the late voice can be elegant, torrential, formal, weary, tender, hopeless, furious. It is always hard-edged and brilliant and, at its best, terrifyingly controlled. Indeed, the tension in Plath's late poetry has much to do with our unease at the specter of so much feeling so tightly reined. We half expect these poems to bolt at any moment, and some, like "The Other," do. Many, however, hold their gait into the very cauldron of morning.

No other voice is quite like this. There are antecedents, of course—I hear a consciousness of Brecht's *Verfremdungseffekt* and of the cool and unfathomable cage of ironies in Kafka's "Ein Hunger Kunstler"—but Plath's combination of passion and distance is unique. She sometimes borrows the ironic perspective of Joyce, and some of the techniques of that perspective, but she dips them into a boil of psychological complexity. We respond simply, empathetically, to pandied little Stephen Dedalus, our own hands curled, crawling, crushed; and that response sets us up for the equally decisive undercutting of Stephen's ensuing triumph. But Plath, who loves us far less than Joyce did, will not bear such intimacy. She fends us off—"I am too pure for you or anyone"—even as her poems beckon.

"Cut," with its wry and terrible self-knowledge, its manic and cunningly associative imagery, and its bold, bald gallows humor exemplifies Plath's later voice:

> What a thrill—
> My thumb instead of an onion,

it begins, the nervous brilliance of this start already preparing us for the flirtation with insight that the poem enacts. Through the first five stanzas the performance continues, the tough-girl smile, half grimace, stays fixed:

> The top quite gone
> Except for a sort of a hinge
>
> Of skin,
> A flap like a hat,
> Dead white.
> Then that red plush.
>
> Little pilgrim,
> The Indian's axed your scalp.
> Your turkey wattle
> Carpet rolls

> Straight from the heart.
> I step on it,
> Clutching my bottle
> Of pink fizz.
>
> A celebration, this is.
> Out of a gap
> A million soldiers run,
> Redcoats, every one.

We are watching an entertainment, a tour de force, with the speaker as conscious as we are of her gifts. How the roller coaster of her diction ranges! The casual slovenliness of "What a thrill" and "a sort of hinge // Of skin" gives breathtaking way to the sudden precision of "that red plush." How her images breed! Holding the lacerated hand before her eyes, fingers stiffly spread, she sees the turkey that we traced as children, and the poem grows colonial, with pilgrims and Indians. The frothy thumb becomes a champagne bottle, the Thanksgiving celebration general; and here come the redcoats!

But beneath this manic catalogue, exultation lies down. The act that precipitated the poem is self mutilation, and however the speaker colors it, what "rolls // Straight from the heart" is her blood. Behind a distancing gallows humor that casually accepts, there is revulsion. And the poem, as if hearing itself, turns:

> Whose side are they on?
> O my
> Homunculus, I am ill.
> I have taken a pill to kill
>
> The thin
> Papery feeling.
> Saboteur,
> Kamikaze man—
>
> The stain on your
> Gauze Ku Klux Klan
> Babushka
> Darkens and tarnishes and when
>
> The balled
> Pulp of your heart
> Confronts its small
> Mill of silence
>
> How you jump—
> Trepanned veteran,
> Dirty girl,
> Thumb stump.

Performance has not ceased here, but grown less jaunty, more intense. The thumb continues its fantastic metamorphoses—the "flap like a hat, / Dead white" has bred a "Gauze Ku Klux Klan / Babushka"—but the violence turns ominous. Admitting she is "ill," the speaker begins to see her intention in the wound. It is an inside job, a little suicide, and the cut thumb is now "Saboteur, / Kamikaze man." In the first half, sentences had been short, jagged, with places to rest. In this last, the poem gains speed and energy, rushing its fourteen-line final sentence toward the shuddering impact of self-hatred. The entertainment, the safely exciting perils of sawmilled heroine, are over. The lumberyard is internal, and no intervention stays the "balled / Pulp" from "its small / Mill of silence." Plath has gathered all her vocal forces toward a stunning convergence. In the end, the Protean thumb is wrestled back to itself, but the speaker's awareness, and our own, has altered. In three intensifying double blows—

> Trépānned véterān,
>
> Dírtȳ gírl,
>
> Thúmb stúmp.

—the poem bangs shut. The wounds of experience, the revulsion toward womanhood, the blunt finality of action—these are the thematic reverberations of the images, and their rhythmic emphasis marks each one a coffin nail.

This supremely heightened close characterizes one inflection of the late voice, that of such poems as "Lady Lazarus," "Poppies in October," "Ariel," "Purdah," "Medusa," "Daddy," "Fever 103°," and "Stings." There is the rapture of exorcism in it, a taut, linguistic violence that strikes us almost like a physical blow. A second inflection is less aggressive, less centrifugal; its intensity is linked not to ecstatic speed but to rigid calm, a sense of foreclosure. There are no roller coasters here. Instead, in poems like "Winter Trees," "Poppies in July," "Edge," and "Words," we approach the realm of archetype, of formal, stylized action. Understatement subsumes the role of volubility, and though behind these lines a heart has broken, no syllable would stir to mourn or mend it.

"Contusion" is such a poem, the titular distinction between it and "Cut" already suggesting a less gaudy, more formal aura. Nothing pours from this wound: the blood is all beneath the surface. "Cut" began with a wryly idiomatic understatement and grew louder and more manic, its images detonating against each other as if to push the curve of binding energy. "Contusion" begins with a momentary flood and then withdraws, its first three stanzas ebbing and ebbing until all that remains is the bleached human desert of the close:

> Colour floods to the spot, dull purple.
> The rest of the body is all washed out,
> The colour of pearl.
>
> In a pit of rock
> The sea sucks obsessively,
> One hollow the whole sea's pivot.
>
> The size of a fly,
> The doom mark
> Crawls down the wall.
>
> The heart shuts.
> The sea slides back,
> The mirrors are sheeted.

Emotion and hope are extinguished here, and we sense that the speaker, emptied of them and not even a presence in the poem, has grown "used to this sort of thing." The drama has gone out of death, leaving a bare and terrible acceptance. In "Death & Co." we can almost heft the foreboding, but the speaker will not go gentle. In "Contusion," the movement is toward entropy. Reversing the flight of "Ariel," the poem returns to "Stasis in darkness."

Yet all is elegance in this quietude, and, poising that elegance against the certainty of extinction, Plath generates a great intensity. Inevitability has replaced astonishment, and the architectural purity of image, lent weight by the weariness of these end-stopped lines, makes everything grave. Three foci—"the spot," "a pit of rock," and "The doom mark" —concentrate the poem's diminishment and support the narrative spaces between stanzas; their progression, from the "dull purple" possibility of life to the crawling certainty of doom, is less tractible and more stark than narration. With the finality of mathematics the concluding tercet draws all three together. The pump that had sent blood beneath the wound now "shuts"; the sea, which had gathered, "slides back"; and in the house of the dead, "The mirrors are sheeted." This is a voice no longer human. It is that of Plath's moon, "bald and wild," with "nothing to be sad about." Already we can hear "Her blacks crackle and drag" in the ritualized, mourning-clothed procession for the dead.

Many of the late poems, of course, are neither as heightened as "Cut" nor as stark as "Contusion," but throughout its range Plath's late voice holds its overtones. It is serious, wounded, isolated, taut. A softness enters it now and again, but it never slackens into familiarity and cannot bound into delight. It is exceptionally strong, wholly uncompromising. And it prepossesses: we hear in it an intimacy with pain that both frightens and fascinates. Plath, like Conrad's Kurtz, knows the depths. "It is what you fear," she tells us; "I do not fear it: I have been there." I think it worth listening to a final, more medial example of this voice, a poem less extreme than the ones just explored. "Morning Song" has more of human situation in it than they do, and more variety of tone. Yet from the strange, estranged beginning to the precise and perfect close, Plath marks everything her own.

The poem begins with a distance. The persona, a new mother, feels unincluded in the happening of her child, uncomfortable at the way it alters her marriage, and threatened by the mortality the child reflects:

> Love set you going like a fat gold watch.
> The midwife slapped your footsoles, and your bald cry
> Took its place among the elements.
>
> Our voices echo, magnifying your arrival. New statue.
> In a drafty museum, your nakedness
> Shadows our safety. We stand round blankly as walls.
>
> I'm no more your mother
> Than the cloud that distils a mirror to reflect its own slow
> Effacement at the wind's hand.

There is a stunned precision here, a control that marries with and intensifies the innocence of the candor. The speaker imagines in mecha-nisms—her analogies are engineered to a schematic sense of cause and effect—and her voice holds back its colors. From the vaguely ominous winding of sex to the ritualized slapping of footsoles, begetting and bearing, it seems, have little of the human about them. Life is a synecdochic "bald cry" in these lines, whether the unspoken cry of orgasm that lies behind abstracted "Love" or the utterance of a child's first self-sustaining breath. This wary disenfranchisement echoes through the extended comparison of the very slow third stanza, leaving the mother to watch, in the mirror of her infant, the diminishment of her own vitality for the increase in its.

But now the poems grows warmer. Admitting the infant to her life, the speaker touches care and then hope; instead of being freighted, she is lightened:

> All night your moth-breath
> Flickers among the flat pink roses. I wake to listen:
> A far sea moves in my ear.
>
> One cry, and I stumble from bed, cow-heavy and floral
> In my Victorian nightgown.
> Your mouth opens clean as a cat's. The window square

> Whitens and swallows its dull stars. And now you try
> Your handful of notes;
> The clear vowels rise like balloons.

The change is a modulation of voice. As the child's delicate breathing becomes palpable, a moth against the rose-patterned wallpaper, the speaker hears in it a revitalizing sound of origins, the suck and spray of "A far sea." She is able to smile at herself, "cow-heavy and floral / In my Victorian nightgown," and then extend the infant's newness to the world: "Your mouth opens clean as a cat's. The window square // Whitens and swallows its dull stars." At the close, the child's "bald cry" has become a "handful of notes," fulfilling the musical promise of the title; and naming that change, as much hers as the baby's, the speaker takes on her own newness, a voice of motherhood.

Here as elsewhere in the late poems, the voice is original and of sustained intensity. At its best, it is marked by a cool grasp of image, an associative audacity, and an elegance at every pitch; it has an austere ease, what in the world of musical performance Paganini's listeners once heard and Horowitz's still can: a virtuosity that in itself would be striking but that in the service of art (not mere bravura) takes our breath away. For Plath, this flowering came late in a fearfully brief season, some twenty-three months before her death. In her apprentice years, she had journeyed among many masters, then taken serious training with Thomas, Roethke, Stevens, and Yeats. The poems of that period are hers and yet not hers: not strong enough to cohere into an important, sustaining body, they expose the fathers behind them and the defenses they enact. Near the end, however, Plath "Step[ped] off seven leagues, like those distances // That revolve in Crivelli, untouchable." Her words became axes, honed and deadly, and a major voice cut itself into the echoing wood of our poetry.

Notes

1. "The Manor Garden," *The Colossus and Other Poems* (New York: Random House, 1968), p. 3. To avoid frequent interruptions, all remaining quotes are identified in the list that follows note 4. There Plath's major books are abbreviated as follows: *The Colossus and Other Poems*, C; *Crossing the Water* (New York: Harper and Row, 1971), *CW*; *Winter Trees* (New York: Harper and Row, 1972), *WT*; *Ariel* (New York: Harper and Row, 1966), *A*.
2. "Maudlin" is included in the British edition of *The Colossus* but not in the American. It was omitted from the latter as too imitative and was not collected here until the posthumous publication of *Crossing the Water*.
3. "Poem for a Birthday" is in seven parts: "Who," "Dark House," "Maenad," "The Beast," "Flute Notes from a Reedy Pond," "Witch Burning," and "The Stones." The British edition

of *The Colossus* includes it, but the American edition has only "Flute Notes from a Reedy Pond" and "The Stones," printed as separate poems; the remaining five parts of the original are in America printed as separate poems in *Crossing the Water*. The omission of the complete birthday sequence in the American *Colossus* was based on Roethke's overpresence.
4. See chapter 9, "Plath's Cosmology and the House of Yeats," for Guttenberg's demonstration of this.

List of Quotations

p. 117 "It is no night . . ."/ *C*, p. 22.
"Stone, stone . . ."/ *C*, p. 23.
"the Valves . . ."/ *The Complete Poems of Emily Dickinson*, ed. T. H. Johnson (Boston: Little, Brown, 1960), p. 143.
"The heart shuts."/ *A*, p. 83.
p. 118 "Today bright . . ."/ Sylvia Plath, "Notes on Zarathustra's Prologue," *Crystal Gazer* (London: Rainbow Press, 1971), p. 6.
"the expensive . . ."/ W. H. Auden, "Musée des Beaux Arts," *Collected Shorter Poems, 1927-1957* (New York: Random House, 1966), p. 123.
"Yet desolation . . ."/ "Two Views of a Cadaver Room," *C*, p. 6
"In the room . . ."/ T. S. Eliot, *Collected Poems, 1909-1962* (New York: Harcourt, Brace, 1963), p. 3.
"In their jars . . ."/ "Two Views of a Cadaver Room," *C*, p. 5.
"Walks there not . . ."/ *C*, p. 51.
"All the night . . ."/ *C*, p. 15.
p. 119 "All out-of-doors . . ."/ *The Poetry of Robert Frost*, ed. E. C. Lathem (New York: Holt, Rinehart, and Winston, 1964), p. 108.
"can't keep a house . . ."/ Ibid.
"The small birds . . ."/ "The Manor Garden," *C*, p. 4.
"Better to go down . . ."/ "Provide, Provide," *The Poetry of Robert Frost*, p. 307.
p. 120 "Loom[ing] . . ."/ "Hardcastle Crags," *C*, p. 15.
"windy boy,"/ "Lament," *The Collected Poems of Dylan Thomas* (New York: New Directions, 1957), p. 194.
"The long wind,"/ "Hardcastle Crags," *C*, p. 15.
p. 121 "Mud-mattressed . . ."/ *CW*, p. 43.
"A place, a time . . ."/ "The Eye-mote," *C*, p. 13.
"My father died . . ."/ Sylvia Plath, "Ocean 1212-W," in *The Art of Sylvia Plath*, ed. Charles Newman (Bloomington: Indiana University Press, 1970), p. 272.
"closely and . . ."/ "Notes on the Chronological Order of Plath's Poems," in *The Art of Sylvia Plath*, p. 192.
p. 122 "Our own grist . . ."/ *C*, p. 29.
"suck / Blood . . ."/ *C*, p. 30.
"The spirit . . ."/ *The Collected Poems of Theodore Roethke* (Garden City, N. Y.: Doubleday, 1966), p. 4.
"He dipped . . ."/ Ibid., p. 6.
"bracelet of . . ."/ "The Relique," *Donne's Poetical Works*, ed. H. J. C. Grierson (Oxford: Oxford University Press, 1912), 1: 62.
"image kept . . ."/ "The Premonition," *The Collected Poems of Theodore Roethke*, p. 6.
"Mother . . ."/ *C*, p. 30.
p. 123 "Stop the larks . . ."/ "I Need, I Need," *The Collected Poems of Theodore Roethke*, p. 76.
"He won't be . . ."/ "The Beast," *CW*, p. 52.
p. 124 "Any touch . . ."/ *C*, p. 30.

"The dark's..."/ *CW*, p. 52.

"The police..."/ "The Other," *WT*, p. 21.

"ghostlier..."/ "The Idea of Order at Key West," in *The Palm at the End of the Mind: Selected Poems and a Play by Wallace Stevens*, ed. Holly Stevens (New York: Knopf, 1971), p. 99.

"the black man..."/ "Daddy," *A*, pp. 50-51.

"blunt..."/ *C*, p. 8.

"It was not..."/ *C*, p. 7.

p. 125 "the noise..."/ "The Tell-Tale Heart," in *The Portable Poe*, ed. Philip Stern (New York: Viking, 1959), p. 295.

"Main Street's..."/ *C*, p. 7.

"white..."/ *C*, p. 8.

"like a..."/ Stevens, *The Palm at the End of the Mind*, p. 387.

"It was not..."/ Ibid., p. 388.

"hoisted..."/ "Night Shift," *C*, p. 8.

"The time of year..."/ Stevens, *The Palm at the End of the Mind*, p. 51.

"fear / Of..."/ *CW*, p. 42.

"the necessary..."/ Stevens, *The Palm at the End of the Mind*, p. 354.

"A certain minor..."/ *CW*, p. 41.

p. 126 "Day creeps..."/ Stevens, *The Palm at the End of the Mind*, p. 163.

"Everything is..."/ Ibid., p. 164.

"The the."/ Ibid.

"The sea..."/ "A Winter Ship," *C*, p. 44.

"We wanted..."/ *C*, p. 45.

"every winch..."/ *C*, p. 45.

p. 127 "The sun..."/ *C*, p. 45.

"The brawling..."/ *The Collected Poems of W. B. Yeats* (New York: Macmillan, 1956), p. 40.

"During a..."/ *C*, p. 66.

"Scrupulously..."/ *C*, p. 66.

"She withdrew..."/ *C*, p. 67.

"Nine bean-rows..."/ "The Lake Isle of Innisfree," in *The Collected Poems of W. B. Yeats*, p. 39.

"where motley..."/ "Easter 1916," in *The Collected Poems of W. B. Yeats*, p. 176.

p. 128 "a burgeoning..."/ *C*, p. 67.

"Irrefutable..."/ *CW*, p. 9.

"fixed"/ *A*, p. 85.

"a child..."/ Interview with Peter Orr.

"but now..."/ *The Collected Poems of W. B. Yeats*, p. 185.

"Mule-bray..."/ "The Colossus," *C*, p. 20.

p. 129 "pithy and..."/ "The Colossus," *C*, p. 21.

"Dead hands..."/ "Ariel," *A*, p. 26.

"Now they ball..."/ "Wintering," *A*, p. 68.

"The pure gold..."/ "Lady Lazarus," *A*, p. 8.

"turning..."/ "Witch Burning," *CW*, p. 53.

"She wrote..."/ "Notes," in *The Art of Sylvia Plath*, p. 193.

"Father Fear"/ "The Lost Son," *The Collected Poems of Theodore Roethke*, p. 56.

p. 130 "I am too..."/ "Fever 103°," *A*, p. 54.

"What a thrill..."/ *A*, pp. 13-14.

p. 133 "Colour floods..."/ *A*, p. 83.

"Stasis in..."/ "Ariel," *A*, p. 26.

"bald and wild,"/ "The Moon and the Yew Tree," *A*, p. 41.

"nothing to be sad..."/ "Edge," *A*, p. 84.

"Her blacks..."/ "Edge," *A*, p. 84.

"It is what..."/ "Elm," *A*, p. 15.

p. 134 "Love set..."/ *A*, p. 1.

p. 135 "Step[ped] off..."/ "Gulliver," *A*, p. 35.

Barnett Guttenberg

Plath's cosmology and the house of Yeats

"Well, here I am! Safely in Yeats's house!" So opens Plath's letter to her mother from London announcing success in renting an apartment in a house where Yeats had lived.[1] The coincidence is perhaps without meaning (although Plath would probably have thought otherwise). The enthusiasm, however, is not, for she had long been an admirer of Yeats's poetry. In a letter to her mother in 1956, he is "my beloved Yeats";[2] questioned in 1958 as to whom she was reading, she answered, "Yeats, Ted Hughes continually, Yeats, Eliot, John Crowe Ransom especially . . . Lowell . . . Shakespeare, Chaucer . . . Wyatt . . . Hopkins . . . I think Yeats I like very much."[3] Perhaps the broadest explanation for Plath's approval of Yeats, apart from the uncompromising career itself, can be found in the introduction to his edition of Blake's poetry: "The chief difference between the metaphors of poetry and the symbols of mysticism is that the latter are woven together into a complete system." In feeling the need to hammer his thoughts into unity, Yeats was taking his first step toward the "complete system" that he would ultimately achieve with *A Vision*. Plath hammered her thoughts into the unity of such a system early, and in spite of significant departures from Yeats—the inevitable and insistent "swerve," in Bloom's view—a consistent, and in many respects Yeatsian, pattern lends continuity to the body of work and looms larger than any of its constituent parts.

Plath's "complete system" is specifically Yeatsian in its dialectic of flesh and spirit, this world and the other, which appears in its simplest form in a poem like "The Ghost's Leavetaking." Here the act of awakening becomes the "joint between two entirely / Incompatible modes of time," where for the moment "the raw material / Of our meat-and-potato thoughts assumes the nimbus / Of ambrosial revelation." The tone seems playful. The "ghost" consists of "sleep-twisted sheets"; after the momentary appearance on earth, it disappears into its own realm, "and God knows what is there." The subject, however, proves serious, for the broken link between the material world and that "otherworld" of revelation remains central to Plath's poetry.

Plath's system is again specifically Yeatsian in the ambivalence that characterizes each pole of the dialectic. The otherworld figures frequently —as it does in "The Ghost's Leavetaking"—as a holy Byzantium, spiritual and archetypal. It is the Platonic source, holding the "myth of origins / Unimaginable" ("Full Fathom Five"); pregnant women, absorbed in their creation, "step among the archetypes" ("Heavy Women"); water drained from ponds is "Threading back, filament by filament, to the pure / Platonic table where it lives" ("Private Ground"). Yet the otherworld poses its dangers. The fatal Lorelei, with their song of "a world more full and clear / Than can be" prove "deranging" ("Lorelei"). Those who listen are lost in self-absorption, "wrapped up in themselves," and the slightest encounter with the mundane world reveals these wrappings to be the bubbly stuff of dreams, trivial, extraneous, and evanescent: "Balloons tied by a string / To their owners' wrists, the light dreams float / To be let loose at news of land" ("On Deck").

The physical world has a similar dual nature. On rare occasion, and particularly in the past, it involves simple order and harmony: a "labor of love" and "graciousness" ("Point Shirley"). It involves the sensual time of "ticks blown gold," rather than the abstract time of "dry ticks" ("Two Sisters of Persephone"). Increasingly, however, the physical appears not as the harmoniously and sensually substantial, but as crude and impure substance; to the suicidal narrator of "Suicide off Egg Rock," his body seems "beached with the sea's garbage."

Plath's ambivalent Yeatsian dialectic takes its shape around Yeats's central symbols, the sun and the moon. The moon, for Plath as for Yeats, symbolizes the archetypal and eternal. "Lorelei" begins with "a full moon";

the ghost in "The Ghost's Leavetaking" brings "obscure lunar conundrums"; the dream-balloons in "On Deck" are "moony balloons." The sun, for Plath as for Yeats, symbolizes the mundane. The sister who chooses "ticks blown gold" has "freely become sun's bride" ("Two Sisters of Persephone"); to the narrator of "Suicide off Egg Rock," who sees himself as a victim of life, "Sun struck the water like a damnation." The symbols of sun and moon, for both Plath and Yeats, are consistent structural elements; they extend throughout the poetry to the "red eye" of "Ariel" and the "head a moon" of "Fever 103°."

A full array of imagery fans out from sun and moon to further shape the dialectic. Comparatively few images define the otherworld, presumably because only "God knows what is there." The water that carries one from "that country" to Byzantium appears consistently: "On Deck" takes place on water, the Lorelei sing from water, and, in "Full Fathom Five," the "myth of origins / Unimaginable" calls from water. A related image is the color blue. The twists of the road in "Hardcastle Crags" are "moon-blued," and in "Two Views of a Cadaver Room," Breughel's lovers are preserved from the destructive panorama, "He, afloat in the sea of her blue satin / Skirts."

The imagery of the solar realm includes all the physical products of earth, such as fruit and flower, over which the sun holds dominion. Thus, the sun in "The Bull of Bendylaw" is "the florid sun." The discontented lover in "Leaving Early" begins by complaining, "Lady, your room is lousy with flowers," and ends by asking, "Lady, what am I doing / . . . Knee-deep in the cold and swamped by flowers?" The swamp is that of social form conjoined with that other flower, the flesh. Thus her velvet pillows are "the color of blood pudding," while her geraniums "stink of armpits" and are "musky as a lovebed." The imagery of flesh and flower is linked again when the surgeon ("The Surgeon at 2 A.M.") describes his bower: "It is a garden I have to do with—tubers and fruits / Oozing their jammy substances, / . . . This is the lung-tree." The central flower in Plath's garden of fleshly delights is of course the heart, "a red bell-bloom."

Within Yeats's unending dialogue between flesh and spirit, the solar realm, even when presented as a world well lost, retains its attractions. Thus, although the time of youth, when "I swayed my leaves and flowers in the sun," consisted of "lying days," and although the spiritual realm beckons persuasively, the process of gaining it, in which "Now I may wither into truth," seems both dubious and destructive. The golden apples of the sun hold their allure for Yeats even under repudiation, so that the narrator of "Sailing to Byzantium," translated into the realm of artifice, chooses to sing of earthly flux. While the golden apples grow ever more appetizing to the aging Yeats, they take on an increasingly obscene and repulsive tinge for Plath; they are "gold-ruddy balls" whose "Golds bleed and deepen, the mouths of Thermopylae" ("Letter in November"). Here is the area of Plath's most significant "swerve" from Yeats; much of her secondary solar imagery involves a *contemptus mundi* that even the Yeats of *The Tower* did not fully share.

The obscenity of the physical derives, for Plath, from the cyclical, limiting invariability of whatever is begotten, born, and dies—of the "dirty girl." For Plath, that cycle holds all things in thrall: the surgeon proclaims, "I am the sun, in my white coat, / Grey faces, shuttered by drugs, follow me like flowers" ("The Surgeon at 2 A.M."). A minor group of images that embody that limitation includes hooks, thorns, and walls.

A more important cluster of images presents the invariability of the cycle in terms of repetition, and notable among these is the thoughtless round of the mechanical: the prospective suicide in "Suicide off Egg Rock" is oppressed by his own body, "A machine to breathe and beat forever." The central image that reflects the cycle of unalterable biological law and the fragmentation caused by the engine of that law—the "indefatigable fact" of "Night Shift"—is the mirror. Thus the head of the insomniac, who "can feel daylight, his white disease, / Creeping up with her hatful of trivial repetitions," is "a little interior of grey mirrors" ("Insomniac"). Images of repetition recur continually, and the resulting welter of repetition imagery itself contributes to the pattern of repetition. Verbal repetition takes a similar place in the formal fabric of the poetry as part of the mirror pattern; the suicide-to-be feels his blood "beating the old tattoo / I am, I am, I am."

Plath frequently focuses on the destructiveness of the natural cycle, and presents that destructiveness in terms of "the gross eating game" ("All the Dead Dears") that is so largely embodied in the hog who, "stomaching no constraint, / Proceeded to swill / The seven troughed seas and every earthquaking continent" ("Sow"). The mirror-narrator of "Mirror" announces, "Whatever I see I swallow immediately." The flowers in "The Beekeeper's Daughter" constitute "a garden of mouthings," while the disgruntled lover in "Leaving Early" hears "cut flowers / Sipping their liquids from assorted pots." The equally disgruntled wife in "Zoo Keeper's Wife," remembering courtship by her "marrowy sweetheart," recalls that "Your two-horned rhinoceros opened a mouth / Dirty as a bootsole and big as a hospital sink / For my cube of sugar: its bog breath / Gloved my arm to the elbow." An ultimate consumer in this "eating game" is the earth itself; thus, in "The Ghost's Leavetaking," the ghost vanishes into the air and "not down / Into the rocky gizzard of the earth." The narrator of "The Stones," on the other hand, "entered / The stomach of indifference" and "became a still pebble," and the narrator of "Dark House" feels herself comfortably absorbed into "marrowy tunnels":

"It is warm and tolerable / In the bowel of the root. / Here's a cuddly mother."

Related to the earthy landscape that literally devours is the fiery landscape that consumes with flame. Thus the poem "Widow" begins, "Widow. The word consumes itself— / Body, a sheet of newsprint on the fire / . . . Over the scalding, red topography / That will put her heart out like an only eye." The imagery of eating and burning is drawn together in "Suicide off Egg Rock." The prospective suicide who observes how "Flies filing in through a dead skate's eyehole / Buzzed and assailed the vaulted brainchamber" is seeing the flies of hell; as he watches the feast, he "smoldered" on the beach of the modern world, an inferno of "public grills, ochreous salt flats, / Gas tanks, factory stacks—that landscape / Of imperfections." With these hell-fires, the imagery of physical destruction circles back to its center, the sun, as it "flamed straight down" ("The Babysitters") and "struck the water like a damnation" ("Suicide off Egg Rock").

In his dedication to *The Secret Rose*, Yeats wrote, "These stories have but one subject, the war of spiritual with natural order"; in Plath's poetry, that war continues. Complicating the battle in Yeatsian fashion, each pole of the dialectic is itself ambivalent; the lunar sphere is stonily abstract as well as archetypal, while the solar sphere is colorful and harmonious, brutish and destructive. From the first, Plath uses a pattern of recurrent imagery to provide her dialectic with the cohesiveness of a Yeatsian "complete system," and her central sun-moon imagery, together with much of the supporting imagery, is distinctly Yeatsian. The imagery farthest from Yeats defines the destructiveness of the physical world. That imagery grows increasingly important in the final phase; whereas the aging Yeats frantically embraces the flesh, Plath, only thirty in her last phase, savagely renounces the physical. Yet even the imagery of destructiveness is not altogether alien to Yeats, who remarks often enough on the broken body, and who recognizes, too, that "mirror on mirror mirrored is all the show."

The dialectic presented through the pattern of lunar and solar imagery involves opposition; but because fair and foul are near of kin, Yeats's golden bird returns to earth, and similarly, Plath's antithetical figures are caught in a more complex interdependence than one of simple conflict. The spirit in "Ouija" cannot get free of the flesh; the separated spirit and flesh in "Widow" yearn for each other; the flesh and its spiritual cast in "In Plaster" loathe and need each other. Perhaps most important in this dialectical interdependence, for Plath as well as for Yeats, is the way in which each side of the polarity feeds on the other, a pattern in Yeats's poetry that Plath noted with express approval. In the letter to her mother glossing her early poem "Pursuit," she writes, "Another epigraph could have been from my beloved Yeats: 'Whatever flames upon the night, Man's own resinous heart has fed.' The painter's brush consumes his dreams, and all that."[4] Yeats's interpenetrating gyres have a general relevance for Plath, who clearly accepts Yeats's pronouncement that all things are from antithesis, "all things dying each other's life, living each other's death." For Plath as for Yeats, the complete system is centrally concerned with the dying of sun into night, of moon into day. Metaphysically, that concern involves the dying of eternity into time and of time into eternity: incarnation and transfiguration, together with their enactment in Christian myth.

"Flute Notes from a Reedy Pond" articulates the possibility—even while denying it—of a dying into eternity:

> This is not death, it is something safer.
> The wingy myths won't tug at us any more:
>
> The molts are tongueless that sang from above the water
> Of golgotha at the tip of a reed,
> And how a god flimsy as a baby's finger
> Shall unhusk himself and steer into the air.

The representation of death as golgothan passageway, evident as early as "Lorelei"—"Stone, stone, ferry me down there"—finds an early center in the figure of the dead father. He is the central presence of *The Colossus*, as the title attests, because he is a potential emissary from the other world and because, as such, he does not do. Despite the efforts described in the poem "The Colossus," he remains a function of the physical world, his tongue phallic and solar, his sounds those of the barnyard. The father, notwithstanding "acanthine" hair suggestive of Golgotha, fails as a "mouthpiece of the dead," a point of connection with the spiritual realm; the poem ends with the narrator "married to shadow," no longer even listening for the ferry that crosses Stygian waters. In "Full Fathom Five" the father surfaces from those waters, transformed with Shakespeare's help into an emissary of sorts. Although the narrator makes an unqualified choice of realms—"Father, this thick air is murderous. / I would breathe water."—the father remains "inscrutable"; an underlying irony is that the father's transformation in *The Tempest* is wholly imaginary.

The spirits that sang to Prince Ferdinand through Ariel and to Yeats through automatic handwriting will not sing to Plath, and so her attention in the early poetry turns increasingly to death itself as the passageway to the eternal. The intestine of the world's destructive process becomes a symbol of that passageway; since death is potential rebirth, however, that rocky gizzard and the womb stunningly coalesce. In "Dark House," the narrator, who has descended into the "marrowy tunnels" of the earth-self, calls them "the bowel of the root"; at the same time, they are "a cuddly mother," and the narrator says, "Any day I may litter puppies / Or mother a horse." In "Metaphors," the narrator explains her obvious pregnancy by saying, "I've eaten a bag of green apples." The juxtaposition of womb and intestine with its suggestion of rebirth through excretion is startling and unYeatsian, but not unprecedented. Dante is reborn from the Inferno of the devil's intestine through Satan's rectum. Plath, in fact, draws together her images of the world as hell and the world as intestine in the concluding lines of "The Beast." "I housekeep in Time's gut-end," the narrator says. Then, alluding to the serene assertion of order and identity with which the Duchess of Malfi rises above her imminent destruction—"I am Duchess of Malfi still"—she adds, "Duchess of Nothing, / Hairtusk's bride." Devil, intestine, and death come together here, although with little hope of an emergence into eternity. The death into eternity makes something of an appearance in "Witch Burning" through the related image of the consuming fire, when the burning witch cries, "My ankles brighten. Brightness ascends my thighs. / I am lost, I am lost, in the robes of all this light." This burning provides a wholly ambiguous consummation, both hellish and heavenly: sexual, destructive, purifying. When Plath examines the possibility of the solar sphere dissolving into its lunar counterpart, she finds no more than this uncertain consummation and the magnificently ambiguous product of the womb-intestine; she cannot share in the triumphant transcendence of *The Tower.*

The dying at the other side of the antithesis, which Plath, presumably because of her own pregnancies, seems to find even more interesting than does Yeats, involves incarnation, the dissolving of lunar sphere into solar. As pregnant women "step among the archetypes" and "listen for the millennium, / The knock of the small, new heart," dusk hoods them in "Mary-blue" ("Heavy Women"). From the dark passageway, an annunciation: "Head, toe, and finger / Come clear of the shadow" ("The Manor Garden"). In these poems of incarnation, however, Plath invariably finds the brightness of that annunciation overshadowed by the destructiveness in store. As early as "The Manor Garden," the birth is "a difficult borning," a long dying into the consuming world. In that poem, as "The worms quit their usual habitations"—presumably corpses—"the small birds converge, converge / With their gifts"; diner becomes dinner in a reversal that will be reversed again when the fledgling at the other end of his earthly sojourn turns into food for worms. The path leads inevitably from Bethlehem to Golgotha; the "golden child" is he whom "the world will kill and eat" ("Mary's Song"). The "difficult borning" is a birth into the "eating game," into the destroying world where "a blue mist is dragging the lake" for its foetus and corpse-to-be, into "crowns of acanthus." Similarly, the pregnant women listen for their millenium under "thorn trees," "While far off, the axle of winter / Grinds round, bearing down with the straw, / The star, the wise grey men": natal gifts, fatal judgment.

With Yeats's system restructured in largely negative terms, with the Yeatsian remoteness of the lunar realm made absolute and balanced by the increasingly absolute destructiveness of the solar realm, the predicament of the poet, the central narrator in each body of poetry, becomes staggering; certainly it allows little opportunity for the characteristic Yeatsian tone of triumph. Plath's qualified response to that predicament, like Yeats's, involves the act of perceiving, to which the antithetical vision also applies. For Yeats, the sun and the moon primarily represent objectivity and subjectivity, respectively. For Plath, the crowd, "riding to work in rows, as if recently brainwashed," has "eyes mica-silver and blank": mirror eyes, solar eyes ("Insomniac"). The snakecharmer, in contrast, creates the world with "moon-eye" ("Snakecharmer"). Candle flames are another symbol of the imagination; "Nun-souled, they burn heavenward" ("Candles"). The imagination is the light and breath of the spirit; its flight, as in the god who can "steer into the air" in response to the tug of "wingy myths," is in contrast to the stony, static, circularity of the entire round, lunar and solar. It is Ariel, winged horse and bright spirit. With its aid, the poet must make contact with the otherworld, traversing the dark passageway that leads through the mirror to the "wingy myths." The apparently insurmountable fall from lunar grace, the icy divinity who "does not hear what the sailor or the peasant is saying" because "She is in love with the beautiful formlessness of the sea" ("Finisterre"), become matters of anguish.

The poet who bears the myths must then, as mother, tree "full of otherworldliness," deliver them from the dark passageway and embody them in the world, or they will remain as removed from mundane concerns as the icy divinity of "Finisterre." The incarnation succeeds in "Black Rook in Rainy Weather," where "the long wait for the angel" has been rewarded with the "celestial burning" that can "Leap incandescent / Out of kitchen table or chair." It succeeds in "The Eye-mote" when the narrator's vision balances the running horses against the static world: "Tails streaming against the green / Backdrop . . . / Holding the horses, the clouds, the leaves / Steadily rooted though they were all flowing / Away to the left like reeds in a sea." A detached subjectivity, however, prevails in "Watercolor of Grantchester Meadows," where the "moony" lovers are unaware of the rapacious owl, and in "Two Views of a Cadaver Room," where the lovers, lost in themselves despite the flaming world around them, are unaware that death is the accompanist to their song, all three fiddling while the world burns. Even where subjectivity is more clearly the creative imagination in the symbolic illumination of the "nun-souled" candle flames, there is the possibility of self-delusion; the candles, although they "mollify the bald moon," are "taken in by their own haloes." The poet-mother, then, runs the risk of self-absorption, like the "smug" pregnant women of the ironic "Heavy Women," who "Settle in their belling dresses," lost in themselves.

The poet's mothering task is not completed by making the Word incarnate in the world; the Word must also be made incarnate in the word. The analogy implicit as early as "The Manor Garden" between flesh and word, child and poem, becomes explicit in "Stillborn," where the narrator grieves that the newborn poems "do not live," even though "They grew their toes and fingers well enough." The newborn child fallen into the rocky gizzard of the world is the real child, then, but it is also the poet's child, the poem, and the mourning over delivery to the "wise grey men" extends to both.

The solar world not only destroys the child, but also puts out the engendering light of the candle, the eye of life and imagination, as part of its great devouring process. Thus the landscape in "Hardcastle Crags," both solar and lunar, is stony, and "Enough to snuff the quick / Of her small heat out." The horror of "Sow" is that the hog consumes the "seven troughed seas" as well as the land. The narrator says, "our marvel blazoned a knight, / Helmed, in cuirass, // Unhorsed and shredded in the grove of combat / By a grisly-bristled / Boar." The hero is defeated by such gross animality. Worse yet, even the imagining of such a battle and defeat is defeated by the new breed of hero, breeder of the "great sow," the farmer, who "with a jocular fist thwacked the barrel nape, / And the green-copse-castled // Pig hove, letting legend like dried mud drop."

In "The Eye-mote," the destructive landscape "unaltered by eyes" ("Hardcastle Crags") has been brought to balance by an act of creative perception until the sun, "holding," "striking," destroys the vision with a splinter in the eye, a splinter that is the sun itself. "Abrading my lid, the small grain burns: / Red cinder around which I myself, / Horses, planets and spires revolve." The result is a fall from harmony into duality: on the one hand, lunar Eden, where the horses have become "outlandish" and "unicorns," "Beasts of oasis, a better time"; on the other hand, the surrounding solar wasteland, a landscape with its color burned out, "a bad monochrome." The stricken poet-narrator imagines himself Oedipus "Before the bed, before the knife, / Before the brooch-pin and the salve": Oedipus the hero, answerer of the riddle, savior of the wasteland: Oedipus before his fall, before being "Fixed . . . in this parenthesis."

Plath more typically views the poet-seer's fate not in terms of savior Oedipus but of savior Christ and the self-sacrifice inherent in his journey from Bethlehem to Golgotha. In "Two Sisters of Persephone," the sister choosing life comes out of her lunar darkness to mate with the sun. The result is incarnation; she "Grows quick with seed" and "bears a king." In her startling courtship, she is "Lulled / Near a bed of poppies"—solar flowers of sexuality and death—and "sees how their red silk flare / Of petalled blood / Burns open to sun's blade." It is on that "green altar" that she has "Freely become sun's bride." In order to bear her child-poem, the lunar mother gives herself to the sun in a ritual of self-sacrifice; the child lost in the rocky gizzard of the world is child-poet as well as child-poem.

In "Candles," the theme of self-sacrifice relates more explicitly to the imagination and to the Yeatsian antithesis. On the one hand is the descent of eternity into time in the form of the yet-uncorrupted child, asleep, still in touch with the eternal source. On the other are the candles, with their "upside-down hearts" of flame dedicated to the spiritual. The child and the candles are antithetical figures of ascent and descent, but the moment is one of apparent harmony, with the polar spheres held in counterpoise; the purity of the infant is one with the purity of the "nun-souled" candle flames, so that "the mild light enfolds her" in a lovely embrace.

The equilibrium, however, is temporary. The candles, as counterparts of the child, represent the fate of the self committed to the eternal. They sacrifice themselves; man's own resinous heart fuels the hearts of flame. They are "taken in by their own haloes" in that they are self-deceived, and in that they are consumed in the process of giving light. Thus, they are "wax fingers," "Grown milky, almost clear, like the bodies of saints." The poem's harmony dissolves with the child's as the meditation on the burning candle leads the narrator to ask, "How shall I tell anything at all / To this infant still in a birth-drowse?" Her eyes not yet open to the world, she cannot begin to understand the consuming process that awaits, or the macabre ambiguity with which "the mild light enfolds her." Within that enfolding light, "The shadows stoop over like guests at a christening," as ambiguous as the wise grey men who conclude "Heavy Women"; in each case, they attend on an incarnation and point toward a destruction.

In "Candles," Plath alludes pointedly to Yeats's poem "Coole Park and Ballylee, 1931" through the well-known phrase "the last romantics." Yeats's poem, too, plays on the counterpoise of destruction and grace evident in Plath's enfolding light. The "last romantics," with their theme of "traditional sanctity and loveliness," stand opposed to the groping stick, the dying swan, and the darkening flood. The beautiful people, despite the elegiac tone and the battering by time, have won a victory. Their artistic achievement is judged secure. In addition, there is the underlying sense that the era of loveliness will return; Yeats carefully points out in his first stanza that the water of the soul, although presently a "darkening flood," runs alternately underground and overland. Plath, with "Candles," offers a sharp rejoinder that all of her poetry develops. Even amid the deceptive Yeatsian tone of harmony, there is no victory: neither spiritual achievement nor the promise of restoration. Grace is subsumed into destruction; as the image of kindly light dissolves into the image of consuming flames, grace seems a dubious entity. Plath's "last romantics," the candles, are not only "ephemerids," together with their flames, but are also self-deceived, self-absorbed, and self-destructive.

Plath's late poems, despite their profound change in form, continue to elaborate the complete system of antithetical spheres and supporting imagery so firmly established by their predecessors. The solar realm proves increasingly destructive, the lunar realm increasingly inaccessible, and the plight of the poet narrator, caught between what cannot be reached and what cannot be borne, increasingly intolerable. The poems continue to focus on a deathly incarnation and a problematical trans-figuration. Thus, in the transitional "Widow," the widow, shading into the solar black widow spider who has devoured her husband with his "moon-white...moth-face," yearns for his return so that she can devour him again. In a conclusion indebted to the dream-scene from *Wuthering Heights*, in which Catherine's ghost struggles with the slow-witted Lockwood at the window, the widow fears that

> His soul may beat and be beating at her dull sense
> Like blue Mary's angel, dovelike against a pane
> Blinded to all but the grey, spiritless room
> It looks in on, and must go on looking in on.

While the flesh yearns for its consummation with spirit, the spirit, liberated, remains drawn to flesh and its promise of a dying into time, of incarnation. The union involves destruction; the separation involves an unsuccessful annunciation, a failure to embody the divine in the temporal.

The later poems of incarnation continue to concentrate on the har-rowing journey in store. The world of the "eating game" consumes the child, so that eternity is lost in time; in "Morning Song," "The window square // Whitens and swallows its dull stars." Some of these poems, like "Mary's Song," offset birth with death, structuring themselves around the antithesis. In "Nick and the Candlestick," a poem of apparent affirma-tion, the child borne from the dark passageway by the miner-mother is "the one / Solid the spaces lean on, envious." The poem ends triumphantly with "You are the baby in the barn," and the title alludes to Jack's leap over the fleshly tallow of the candle. Yet the burning candle once again serves as an antithetical image of death, and with the baby finally located in the barn, Golgotha is in effect counterpoised against Bethlehem. In the Yeatsian conflation of "Winter Trees," the trees, envisioned as Ledas "full of otherworldliness," blend into Marys and pietas. In "Brasilia," the entire antithesis oscillates within the image of "the dove's annihilation," which connotes on the one hand a fatal annunciation and on the other a Crucifixion and uncertain ascension: "the high / Precipice that emptied one man into space" ("Mary's Song").

The frantic tone of the late poems reflects the increasingly agonized existence of a consuming world and an imprisoning dialectic: of a moon that "is no door" ("The Moon and the Yew Tree"). There is still a fear of ultimate emptiness, as in the earlier "Blackberrying"; to the narrator of "Sheep in Fog," the far fields of dark passage "threaten / To let me through to a heaven / Starless and fatherless." More often, the poems of death take on a note of suicidal defiance, as in the earlier "Mussel Hunter at Rock Harbor," where the narrator finds "the husk of a fiddler-crab" that had "strangely strayed above // His world of mud" and "saved / Face, to face the bald-faced sun." A similar note of suicidal defiance appears in "Daddy." The concluding words, "I'm through," involve not only the obvious defiance of "I'm through with you," but also the suicidal "I'm finished," so that the final statement is one of ambiguous repudiation and submission.

The agonized sense of imprisonment and destruction leads, in the late poems, to a dream of revenge, a second coming. Earlier poems occasionally offer the impersonal revenge of the sea. At the end of "The Bull of Bendylaw," the bull of the sea is triumphant; "the king's tidy acre is under the sea / And the royal rose in the bull's belly / And the bull on the king's highway." In the later poem "The Couriers," the narrator praises "A disturbance in mirrors, / The sea shattering its grey one." In these culminating poems, however, the narrator reappears in the solar realm transformed into avenging goddess: a vengeful Diana or Kali or Ishtar. Thus, in "Stings," the narrator, dealing with bees, says, "I / Have a self to recover, a queen." That self, "With her lion-red body, her wings of glass," like Yeats's great beast, "is flying / More terrible than she ever was, red / Scar in the sky, red comet / Over the engine that killed her." In "Lady Lazarus," a similar great beast comes back; the narrator, consumed in the Nazi ovens of life, warns the apparently interchangeable "Herr God, Herr Lucifer" that "Out of the ash / I rise with my red hair / And I eat men like air."

Lady Lazarus's phoenix-like "comeback in broad day" suggests, more generally, Plath's increasing concern with Yeats's sources in the Eastern occult and with Eastern versions of renewal as forms of escape. Reincarnation figures in the late poems, as does the pattern of *samsara*, the great wheel, so important to Yeats, from which the dead are reborn.

"Getting There" deals with that journey from birth to rebirth. The narrator says, "I fly to a name, two eyes / . . .the face at the end of the flare." The body of "this woman" is an intervening obstacle, but finally, unhusked from the Golgotha of her previous lives—"old bandages, boredoms, old faces"—the quintessential She can "Step. . .from the black car of Lethe, / Pure as a baby." In "Totem," however, the wheel of reincarnation is viewed more characteristically, not as delivery round from birth to birth, but as treadmill:

> There is no terminus, only suitcases
>
> Out of which the same self unfolds like a suit
> Bald and shiny, with pockets of wishes,
>
> Notions and tickets, short circuits and folding mirrors.

For Yeats, in his enthusiasm for reincarnation, dying is "a second wind." For Plath, the great wheel represents the ultimate web of repetition, where waits the well-armed spider: "Death with its many sticks."

In the late poems, Plath also considers renewal through transcendence or *nirvana*, the escape from that round of reincarnation that occurs, in Hindu and Buddhist belief, through a process of self-renunciation that results in enlightenment. "Fever 103°" seems to describe just that process; the narrator, "selves dissolving, old whore petticoats," becomes a "pure acetylene / Virgin" ascending "To Paradise." Even amid the feverish unreality of this escape, however, there is fear of being caught in the wheel of death and rebirth. With the self dissolved, "a snuffed candle," in the burning-away process of *nirvana*, the individual manifestations of that self fall away like smoke; the narrator says, "the low smokes roll /From me like Isadora's scarves, I'm in a fright // One scarf will catch and anchor in the wheel."

Nirvana is still more severely undercut in "Ariel." As the ferry of Buddhist doctrine moves across the river of *samsara* toward the shores of light, it pulls away from the shores of facticity, whose objects, from this enlightened point of view, dissolve, figments of imperception. The major part of "Ariel" describes such a journey, with the phenomenal world, if not quite illusory, fragmentary and immaterial. The title, of course, conjoins Plath's stallion with Shakespeare's sprite, who finally gains release from his bondage to the mundane. The image of the arrow, very possibly derived from Yeats, underscores the theme of transcendence. Yeats found his dream—"a naked woman of incredible beauty, standing upon a pedestal and shooting an arrow at a star"—readily comprehensible. The star is solar: examined closely, it is "a little golden heart," and is ultimately Apollo the sun god; the arrow shot into the unknown symbolizes rebirth.[5] Plath's arrow, "the stake in the fat black heart," the stake in the eye of the devouring Polyphemus, seems to mean death for the newborn sun and its conflagrations, an end to solar vision.

Yet the image of the arrow, as Plath develops it, has a typical ambiguity. Flying is verbally linked with suicide; transcendence is juxtaposed with self-immolation. The arrow of self is Ahab's harpoon, and the death of the sun is the death of the self. The flight ends in the sun, around which everything finally turns: "I myself, / Horses, planets, and spires" ("The Eye-mote"). The force that drives the dew (which is "at one with the drive" of the arrow) drives the moon-moth in "Widow" in what is an awful "at-one-ment," an even more appalling consummation than that of "Witch Burning." For "Ariel," finally, offers no prospect of *nirvana*. There are no sacred, if ambiguous, "robes of light"; the tone, in the end, is again one of suicidal defiance.

In conclusion, Plath builds a complete system, with a Yeatsian antithetical vision and consistent clusters of Yeatsian imagery. In addition, she seems to offer a series of rejoinders on various points of disagreement. For Yeats, the antithetical vision yoking here and there means possibility. Yeats's narrator, beleaguered by love, by age, by history, by abstraction, by his own public role, exults in his victory over these adversaries. In "Sailing to Byzantium," he vanquishes that country of unheedful spawning; in "The Circus Animals' Desertion," he lies down victorious "where all the ladders start, / In the foul rag-and-bone shop of the heart"; in "Coole Park and Ballylee, 1931," he goes down dignified, secure in the knowledge of loveliness achieved and the prospect of loveliness restored. Both life and history afford fair vistas. The wheel of reincarnation offers still another set of possibilities, and glittering afar is the *nirvana* of golden birdhood. The poems, then, are predominantly poems of triumph. In "The Lamentation of the Old Pensioner," the old man cries, "I spit into the face of Time, / That has transfigured me"; however one interprets time's transfigurations here, the old pensioner's cry is clearly much more than mere "lamentation."

In Plath's poetry, irony flows in the other direction, for reality proves even worse than appearance or expectation. The complete system is, in the end, not one of counterpoise, but of complete hostility, and the adversaries, solar and lunar, are equally invincible. Birth is a momentary manifestation of the eternal, but one is born only to be broken on the solar wheel of life. There are no ladders, and the dark passageway opens on a dubious consummation: revenge, repetition, or emptiness, as time bleeds into space. Plath's winding stair opens "onto nothing at all"; it is a "coiled-spring stair" ("Widow"). In a mechanical and deterministic universe, the wheel of reincarnation seems a mere macrocosmic counterpart of the sun's iron wheel. As dismay at the great sow of the world hardens into revulsion and the lunar realm resists all overtures, the plight of the poet-narrator intensifies and crystallizes in poems of impossibility.

The early poetry, with its attempt to incorporate the Word into the word-flesh of conventional form, is rejected as genteel "talk, talk, talk" ("The Applicant"); the late poetry, instead, is the subjective and literal burning cry, child-poem and child-poet "the pure gold baby / That melts to a shriek" ("Lady Lazarus"). The role of the poet is not Yeatsian and imperial, for the creative flame burns self-sacrificially. The poet is "The Hanging Man," Christ and Prometheus. The crime has been the delivery of the purifying flame into the world; the punishment is life.

Notes

1. 14 December 1962, *Letters Home: Correspondence 1950-1963*, selected and edited with commentary by Aurelia Schober Plath (New York: Harper and Row, 1975), p. 488.
2. 9 March 1956, Plath, *Letters Home*, p. 223.
3. Reading in Springfield, Massachusetts, 18 April 1958. Quoted by Edward Butscher in *Sylvia Plath: Method and Madness* (New York: Seabury Press, 1976), p. 228.
4. 9 March 1956, Plath, *Letters Home*, p. 223.
5. W. B. Yeats, *The Autobiography of William Butler Yeats* (New York: Doubleday Anchor, 1958), pp. 248-49, 380-83.

3. Personal and public contexts

Marjorie Perloff

Sylvia Plath's "Sivvy" poems: a portrait of the poet as daughter

1

On 6 February 1961, just ten months after the birth of her first child, Frieda, and in the third month of her second pregnancy, Sylvia Plath had a miscarriage. She wrote to her mother that day:

> I do hope the sad news in my last letter didn't cast you down too much. I foresaw how you'd enjoy sharing the good news with all our friends and relatives and only hope it hasn't been too hard to contradict our optimistic plans [for Mrs. Plath to come to England to help with the babies]. I hadn't told anyone over here, thank goodness, so I don't have to suffer people commiserating with me, which I couldn't stand just now.... All I can say is that you'd better start saving for another trip another summer, and I'll make sure I can produce a new baby for you then![1]

The loving daughter who writes so solicitously to her mother, promising to "produce a new baby" for her as soon as possible, had already begun a novel in which that mother is mercilessly portrayed as the interfering, rigid, and wholly uncomprehending Mrs. Greenwood, a threatening presence whom Esther (Sylvia) must reject. No wonder *The Bell Jar* was published under a pseudonym, and even then Sylvia wrote to her brother Warren that "this must never be published in the United States."[2]

But which is the "real" Sylvia Plath: the girl who wrote the letter cited above or the author of *The Bell Jar*? The obvious answer (and it is one I have given myself) is that Plath had a schizoid personality,[3] a divided self—the "poetic" or inner self that composed *The Bell Jar* and *Ariel* was thoroughly masked when she presented herself to others. But what is less well understood, and what *Letters Home* reveals, is that the various roles Plath assumed—Dutiful Daughter, Bright and Bouncy Smith Girl, Cambridge Intellectual, Adoring Wife and Mother, Efficient Housekeeper—were so deeply entrenched that they determined the course not only of her life but also of her writing. If, as Karl Miller so rightly observes, Plath's letters to her mother were "bent on withholding her 'true' condition,"[4] so, the correspondence suggests, were the poems written prior to the final crisis in her life, poems that emerged, in large part, from Plath's false-self system. It was not until the summer of 1962, when Aurelia Plath became an inadvertent witness to the actual dissolution of the Plath-Hughes marriage, that Sylvia finally stopped "producing" poems as she had produced babies, in order to please and impress her mother, and, by extension, "all our friends and relatives," editors, and contest judges. Significantly, the first letter written after the final rupture with Ted Hughes (23 September 1962) is also the first one signed "Sylvia" rather than "Sivvy."[5] A subsequent letter, dated 9 October, in which Plath writes: "The horror of what you saw and what I saw you see last summer is between us and I cannot face you until I have a new life," is signed with the initial "S." She was never to face her mother again. Rather, "the horror of what I saw you see" was exorcized in the *Ariel* poems, the bulk of which were written in the four short months that now remained. Read in the perspective of the letters, *Ariel* is seen to be a book that had to be posthumous. Alive, Sylvia Plath could never have tolerated the pain and humiliation of exposure; she could not have permitted her mother, for whom she had been writing so assiduously, to see the self revealed in poems like "Lesbos" and "Medusa."

In coming to terms with the transformation of "Sivvy," the carefully controlled voice of the earlier poetry and prose, into the Sylvia of the *Ariel* poems, the "I" whom Robert Lowell called "something imaginary, newly, wildly and subtly created—hardly a person at all,"[6] *Letters Home* is a centrally important document. Reviewers have tended to minimize its value because the selection of letters is so severely slanted: Aurelia Plath evidently omitted all those letters that she felt might put her daughter in the wrong light, and after she had made her excisions, Ted Hughes, whose legal property the letters are, made further extensive cuts.[7] But the irony is that despite the fractured state of the final manuscript, the portrait of Sylvia that emerges is peculiarly consistent.

One learns, to begin with, that Sylvia Plath did not just happen to be a schizophrenic girl who had a genius for poetry. In many ways, hers was a representative case of the American Dream gone sour; indeed, if Sylvia Plath had not existed, she might have been invented by Scott Fitzgerald. For as in the typical Fitzgerald story, it all looked in the beginning so promising, so hopeful. Aurelia Plath's introduction to *Letters Home* is prefaced by a charming family photograph: a young and quite pretty Aurelia is sitting on the grass, holding an adorable little Sylvia on her lap. Reclining next to her is the tall handsome father, Otto Plath. It is an idyllic scene, especially within the context of Aurelia Schober's early life. An immigrant of humble Austrian parentage, Aurelia remembers a poignant scene when, as a little girl, she stood in the schoolyard during recess, trying to understand what the other children were shouting to one another:

> The two words I heard most frequently were "Shut up!" so when I went home at the end of the school day and met my father, I answered his greeting proudly and loudly with "Shut up!" I still remember how his face reddened. He took me across his knee and spanked me. Weeping loudly over that injustice, I sobbed out, *"Aber was bedeutet das, Papa? Was bedeutet das?"* (What does that mean?) Then he realized I had not understood what the words meant; he was sorry, hugged me, and asked me to forgive him. It was my first and last spanking. (*LH*, p. 4)

To transcend her immigrant status, to learn *what the words meant* —this was Aurelia Schober's unflagging aim. In high school, she was extremely bookish, reading her way through Austen, Eliot, Dickens, Hardy, Melville, and James. Later she added Rilke and Hesse to her list of favorite writers. Although she obediently began her studies in the business school of Boston University, she persuaded her father to let her switch to modern languages and prepared for a teaching career in high-school English and German. She did teach for a year at Melrose (Massachusetts) High School and then decided to go on to a Master's Degree in English and German—surely an unusual choice for a girl of her time and class. It was here that she became a student of Professor Otto Plath, a distinguished entomologist, who was giving the course in Middle High German that year. Twenty-two years Aurelia's senior, Otto Plath was a difficult and moody man. His widow is discreet in talking about their courtship, but she was evidently swept off her feet by his learning, wisdom, and virile good looks. Within two years, they were married. She immediately yielded to his wish and became "a full-time homemaker." She also gave him, exactly according to the schedule set forth by him, two children: first Sylvia (1932) and then Warren (1935).

Although Aurelia and Otto were originally drawn to one another because of their mutual literary and scientific interests, after their marriage she subordinated herself totally to her superior husband, in keeping with her Germanic upbringing. It was not an amusing household:

> Otto soon found the study he set up for himself in our apartment too gloomy as it faced north, so he moved all the materials he needed for the writing of "Insect Societies" into the dining room, where they remained for nearly a year. The seventy-plus reference books were arranged on top of the long sideboard; the dining table became his desk. No paper or book was to be moved! I drew a plan of the arrangement and managed to have friends in occasionally for dinner the one evening a week that my husband gave a course at Harvard night school, always replacing every item correctly before his return.
>
> Social life was almost nil for us as a married couple. My dreams of "open house" for students and the frequent entertaining of good friends among the faculty were not realized. During the first year of our married life, all had to be given up for THE BOOK. After Sylvia was born, it was THE CHAPTER. (*LH*, pp. 12-13)

Countless elegies have been written for Sylvia Plath, but who weeps for her mother, leading what must seem to us today a painful and demeaning life? Otto Plath became ill in 1936 but refused to consult a doctor. When he finally gave in and let himself be examined, it turned out that he had diabetes mellitus, a disease that could have been arrested if diagnosed early. It was, accordingly, his stubborn neglect that led to his protracted illness and his premature death in 1940. At thirty-four, Aurelia Plath found herself a widow with very little money and two small children to support. Having given up her career for Otto, she did not find work easily. Her parents moved in with her so as to help with the children, and she managed to get a job as a substitute teacher at a distant high school, rising at 5:30 every morning to meet her first class.

From then on, Aurelia Plath worked tirelessly to give her children everything America had to offer to the best and the brightest, for Sylvia and Warren *were* the best and the brightest. In Wellesley, Massachusetts, where the family moved so that the children could take advantage of the excellent public school system, Sivvy got the best grades and won all the prizes. She took music and dance lessons, joined the Girl Scouts, belonged to the local Unitarian Church group, and went to good summer camps. Everything had to be "normal" and wonderful, and for a time it seemed that the mother's self-sacrifice was wholly worthwhile. Sivvy was pretty and popular and won a full scholarship to Smith; Warren, who went to Exeter, later won a coveted National Merit Scholarship to Harvard. Within a few weeks of entering the freshman class at Smith, Sivvy was writing to her mother:

> How can I ever, ever tell you what a unique, dreamlike and astounding weekend I had! Never in my life, and perhaps never again, will I live through such a fantastic twenty-four hours.... Picture me then in my navy-blue bolero suit and versatile brown coat, snuggled in the back seat of an open car, whizzing for two sun-colored hours through the hilly Connecticut valley! The foliage was out in full tilt, and the hills of crimson sumac, yellow maples and scarlet oak that revolved past—the late afternoon sun on them—were almost more than I could bear.
>
> At about 5 P.M. we rolled up the long drive to "The Elms." God!... Great lawns and huge trees on a hill, with a view of the valley, distant green cow pastures, orange and yellow leaves receding far into the blue-purple distance.
>
> A caterer's truck was unloading champagne at the back. We walked through the hall, greeted by a thousand living rooms, period pieces, rare objects of art everywhere. (*LH*, p. 75)

It sounds like *Gatsby* rewritten for the daytime serials. But Aurelia Plath, herself only in her mid-forties, who had promised Sylvia the day her father died that she would never remarry (*LH*, p. 25), must have been delighted. Confident in what she calls "a sort of psychic osmosis" (*LH*, p. 32) between herself and Sylvia, she vicariously enjoyed her daughter's pleasures, sympathized with her "problems" (difficult courses, unsatisfactory blind dates, rejection slips) and gloried in her accomplishments, which were considerable. True, after her junior year when she was Guest Editor for *Mademoiselle* in New York, Sylvia underwent the breakdown described in such different terms in *The Bell Jar*, and Mrs. Plath knew something was terribly wrong. But then there were the reassuring letters from Sivvy's scholarship sponsor, the "famous writer," Olive Higgins Prouty, who told Aurelia that Sylvia's doctor had fortunately found "no trace of psychoses" (*LH*, p. 126) and that she herself had had a similar "nervous breakdown" as a young girl and had profited from the experience, becoming stronger and wiser. And indeed, Sivvy did recover after a few months at McLean's, made a dazzling return to Smith, won a Fulbright to Cambridge, met and married the man of her dreams, and became, for a time, the perfect Successful Girl Poet Married to Tall and Handsome Successful Poet. No wonder her mother was proud of her and tried to ignore the danger signals—and there were many, even in the early days at Smith.[8] In letter after letter, Sivvy continued to confirm her mother's fondest dreams, describing her marital bliss, her joy in the babies, her cooking and sewing triumphs, her daffodil garden in Devon, her own and Ted's ever increasing literary successes. When, on 11 February 1963, the American Dream turned to dust, everything Mrs. Plath had worked for suddenly vanished. For weeks, she refused to believe that Sylvia's death was really a suicide.

But what of Sylvia herself? What sort of influence did Aurelia Plath exert over her daughter's development as a poet? The letters reveal that she was by no means the negative presence Mrs. Greenwood is in *The Bell Jar*. Sylvia both feared and worshipped her widowed mother who lived only for her children and especially for her. In May 1953, shortly before her first breakdown, Sylvia wrote to Warren:

> You know, as I do, and it is a frightening thing, that mother would actually Kill herself for us if we calmly accepted all she wanted to do for us. She is an abnormally altruistic person and I have realized lately that we have to fight against her selflessness as we would fight against a deadly disease. My ambition is to earn enough so that she won't have to work summers in the future.... After extracting her life blood and care for 20 years, we should start bringing in big dividends of joy for her, and I hope that together we can maybe plan to take a week down at the Cape at the end of this summer. (*LH*, pp. 112-13)

This extraordinary letter reveals Plath's peculiar ambivalence about her mother. On the one hand, she recognizes that she must fight against her mother's selflessness as if it were "a deadly disease," but so great is the debt she feels she owes Aurelia that in the next breath she quickly rescinds these words and talks of the "big dividends of joy" she hopes to bring her. And of course these "dividends" were to be more than relaxing summers at the Cape. Aurelia Plath had, after all, a marked literary bent of her own; during Sylvia's early college days, she and her daughter read Auden, Yeats, and Spender together (see *LH*, p. 85), and even after Sylvia had met Ted Hughes, she treated her mother as a kind of collaborator. In a letter of 9 March 1956, for example, she encloses two new poems, "Channel Crossing" and "The Pursuit," with this comment:

> I'll be so eager to hear what you think of these: for myself, they show a rather encouraging growth. "Channel Crossing" is one of the first I've written in a "new line"; turning away from the small, coy love lyric.... "The Pursuit" is more in my old style, but larger, influenced by Blake, I think (tiger, tiger), and more powerful than any of my other "metaphysical" poems; read aloud also. It is, of course, a symbol of the terrible beauty of death, and the paradox that the more intensely one lives, the more one burns and consumes oneself.... The quotation is from Racine's *Phèdre*, where passion as destiny is magnificently expressed. (*LH*, p. 222)

Aurelia Plath evidently took a keen interest in these patient literary explanations. On the other hand, being poor and practical, what she most wanted for her daughter was fame and financial success. Blake and Racine were of course great writers, but in practical terms, success was personified by Olive Higgins Prouty, the author of *Stella Dallas*. To achieve success, one had to master the technique of popular magazine fiction. Under her mother's tutelage, Sivvy carefully studied the "craft" of the short stories in the *Ladies' Home Journal*, the *Saturday Evening Post*, and the *Atlantic Monthly*. As late as September 1961, she told her mother: "I am very encouraged by selling my first women's magazine story; my second hasn't sold yet, but the fiction editor of one of the two women's weeklies here [London] wants to see me and talk over their requirements on the strength of it. . . . I'll get into the *Ladies' Home Journal* yet!" (*LH*, p. 431) Not until Ted had deserted her and she was alone in Devon with the two babies, did she finally reject this literary ideal. On 21 October 1962, she wrote her mother:

> Don't talk to me about the world needing cheerful stuff! What the person out of Belsen—physical and psychological—wants is nobody saying the birdies still go tweet-tweet, but the full knowledge that somebody else has been there and knows the *worst*, just what it is like. It is much more help for me, for example, to know that people are divorced and go through hell, than to hear about happy marriages. Let the *Ladies' Home Journal* blither about *those*. (*LH*, p. 473)

Here Sivvy has finally given way to Sylvia.

But until the last year of her life, Plath's ideal way remained popular success, coupled with the role of wife and mother. Despite her rather vague objections to the atom bomb and to Nixon, she was essentially a conservative. At Smith, her friend Nancy Hunter Steiner recalls, she came into conflict with a girl named Gloria Brown ("Brownie"), who was considered "the leader of the Beatnik fringe" and whom Sylvia despised as a difficult outsider. As Steiner puts it:

> To Brownie, Sylvia was a misguided child who allowed an external force to condition her behavior, even when that force ran contrary to instinct. . . . A crucial and ironic difference marked the attitudes of these two startlingly different young women. Sylvia could not guess that society would ever change; she seemed to see the taboos and tensions of her background as permanent conditions that could never be substantially altered, and she bore them with surface resignation. Brownie, on the other hand, seemed to sense the changes that were already stirring underfoot. She flitted excitedly on the first wave of a new and radical movement, like a prophet who could see ahead into the '60's and '70's, while Sylvia looked back, absorbed in the events and attitudes of the '30's and 40's, unaware of any embryonic alternative to their platitudes and pieties.[9]

We can now understand why Sylvia Plath remained impervious to the influence of such "experimental" poets as Denise Levertov, Allen Ginsberg, and Charles Olson. At Cambridge, she regarded the women dons as "bluestocking grotesques" (*LH*, p. 219) and assured her mother: "Don't worry that I am a 'career woman'. . .I am definitely *meant* to be married and have children and a home and write like these women I admire: Mrs. Moore (Sarah-Elizabeth Rodgers), Jean Stafford, Hortense Calisher, Phyllis McGinley" (*LH*, p. 208). This was precisely Mrs. Plath's own view. Two years after Sivvy's marriage, she confided in her diary:

> We visited Ruth [an old friend of Sylvia's] on Thursday. She had come home with her five-day-old son, a wee, red-faced infant. Her two daughters were entrancing, especially the lively two-year-old, who immediately captured Ted. . . .
>
> I thought the golden, curly-haired one-year-old. . .would attract Sivvy most; but, no, it was the newest one, the wizened little boy. . . . There was such warmth, such yearning in Sivvy's face, my heart ached for her. I'd love to be a fairy godmother, to wave a wand and say, "Here, my darling, is a little house; here is a good woman to help you each morning. Now have your baby; spend your mornings writing, then belong to your family the rest of the time." (*LH*, p. 348)

Symbolically, Mrs. Plath *was* the fairy godmother who waved the wand: within a few months of this incident, Sivvy was pregnant, and after the birth of Frieda, she followed to the letter the blueprint outlined above. Although she did not have a "good woman" to help her, she did arrange things so that Ted took over the baby in the mornings, while she retreated to the study to write. Then she was willing to "belong to [her] family the rest of the time." But one senses an increasing frustration and tension in the letters of this period, no doubt because the composition of poetry could not take place in such a rigidly controlled setting. Having given her mother a "Wunderkind" (*LH*, p. 373) as grandchild, within two weeks she was "eager to begin writing and thinking again" (*LH*, p. 377); and after the birth of Nicholas in January 1962, she alternated within the same letter between rapt motherhood ("I think having babies is really the happiest experience of my life. I would just like to go on and on.") and frustration ("I am enjoying my slender foothold in my study in the morning again. It makes all the difference in my day. I still get tired by teatime and have spells of impatience for not doing all I want in the way of study and reading" (*LH*, pp. 449-50).

In this context, the infidelity of her husband and their consequent separation must have been the electric shock that finally severed the carefully "patched" self. In the winter of 1962, Plath could still be Sivvy, happy mother of two who wrote brilliant poetry in her free mornings. But by that summer she had become, in what seems to me an especially sad irony, a "widowed" young mother with very slender financial means —in short, *she had become her mother.* Even the sex of her two children —first a girl, then a boy—repeated the Sylvia-Warren pattern.

Only now, one gathers, did Sylvia fully grasp the futility of her former goals. And so she had to destroy the "Aurelia" in herself; she now rejected all notions of home, family, marriage, love, hard work. In the demonic *Ariel* poems, she could finally vent her anger, her hatred of men, her disappointment in life. "Dearest Mother" now becomes the dreaded Medusa, and Sylvia tells her:

> I didn't call you.
> I didn't call you at all.
> Nevertheless, nevertheless,
> You steamed to me over the sea,
> Fat and red, a placenta
>
> Paralyzing the kicking lovers. (*A*, pp. 39-40)

But having "killed" her mother, whose identity was so closely bound up with her own, it was inevitable that she would now kill herself.

2

Read against the background of the mother-daughter relationship I have been discussing, the thrust of Plath's earlier poetry becomes much clearer. The question of influence, for example, appears in quite a new light. One reads again and again that Plath was "influenced" first by Hopkins, Yeats, and Thomas, then by Auden and Stevens, later by Lowell, and most profoundly by Roethke and Ted Hughes himself.[10] I find that, on the contrary, Plath was peculiarly impervious to what Harold Bloom has called the anxiety of influence. For her, it was not a case of beginning in the shadow of a strong poet, of absorbing that poet's influence and then swerving away from the predecessor in the act of finding her own voice. Rather, she imitated a series of poets who have little in common with one another beyond their status as "major poets." While still at Smith, she wrote remarkably clever imitations of Emily Dickinson, adopting Dickinson's verse forms, slant rhymes, characteristic images, and "metaphysical" themes. Here is "Admonition":

> If you dissect a bird
>   To diagram the tongue
> You'll cut the chord
>   Articulating song.
>
> If you flay a beast
>   To marvel at the mane
> You'll wreck the rest
>   From which the fur began.

> If you pluck out the heart
>   To find what makes it move,
> You'll halt the clock
>   That syncopates our love. (*LH*, p. 110)

Surely this is the perfect "Sivvy" poem—well crafted, correct, poised, and written on an "interesting" theme: the perils of being too analytical. But the gnomic quality of "Admonition" is all surface; there is nothing behind its pithy propositions, and Emily Dickinson would hardly have placed the flaying of beasts in the same category as the dissection of birds. Indeed, Sylvia Plath herself is oddly absent from this text; it is designed to please magazine editors, who might well be impressed by the "maturity" of its insights, designed for one's "literary" mother.

"Admonition" is still an undergraduate poem, and Sylvia Plath herself soon dismissed it and comparable exercises as juvenilia. But the habit of imitation persisted. One of the first poems written after Plath's meeting with Ted Hughes in the spring of 1956 was "Metamorphosis," reprinted in *The Colossus* under the title "Faun."[11] Sivvy included this poem in an ecstatic letter home in which she talks of "living in the midst of a singing joy which is the best of Hopkins, Thomas, Chaucer, Shakespeare, Blake, Donne, and all the poets we love together." Ted, she explains,

> knows all about the habits of animals and takes me amid cows and coots. I am writing poems, and they are better and stronger than anything I have ever done; here is a small one about one night we went into the moonlight to find owls:
>
> > Haunched like a faun, he hooed
> > from grove of moon-glint and fen-frost
> > until all owls in the twigged forest
> > flapped black to look and brood
> > on the call this man made.
> >
> > No sound but a drunken coot
> > lurching home along river bank;
> > stars hung water-sunk, so a rank
> > of double star-eyes lit
> > boughs where those owls sat.
> >
> > An arena of yellow eyes
> > watched the changing shape he cut,
> > saw hoof harden from foot, saw sprout
> > goat horns; heard how god rose
> > and galloped woodward in that guise. (*LH*, p. 234)

This is a curious blend of Auden, Hopkins, Thomas, and Hughes.

164

Formally and tonally, "Faun" recalls such early Auden poems as "Consider," "Never Stronger," and "No Change of Place," which begins:

> Who will endure
> Heat of day and winter danger,
> Journey from one place to another,
> Nor be content to lie
> Till evening upon headland over bay,
> Between the land and sea
> Or smoking wait till hour of food,
> Leaning on chained-up gate
> At edge of wood?[12]

Like Auden, Plath uses a conventional rhyming stanza in which consonance is frequently substituted for full rhyme ("coot"/"lit"/"sat"); like his, her sentences are long and complex, clausal units regularly overriding line ends, and she creates a tightly packed verse fabric by aligning heavily stressed monosyllables and omitting definite articles and subject pronouns as in "saw hoof harden from foot, saw sprout / goat horns; heard how god rose / and galloped woodward in that guise."

If the stanza form and syntax of "Faun" recall Auden, its heavy compounding, alliteration, and assonance bring to mind the elaborate sound structures of Dylan Thomas as well as the Hopkins of "Inversnaid":

> A windpuff bonnet of fáwn-froth
> Turns and twindles over the broth
> Of a pool so pitchblack, féll-frówning
> It rounds and rounds Despair to drowning.[13]

In a sense she could hardly have intended, Plath was indeed "living in the midst of a singing joy which is the best of Hopkins [and] Thomas." But her immediate source was the poetry of her future husband, who had taken her for walks in the moonlight "amid cows and coots." The diction of "Faun" repeatedly echoes poems that were to appear in Hughes' first book, *The Hawk in the Rain* (1957).[14] "No sound but a drunken coot / lurching home along river bank" recalls Hughes' "Phaetons":

> Angrier, angrier, suddenly the near-madman
> In mid-vehemence rolls back his eye
> And lurches to his feet, (p. 8)

as well as "The Horses":

> With draped manes and tilted hind-hooves
> Making no sound. (p. 9)

Again, the lines "saw hoof harden from foot . . ." are reminiscent of "Meeting":

> A black goat clattered and ran
> Towards him, and set forefeet firm on a rock. (p. 33)

And so on.

In "Faun," Plath wanted to portray the mystery, the strange otherness of the animal world in much the same way Ted Hughes did in such poems as "The Thought Fox," "Horses," and "The Hawk in the Rain." But there is an interesting difference. For Hughes, the world of blind force, of natural violence, *is* the real world; in trying to depict that world in his early poetry, he naturally turned to those poets who had a similar vision: Dylan Thomas and especially D. H. Lawrence. But in Plath's "Faun," the world of night owls seems to be sheer decor. There is, for instance, a peculiar disjunction between the mysterious Northern landscape ("grove of moon-glint and fen-frost") and the "literary" notion of having the young man who can communicate with owls turn into a faun. Again, if a particular metamorphosis is to be the poet's theme, what is the function of the incantatory, spellbinding Thomas-like sound repetitions?

These are issues that must be raised because, in the wake of *Ariel* (1966), it became fashionable to argue that *of course* Plath's genius had always been there, latent in the early poetry. According to Peter Davison, the *Atlantic* editor and poet who had been Sylvia's close friend, the *Ariel* poems would never have come into being without the "long, deliberate, technical training that preceded them. We can only perform with true spontaneity what we have first learned to do by habit."[15] And John Frederick Nims has observed: "We might begin by saying to young writers: Forget *Ariel* for a while; study *The Colossus*. Notice all the stanza-forms, all the use of rhythm and rhyme; notice how the images are chosen and related; how deliberately sound is used. . . . without the drudgery of *The Colossus*, the triumph of *Ariel* is unthinkable."[16]

This is the way we usually regard the development of poets, and in most cases it makes sense: reading, say, Ezra Pound's pre-Raphaelite lyrics and Browningesque dramatic monologues, one finds the roots of the mature style of the *Cantos*. But in Plath's case, the "deliberate technical training" that Davison speaks of was less a move toward *Ariel* than it was a retreat toward safety, the cultivation of a mask. Consider "Epitaph for Fire and Flower," a poem enclosed in a letter to "Dearest darling mother" on 2 October 1956 and subsequently published in *Poetry*, although not included in *The Colossus*. It begins:

> You might as well string up
> This wave's green peak on wire

> To prevent fall, or anchor the fluent air
> In quartz, as crack your skull to keep
> These two most perishable lovers from the touch
> That will kindle angels' envy, scorch and drop
> Their fond hearts charred as any match. (*LH*, p. 274)

This love poem, begun on Plath's honeymoon in Spain, sounds as if Dylan Thomas were trying to rewrite Donne's "The Canonization." The "two most perishable lovers" are so special that nothing can separate them. To break them asunder would be as impossible as stringing up a wave on wire or "anchor[ing] the fluent air / in quartz." Angels envy them and "astounded generations" of museumgoers regard these "statues," locked in their embrace and "Secure in museum diamond," with envy and admiration. But though the lovers try to "outflame the phoenix," "the moment's spur / Drives nimble blood too quick" (an echo of Thomas's "The Force that Through the Green Fuse Drives the Flower"), and "a languor of wax congeals the vein / No matter how fiercely lit." In language reminiscent of Thomas' "A Process in the Weather of the Heart," the poem concludes that "Dawn snuffs out star's spent wick," that no matter how passionate their nighttime love, the "altering light" of morning brings the lovers back to earth, to their daytime selves.

Surely a poem for mothers. The lovers, discreetly referred to in the third person, are capable of "the most scrupulous and utter faithfulness in the world," as Sivvy said of her relationship to Ted in a letter of 18 May 1956 (*LH*, p. 254),[17] but they also know that in the daytime world, there must be an "Epitaph for Fire and Flower." In this neo-metaphysical poem, with its ingenious conceits and elaborate sound structure, Plath seems to define what love is supposed to be rather than what it *is* for her.

One can argue, of course, that Plath was only twenty-four when she wrote "Epitaph for Fire and Flower," that it is an apprentice poem she herself later excluded from *The Colossus*. This would be a valid argument if one could chart a direction in the work of the following four years, if the early poems were indeed moving toward a goal. But what happens is that Plath simply drops the dense metaphoric mode of "Epitaph" and tries out first one style and then another without ever quite renouncing her carefully constructed facade. This is true of "Point Shirley," written in 1959 under the influence of Robert Lowell;[18] it is even truer of the series of seven poems called *Poem for a Birthday*, written at Yaddo in the fall of that year and included in the British edition of *The Colossus* (1960).[19]

If we except "The Stones," the last poem in the series, which Plath did choose to include in the shorter American edition of *The Colossus*, and which, as I have argued elsewhere,[20] is one of her first major poems, we are left with a set of variations on the poems of Theodore Roethke, especially the "mad songs" of *Praise to the End! Poem for a Birthday* has been the subject of extensive psycholiterary study, notably by David Holbrook, who regards the series as the key document in understanding Plath's "regressed libidinal ego," her Electra complex, her longing to return to the womb, her split identity.[21] But Plath's imitations of Roethke are so expert, she so perfectly assumes his voice, his image patterns, his aphorisms, that one must regard with some skepticism the notion that here the poet is revealing her inner mental anguish. The line "My heart is a stopped geranium," for instance, is read by Holbrook as signifying the "lifeless aridity" experienced by the schizoid individual (p. 37); yet in Roethke's "Meditations of an Old Woman," we find the line: "My geranium is dying, for all I can do."[22] Indeed, Roethke, whom Plath herself refers to as "my influence" (*LH*, p. 407), is the central presence of the sequence. Here are the first two stanzas of "Dark House" (the second poem) side by side with their probable sources:

"Dark House"	Roethke, *Collected Poems*[23]
This is a dark house, very big,	It is dark in this wood, soft mocker. (p. 85)
I made it myself,	
	Sat in an empty house
Cell by cell from a quiet corner,	Watching shadows crawl Scratching. (p. 53)
Chewing at the grey paper,	
	Went down cellar
Oozing the glue drops,	Talked to a faucet The drippy water
Whistling, wiggling my ears,	Had nothing to say. (p. 74)
Thinking of something else.	Whisper me over. (p. 74)
	I'm all ready to whistle. (p. 84)
It has so many cellars	Went down cellar. (p. 74)
Such eelish devlings!	Such owly pleasures! (p. 87)
I'm round as an owl,	I know it's an owl. He's making it darker. (p. 72)
I see by my own light.	
	Was it light within?
Any day I may litter puppies.	Was it light within light?
Or mother a horse. My belly moves.	Sit and play Under the rocker

<table>
<tr><td>I must make more maps.</td><td>Until the cows
All have puppies. (p. 71)</td></tr>
</table>

I must make more maps.　　　　　　Until the cows
　　　　　　　　　　　　　　　　All have puppies. (p. 71)

　　　　　　　　　　　　　　　　A deep dish. Lumps in it.
　　　　　　　　　　　　　　　　I can't taste my mother (p. 74)

Despite these borrowings, Plath does not really resemble Roethke. Her use of nature imagery, for instance, seems oddly willed. When she writes, "Pebble smells, turnipy chambers. / Small nostrils are breathing. / Little humble loves!" (*CW*, p. 50), one immediately recalls the climax of "A Field of Light," where Roethke's speaker declares:

> I touched the ground, the ground warmed by the killdeer,
> The salt laughed and the stones;
> The ferns had their ways, and the pulsing lizards,
> And the new plants, still awkward in their soil,
> The lovely diminutives.
> I could watch! I could watch!
> I saw the separateness of all things! (*CP*, p. 63)

For Roethke, this world of "lovely diminutives"—ferns, tendrils, leaf-mold, moss, worms, snails, otters, moles—constitutes a "greenhouse Eden." In such manifestations of plant and animal life, he found the continuity of life and death and understood the organic nature of the universe. It is a vision Plath did not really share. There was no room for wise passiveness in her response to nature; rather, she had to conquer it, to become one with her horse Ariel, flying like an arrow "Into the red / Eye, the cauldron of morning" (*A*, p. 27).[24] Thus when, in the Yaddo poems, she talks of "little humble loves" and "turnipy chambers" or declares "I bed in a fish puddle" (*CW*, p. 52) or "Nightly . . . I enter the soft pelt of the mole" (*C*, p. 50), she is still playing a part, in this case that of a celebrant of dark instinctive life.

In the year following Frieda's birth (April 1960), Plath was evidently too busy to write more than a few poems. The letters of this period are, despite an undertone of frustration, aggressively proud and happy, exulting over Ted's literary triumphs, the joys of motherhood, and the now more and more frequent meetings with famous writers. Thus T. S. Eliot, who invited the Hugheses to dinner in May 1960, is described as "a descended god; he had such a nimbus of greatness about him." "Talk," she tells her mother, "was intimate gossip about Stravinsky, Auden, Virginia Woolf, D. H. Lawrence. I was fascinated. Floated in to dinner, sat between Eliot and Spender, rapturously, and got along very well" (*LH*, p. 381).

This is still essentially the Sivvy of Yale prom days; like that Sivvy, she was, in 1960, still "working very hard" on "women's magazine stories," hoping to write something "good enough for the *Saturday Evening Post.*" "For the first time," she says in this letter (28 November 1960), "I know where I'm going" (*LH*, p. 401). But by the following spring, shortly after her miscarriage, a definite change had occurred. The letters continue to be doggedly cheerful, but they no longer contain copies of new poems or more than passing references to them. Rather, when a particular incident furnishes both the material for a letter and for a poem, a curious splitting takes place. Take, for example, Plath's response to the appendectomy she underwent in March of 1961. Here is Sivvy's description in a long letter home:

> I am writing this to you propped up in my hospital bed less than 24 hours after my operation.... The progress they've made since I had my tonsils out in anesthetics is wonderful. I had an injection in my ward bed which dried up all my saliva and made me pleasantly drowsy. A very handsome young lady anesthetist introduced herself to me and said I'd see her later. She gave me an arm-shot in the anteroom which blacked me out completely. I drowsed pleasantly the rest of the day after I had the shot of painkiller and was ready to see dear Ted when he came during visiting hours in the evening, bearing a jar of freshly squeezed orange juice, a pint of milk, and a big bunch of hothouse grapes....
>
> He is an absolute angel. To see him come in at visiting hours, about twice as tall as all the little, stumpy people, with his handsome, kind, smiling face is the most beautiful sight in the world to me. He is finishing his play and taking admirable care of little Frieda....
>
> I am in a modern wing of this hospital—all freshly painted pink walls, pink and green flowered bed curtains and brand-new lavatories, full of light and air.... The nurses are all young, pretty, and cheerful. (*LH*, pp. 410-411)

And in the next letter:

> I am writing propped up in my hospital bed, six days now after my operation. My stitches are "pulling" and itching, but the nurses say that's a sign I'm healed.... Actually, I feel I've been having an amazing holiday! I haven't been free of the baby one day for a whole year, and I must say I have secretly enjoyed having meals in bed, backrubs, and nothing to do but read (I've discovered Agatha Christie—*just* the thing for hospital reading—I am a who-dun-it fan now), gossip, and look at my table of flowers sent by Ted's parents, Ted, Helga Huws, and Charles Monteith, Ted's editor at Faber.... Now I am mobile, I make a daily journey round the 28-bed ward, stopping and gossiping. This is much appreciated by the bedridden women, who regard me as a sort of ward newspaper.... (*LH*, p. 412)

Sylvia Plath knew very well what her mother wanted to hear, and her cheery, no-nonsense account of her hospital stay is a masterpiece of women's magazine reportage. The poem "Tulips," written concurrently about the same event, is not just different—most of us, after all, try to save face when we talk of our illnesses to our relatives—it virtually turns the prose account inside out. The "freshly painted pink walls" and "pink and green flowered bed curtains" become deathly white: "Look how white everything is, how quiet, how snowed-in" (*A*, p. 10). The "young, pretty and cheerful nurses" now

> pass the way gulls pass inland in their white caps,
> Doing things with their hands, one just the same as another,
> So it is impossible to tell how many there are.
>
> My body is a pebble to them, they tend it as water
> Tends to the pebbles it must run over, smoothing them gently.
> They bring me numbness in their bright needles, they bring me sleep.

The young patient who describes herself in the letter as a "sort of ward newspaper," gossiping with the bedridden women and cheering them up, is, in the poem, a "nobody," who has given her name and her "day-clothes up to the nurses / And my history to the anesthetist and my body to surgeons." The avid who-dun-it fan who adores Agatha Christie becomes "an eye between two white lids that will not shut. / Stupid pupil, it has to take everything in."

But the most interesting difference between letter and poem is Sylvia's response to her husband and baby. In the letter, Ted is "an absolute angel," whose "handsome, kind, smiling face is the most beautiful sight in the world to me," and who brings her delicious things to eat and tales of little Frieda. In "Tulips," however, the speaker declares:

> Now I have lost myself I am sick of baggage—
> My patent leather overnight case like a black pillbox,
> My husband and child smiling out of the family photo;
> Their smiles catch onto my skin, little smiling hooks.

In the late poems, Plath often refers to other people as trying to put their "hooks" into her; in "The Other," for example, we read:

> You come in late, wiping your lips.
> What did I leave untouched on the doorstep—
>
> White Nike,
> Streaming between my walls?

> Smilingly, blue lightning
> Assumes, like a meathook, the burden of his parts.[25]

Here, the "Other" is evidently the hated woman who is the rival for her husband's affections, and so the association with meathooks is not surprising. But to regard the smiles of husband and child in the family photo as "little smiling hooks" is to reject all human love, and indeed, the "amazing holiday" Sivvy writes of to her mother is nothing less than a time of tension between life and death, a time when the death-wish almost wins out. The "flowers" described casually in the letter become the blood-red tulips that "breathe. . .through their white swaddlings, like an awful baby." The implication of the simile is clear: Sivvy adored "little Frieda," but Sylvia subconsciously resented the infant's demanding breathing. In the speaker's imagination, the tulips now loom larger and larger, "A dozen red lead sinkers round my neck":

> Nobody watched me before, now I am watched.
> The tulips turn to me, and the window behind me
> Where once a day the light slowly widens and slowly thins,
> And I see myself, flat, ridiculous, a cut-paper shadow
> Between the eye of the sun and the eyes of the tulips,
> And I have no face, I have wanted to efface myself.
> The vivid tulips eat my oxygen.

The tulips, as I have argued elsewhere,[26] ultimately recall the poet to life; their vivid presence restores, at least for the moment, her sense of having a "face":

> The tulips should be behind bars like dangerous animals;
> They are opening like the mouth of some great African cat,
> And I am aware of my heart: it opens and closes
> Its bowl of red blooms out of sheer love of me.
> The water I taste is warm and salt, like the sea,
> And comes from a country far away as health.

But, as many readers have noted,[27] at the end of the poem "health" is still a far-away country, and the self gives up the white hospital world of numbness and calm only with great reluctance. It is as if she finds it increasingly difficult to live in the world, as if the routine hospitalization has brought out fears and desires that had been latent for years.

To read "Tulips" in the perspective of the two letters cited above is thus a chilling experience. By the middle of 1961, the Sivvy mask was cracking; the more enthusiastic and Pollyanna-like the letters of these months, the more somber and withdrawn the poems. And what is especially

172

interesting is that "Tulips," like the *Ariel* poems that follow, is no longer in any sense an imitative poem; on the contrary, it seems to manifest no influence at all, although it can be said to follow the paradigm established by Keats's "Ode to a Nightingale," in which the longing for "easeful Death" finally gives way to the recognition that the poet cannot escape his "sole self." But whereas Keats's speaker longs to transcend the sense world so as to enter the magic realm of the nightingale, the "I" of "Tulips" is attracted by the purely negative qualities of death — that is, by the peace of nonbeing.

Compared to Lowell's hospital poems, "Tulips" is peculiarly abstract, hallucinatory, non-mimetic. But the Roethke influence disappears as well. In the world of Roethke's "Flower Dump," "everything [is] limp" until "one tulip on top, / One swaggering head / Over the dying, the newly dead" forces its way to the surface, bringing signs of a new life. Plath's tulips similarly signal a return to life, but their power is felt to be as menacing as "the mouth of a great African cat."

It is, I think, the extraordinary *originality* of poems like "Tulips" that makes Sylvia Plath such an important but, paradoxically, limited poet. In *Ariel* and *Winter Trees*, we have a body of work quite unprecedented in twentieth-century American poetry; to find analogues for "Tulips," one would have to turn to, say, Trakl or to German Expressionist painting, in which a vase of flowers can become a similarly threatening presence. But Plath's limitation is that, having finally ceased to be Sivvy, she had really only one subject: her own anguish and consequent longing for death. To a degree, she camouflaged this narrowness by introducing political and religious images: "Daddy" as "Panzer-man"; the poet herself as a Jew being "chuf(fed) off to Dachau, Auschwitz, Belsen," her skin "Bright as a Nazi lampshade"; her enemy as alternately "Herr Lucifer," "Christus" with "The awful / God-bit in him," or "Blubbery Mary," offering a "Communion wafer." But since the woman who speaks throughout *Ariel* hates all human beings just as she hates herself, her identification with the Jews who suffered at Auschwitz has a hollow ring, just as her violent rejection of Christianity is no more than a rejection of herself.

The references to "Hiroshima ash" or "the cicatrix of Poland" are, I believe, no more than Gothic trappings, calling attention to their own cleverness. Thus when the speaker of "Medusa" rejects her mother as a "Ghastly Vatican," the metaphor has a certain accuracy (the power of the vampiric mother is analogous to that of the all-powerful and oppressive Church), but it is also peculiarly reductive in that it allows us to view both terms of the equation in only one way.

Sylvia Plath's real poetic world is rooted in her own private experience. Consider "The Bee Meeting," the first of the extraordinary bee poems, written in the fall of 1962. The prose version of this poem may be found in a letter of 15 June:

> Today, guess what, we became *beekeepers!* We went to the local meeting last week (attended by the rector, the midwife, and assorted beekeeping people from neighboring villages) to watch a Mr. Pollard make three hives out of one (by transferring his queen cells) under the supervision of the official Government bee-man. We all wore masks and it was thrilling. It is expensive to start beekeeping . . . but Mr. Pollard let us have an old hive for nothing, which we painted white and green, and today he brought over the swarm of docile Italian hybrid bees we ordered and installed them. We placed the hive in a sheltered out-of-the-way spot in the orchard—the bees were furious from being in a box. Ted had only put a handkerchief over his head where the hat should go in the bee-mask, and the bees crawled into his hair, and he flew off with half-a-dozen stings. I didn't get stung at all, and when I went back to the hive later, I was delighted to see bees entering with pollen sacs full and leaving with them empty. (*LH*, p. 457)

By the time "The Bee Meeting" was written, Mrs. Plath had witnessed "the horror of what I saw you see" and Sylvia and Ted had separated. Like "Tulips," the poem thus inverts the cheery report home, but "The Bee Meeting" is the more hallucinatory poem, moving into the world of nightmare and fantasy. It begins:

> Who are these people at the bridge to meet me? They are the villagers—
> The rector, the midwife, the sexton, the agent for bees.
> In my sleeveless summery dress I have no protection,
> And they are all gloved and covered, why did nobody tell me?
> They are smiling and taking out veils tacked to ancient hats. (*A*, p. 56)

Here there are no more masks. The self stands exposed, alone and vulnerable in a "sleeveless summery dress," and "nude as a chicken neck." She is terrified of engulfment, of victimization at the hands of those "gloved and covered" others, with their "veils tacked to ancient hats." In the surrealistic scene that follows, the "real" people—rector, midwife, sexton—become interchangeable:

> Which is the rector now, is it that man in black?
> Which is the midwife, is that her blue coat?
> Everybody is nodding a square black head, they are knights in visors,
> Breastplates of cheesecloth knotted under the armpits.
> Their smiles and their voices are changing. I am led through a beanfield.

As the helpless speaker becomes the victim of the villagers, they are dehumanized: "Strips of tinfoil winking like people, / Feather dusters fanning their hands in a sea of bean flowers." The tortured "I" tries to learn what is happening:

174

Is it some operation that is taking place?
It is the surgeon my neighbours are waiting for,
This apparition in a green helmet,
Shining gloves and white suit.
Is it the butcher, the grocer, the postman, someone I know?

But she never finds out. Nor can she run away: "I cannot run, I am rooted." Meanwhile, the "outriders" begin to come out of the hive in further pursuit. "If I stand very still," the speaker says, "they will think I am cow parsley, . . .// . . .a personage in a hedgerow." But the longing to be invisible and hence impervious is not fulfilled; for a moment, the villagers are distracted by their hunt for the queen bee, but in the final sequence, the speaker sees that she herself is the virgin destined to take the queen bee's place, that she is the one "they," whether the bees or the bee-keepers, have been after:

I am exhausted, I am exhausted—
Pillar of white in a blackout of knives.
I am the magician's girl who does not flinch.
The villagers are untying their disguises, they are shaking hands.
Whose is that long white box in the grove, what have they
    accomplished, why am I cold?

This scene of public humiliation, the villagers "untying their disguises" and "shaking hands" as if to congratulate one another, recalls Kafka's *The Trial*, as does the poet's sudden terrible realization that "they" have all along been planning her death, a death now prefigured in the appearance of "the long white box in the grove," which is her own coffin. The underlying note is one of *fear*, a terrible, nameless fear that is, in Laingian terms, the fear of total self-dissolution and hence "death."

The bee poems thus mark, both literally and figuratively, a dead end. For years, Sivvy had been trying to tell herself that she was "milkweed silk, the bees will not notice," that perhaps no one would ever "notice" the inner Sylvia. But now she admits that "I could not run without having to run forever." There is, finally, no future. Thus, when in "Medusa," she tells the female monster (a terrifying projection of the mother imago), "Off, off, eely tentacle! // There is nothing between us" (*A*, p. 40),[28] she is paradoxically cutting herself off from the "Old barnacled umbilicus" that had, in fact, kept her alive thus far. The first shock of recognition produced by Sylvia Plath's sudden "independence" from her husband and her mother was the stimulus that gave rise to the *Ariel* poems. But given the "psychic osmosis" between herself and Aurelia Plath (*LH*, p. 32), given the years of iron discipline during which Sylvia had been her mother's Sivvy, the touching assertion that "There is nothing between us" could only mean that now there would be nothing at all.

Notes

1. Sylvia Plath, *Letters Home: Correspondence 1950-1963*, selected and edited with commentary by Aurelia Schober Plath (New York: Harper and Row, 1975), p. 409. Subsequently noted as *LH*.
2. See Lois Ames, "Sylvia Plath: A Biographical Note," *The Bell Jar* (New York: Harper and Row, 1971), p. 295.
3. Marjorie Perloff, "On the road to *Ariel*: The 'Transitional' Poetry of Sylvia Plath," *Iowa Review* 4 (Spring, 1973): 94-110. Reprinted in *Sylvia Plath: The Woman and the Work*, ed. Edward Butscher (New York: Dodd, Mead, 1977), pp. 125-42.
4. "Sylvia Plath's Apotheosis," *New York Review of Books* 23 (24 June 1976): 3.
5. There are a few exceptions to this rule. For instance, a handwritten note from Nice (7 January 1956) describing a trip to the Matisse Chapel at Vence, is signed "Sylvia" (see *LH*, pp. 204-5), but here Plath was writing an open postcard and hence observing the formalities.
6. "Foreword," *Ariel* (New York: Harper and Row, 1966), p. ix.
7. In "Book Ends," *New York Times Book Review*, 14 September 1975, the editors explain how *Letters Home* was in fact assembled. Because Plath left no will when she died, her literary estate passed to her husband, Ted Hughes. Aurelia Plath thus had to apply to her former son-in-law and to his sister Olwyn Hughes (Plath's literary executor) for permission to quote from the seven-hundred-odd letters Sylvia had written home between 1950 and 1963. The manuscript took two years to assemble; Ted Hughes read it a first time without objection, but before publication he changed his mind and insisted on so many excisions that, according to the *Times*:

   > editor [Fran] McCullough returned with a "fractured" manuscript.... A lot of Mr. Hughes's deletions had to do with protecting the privacy of the couple's two children, removing private domestic details and excising some tart references by Miss Plath to contemporaries; he also removed some glowing descriptions of himself in early love letters. At this point, Harper and Row's lawyers took charge, simply restoring those that presented no libel or invasion of privacy problems and discarding those that possibly did. (p. 37)

8. See especially the letter of 19 November 1952 (*LH*, pp. 97-99), in which Sivvy is in despair because of a chemistry course that, she claims, is destroying her life; she admits she has "practically considered committing suicide" to get out of it.
9. Nancy Steiner, *A Closer Look at Ariel: A Memory of Sylvia Plath* (New York: Harper's Magazine Press, 1973), pp. 78-79.
10. The best source for the study of Plath's declared influences is Ted Hughes's "Notes on the Chronological Order of Sylvia Plath's Poems," in *The Art of Sylvia Plath: A Symposium*, ed. Charles Newman (London: Faber and Faber, 1970), pp. 187-95. Hughes tells us, for example, that "Point Shirley" was a deliberate exercise in Robert Lowell's early style and that "Poem for a Birthday" was written shortly after Plath had begun reading "closely and sympathetically for the first time—Roethke's poems" (pp. 191-92). For an interesting if not quite convincing comparison of Plath to Emily Dickinson, see Charles Newman, "Candor Is the Only Wile: The Art of Sylvia Plath," in the same collection, pp. 21-55. Anthony Libby gives a valuable account of the shared myth and "mysticism" in the poetry of Plath and Hughes in "God's Lioness and the Priest of Sycorax," *Contemporary Literature* 15 (Summer, 1974): 386-405.
11. See *The Colossus and Other Poems* (New York: Knopf, 1962), p. 17. Subsequently cited as *C*.
12. W. H. Auden, *Collected Shorter Poems, 1927-1957* (London: Faber and Faber, 1966), p. 23.
13. *The Poems of Gerard Manley Hopkins*, ed. W. H. Gardner and N. H. MacKenzie, 4th ed. (London: Oxford University Press, 1970), p. 88.
14. When Plath wrote "Faun," Hughes had already written most of the poems that were included in *The Hawk in the Rain* (New York: Harper, 1957). Plath herself typed up the manuscript before 21 November 1956 (see *LH*, p. 287), and it was promptly submitted to Harper's for the Poetry Center First Publication contest, which it won. See *LH*, pp. 296-97.

15. "The Last Poetry of Sylvia Plath," *Atlantic*, August, 1966, 76-77.

16. John Frederick Nims, "The Poetry of Sylvia Plath: A Technical Analysis," in Newman, ed., *The Art of Sylvia Plath: A Symposium*, p. 136.

17. Interestingly, Plath seems to have written more letters to her mother during her courtship with Ted Hughes and the first year of her marriage (see pp. 221-318) than at any other time, although it is, of course, possible that Aurelia Plath chose to include more letters from this period than from other less happy ones. One has, in any case, the impression that falling in love and marrying made it possible for Sivvy to be equally loving toward her mother; the loss of Ted created exactly the reverse situation.

18. The opening of Plath's poem echoes Lowell's *Lord Weary's Castle*, especially "In Memory of Arthur Winslow" and "The Quaker Graveyard in Nantucket":

> From Water-Tower Hill to the brick prison
> The shingle booms, bickering under
> The sea's collapse.
> Snowcakes break and welter. This year
> The gritted wave leaps
> The seawall and drops onto a bier
> Of quahog chips,
> Leaving a salty mash of ice to whiten
>
> In my grandmother's sand yard. She is dead,
> Whose laundry snapped and froze here, who
> Kept house against
> What the sluttish, rutted sea could do. (*Colossus*, p. 24)

19. The seven poems included in the British edition (London: Heinemann, 1960) are: "Who," "Dark House," "Maenad," "The Beast," "Witch Burning," "Flute Notes from a Reedy Pond," and "The Stones." In a letter of 1 May 1961, Plath explains that Alfred A. Knopf, who planned to bring out the book in America, wanted her to leave out about ten poems. "By a miracle of intuition," she writes, "I guessed...the exact ten they would have left out" (*LH*, p. 417), and she omitted all the poems in the *Birthday* series except for "Flute Notes" and "The Stones," evidently because she sensed that the others were too imitative. Ted Hughes confirms this view: "STONES was the last [of the sequence] and the only one not obviously influenced by Roethke. It is full of specific details of her experience in a mental hospital, and it is clearly enough the first eruption of the voice that produced ARIEL.... That was the end of the first phase of her development. When she consolidated her hold on the second phase, two years later, she dismissed everything prior to THE STONES as Juvenilia, produced in the days before she became herself" (Newman, ed., *The Art of Sylvia Plath: A Symposium*, p. 192). The remaining poems in the sequence were reprinted in the posthumous *Crossing the Water* (New York: Harper and Row, 1971), subsequently noted as *CW*.

20. See *The Poetic Art of Robert Lowell* (Ithaca, N.Y.: Cornell University Press, 1973), pp. 179-84.

21. David Holbrook, *Sylvia Plath: Poetry and Existence* (London: Athlone Press, 1976), pp. 23-64.

22. *The Collected Poems of Theodore Roethke* (New York: Doubleday, 1966), p. 163. "Meditations of an Old Woman," like "The Lost Son" and *Praise to the End!*, were included in the first "Collected Poems" of Roethke, *Words for the Wind*, which appeared in 1958, the year before Plath wrote *Poem for a Birthday*.

23. I have double-spaced the first two stanzas of Plath's "Dark House" and set them side by side with their probable Roethke sources, mostly from *Praise to the End!*, single-spaced. The page references are to Roethke's *Collected Poems* (1966).

24. I realize that I am retracting certain things I said in my first essay on Plath, "Angst and Animism in the Poetry of Sylvia Plath," *Journal of Modern Literature* 1 (1970): 57-74. When I first read *Ariel*, the connection between Plath and such oracular nature poets as Roethke and Lawrence seemed to me a very real one. But after the publication of *Crossing the Water, Winter Trees* (1971), and *Letters Home*, I have come to believe that the connection is more apparent than real, that Plath did not and could not "identify imaginatively with the life of animals and plants" (see "Angst and Animism," p. 57).

25. Sylvia Plath, *Winter Trees* (London: Faber and Faber, 1971), p. 22.
26. See Perloff, "Angst and Animism," pp. 69-70; and Perloff, "On Sylvia Plath's 'Tulips'," in "Sylvia Plath's 'Tulips': A Festival, *Paunch* 42-43 (December, 1975): 105-9.
27. The participants in the symposium cited above—Arthur Efron, Brian Carapher, M. D. Uroff, Robin Reed Davis, and myself—all seem to agree on this point, although our readings are otherwise very different.
28. For an excellent analysis of "Medusa" in the context of the mother-daughter relationship depicted in *Letters Home*, see Gene Ballif, "Facing the Worst: A View from Minerva's Buckler," *Parnassus: Poetry in Review* 5 (Fall/Winter, 1976): 231-59. Ballif's essay, which appeared after I had completed my own, shares many of my views, although the author's reading of the earlier Plath poetry is more sympathetic than mine.

Murray M. Schwartz and Christopher Bollas

The absence at the center: Sylvia Plath and suicide

> It is a terrible thing
> To be so open: it is as if my heart
> Put on a face and walked into the world.
>
> Sylvia Plath, "Three Women"

Since her death in 1963, Sylvia Plath's life and work have provoked a vast and varied commentary. Some writers have attempted to separate her life and suicide from her art; others have devised metaphoric explanations for the concrete reality of her tragedy. Some, like A. Alvarez, have stated both alternatives. Writing in 1970, Alvarez sees the risk of suicide as a by-product of poetic commitment:

> It is *as though she had decided* that, for her poetry to be valid, it must tackle head-on nothing less serious than her own death, bringing to it a greater wealth of invention and sardonic energy than most poets manage in a lifetime of so-called affirmation.
>
> If the road had seemed impassable, she proved that it wasn't. It was, however, one-way, and she went too far along it to be able, in the end, to

This chapter first appeared in *Criticism, a Quarterly for Literature and the Arts*, 18:2 (Spring, 1976): 147-72. Reprinted with permission of Wayne State University Press. © 1976 Wayne State University Press.

turn back. *Yet her actual suicide. . .is by the way;* it adds nothing to her work and proves nothing about it. It was *simply a risk* she took in handling such volatile material.[1] (Emphasis added.)

This vision of the poet is perhaps more comforting than Alvarez, and others who have carefully explicated the themes and images of "extremist" poets, would wish to admit. He implies the conscious choice of the artist in an obsession with death, minimizes anxiety, and adopts an "as if" tone that can substitute for a searching out of true motives. The catastrophic act is to be dissociated from her work in almost casual phrases: "by the way," "simply a risk." Such a critical attitude permits one to dignify the very obsession that, as Alvarez himself points out, has led an astonishing number of twentieth-century artists to suicidal ends. The poet becomes, then, a reflection of "our" collective concerns, and, as such, a bizarre ego ideal for a brutalizing and fragmented Western culture. But the "volatile material" of Sylvia Plath's art is, first and most intensely, *hers.* Her suffering, as Alvarez realized in his sensitive personal account in *The Savage God*,[2] created the poems poured out in the months before her suicide, not Nazi concentration camps. To understand her suicide, we need to understand her work and her life as a unity.

We shall approach Plath's art as an expression of personal style, her way of being in the world, and we shall view her suicide as a *convergence* of actions, inner and outer. We shall attempt to go beyond the charting of manifest associations and stylistic elements that characterizes most writing about her life or art, seeking instead to reconstruct determining motives that explain our experience of her forms of symbolic action. As Elizabeth Hardwick has said, "Her fate and her themes are hardly separate and both are singularly terrible."[3] We shall follow David Holbrook's insight that an incapacity to love was at the heart of Plath's experience.[4] She was almost always confined to a world in which "Love is the bone and sinew of my curse" ("The Stones," *C*).[5] We view this incapacity to love as a consequence of Plath's failure to integrate her inner world sufficiently to make a coherent sense of personal identity possible. In other words, the unity we seek to define is the unity of a person who announces in her works an absence at the center of her being. Answering the "Why?" of her suicide involves: (1) a description of her characteristic modes of experiencing and representing inner and outer realities; (2) a charting of her relations to father and mother as these figures metamorphose in her art; (3) an identification of her developmental failures; (4) an identification of the motivational strands bound up in the act of suicide.

We assume that in her writing Plath projects her own psychic and somatic states, her self images, and a representation of her world of self-other relations. Her works record, for instance, a consistent spectrum of feelings. Syntonic feelings are "fullness," "purity," "warmth," and "peace." Asyntonic feelings are "flatness," "thin papery" feelings, "dead and moneyless" sensations, and "leaden slag" feelings. The repetitive nature of her object world, the fact that certain object relations and affective states keep recurring, suggests to us that Plath was unable to repress profoundly disturbing memories even through the actions of obsessive-compulsive defenses. We can see an attempt to defend against unwanted internal stimuli in "Lesbos" (A), where Plath's response to an intrusion of murderous impulses is to mobilize a compulsive action.

> Now I am silent, hate
> Up to my neck,
> Thick, thick.
> I do not speak.
> I am packing the hard potatoes like good clothes,
> I am packing the babies,
> I am packing the sick cats.

The ritual is *machinelike*, an exaggeration perhaps of her true defensive functioning, but nonetheless a poignant depiction of how she feels she must exert self control. Not surprisingly the defense becomes the enemy, the machinelike self receives a brutal and haunting attack from Plath in "The Applicant" (A):

> But in twenty-five years she'll be silver,
> In fifty, gold.
> A living doll, everywhere you look.
> It can sew, it can cook,
> It can talk, talk, talk.

In *The Colossus* Plath could project her conflict on to a partially stable landscape, and as in poets before her this process could serve to represent and work through conflict. But the landscape we experience in *Ariel* is almost without exception terrifying and so loaded with psychotic content as to obliterate the possibility of a supportive structure of external reality. Plath created in her poetry a world in which she could no longer find the possibility of survival.

In both collections, however, certain objects that formed a part of Plath's personal world, though maintaining a familial form, nonetheless undergo a series of affective metamorphoses. A stone can be a symbol of the self, a breast, or a ticket to oblivion beneath a watery surface. The sea can be a mirror, a raging bull, or a graveyard. In many cases Plath changed her objects in order to portray some specific conflict. Familiarity with the placement and use of the objects leads us to recognize in time the strangely theatrical nature of the conflict. Something of the eerie feeling we get when we read *Hamlet*, *Lear*, *Othello*, and *Macbeth* and intuit that we are seeing the same dyadic and triadic conflicts in new costume, new forms, and new perspectives emerges when we read Plath's poetry.

We imagine Plath's object world as a theater; each action derives its content and statement from the poet's ordering of her objects. In perhaps the most crucial repetoire of objects in her poetry we see the sea, the sun or the moon, and the poet somewhere in the proscenium. We experience an action that seems an encoded message. Each time some object is dragged across the stage by another object, and the atmosphere of the theater seems informed by the psychic mood of its director. In "The Manor Garden" (C), "a blue mist is dragging the lake." The moon "drags the sea after it like a dark crime" in "The Moon And The Yew Tree" (A), and the sun's cells are found "dragging their Jesus hair" in "Medusa" (A). In "Moonrise" (C) the boney mother drags the "ancient father at the heel," and in "Elm" (A) the poet becomes the moon's victim: "The moon, also, is merciless: she would drag me / Cruelly, being barren." In "Lesbos" (A) the drama becomes even darker:

> That night the moon
> Dragged its blood bag, sick
> Animal
> Up over the harbor lights
> And then grew normal,
> Hard and apart and white.

In "Getting There" (A) she represents the same content, but now *she* represents a condensation of the moon and what the moon drags with it, and the landscape is a Russian terrain:

> It is Russia I have to get across, it is some war or other.
> I am dragging my body
> Quietly through the straw of the boxcars.

Another repeated action is one of departure and destination. In "Departure" (C) the poet mourns the loss of her seaside landscape. She has been placed on a train, separated by its motion from her revered origins, but *where* is this train going? In *Three Women* the Secretary says:

> Trains roar in my ears, departures, departures!
> The silver track of time empties into the distance,
> The white sky empties of its promise, like a cup.

Departures are related to the departure from the beautiful fusion with the world at age two and a half, when her brother *arrived* to destroy her sense of unity, the departure from the father when he left her in death, the departure from the seaside landscape.[6] Torn from an object world that must have supplied her with psychic nourishment, the train that takes her away becomes a persecutory vehicle that catches her in some inexorable drive that cannot be undone, and it merges in her language with her own driving rage. With a deep sense of no destination in her life, with the vision that life is but an endless line of telephone poles reaching into infinity, or a silver track of time glistening on forever, the desire for destination becomes a form of madness:

> The train is dragging itself, it is screaming —
> An animal
> Insane for the destination,
> The bloodspot,
> The face at the end of the flare. ("Getting There," A)

Plath imagined two ways out of this insanity: rebirth or self-destruction. At the end of "Getting There" she is born out of the train metamorphosed. She moves from madness through rebirth to infantile purity:

> The carriages rock, they are cradles.
> And I, stepping from this skin
> Of old bandages, boredoms, old faces
>
> Step to you from the black car of Lethe,
> Pure as a baby.

But there is to be no rebirth. The engine that was the black car of death in "Getting There" is Plath's living self in "Totem" (A). It is a self that begins to destroy its own direction:

> The engine is killing the track, the track is silver,
> It stretches into the distance. It will be eaten nevertheless.

For Plath the only way to stop the running that she feels is useless was for the train (herself) to be derailed. In the final weeks of her life she denied the hope of some terminal stasis free from madness.

> There is no terminus, only suitcases
> Out of which the same self unfolds like a suit
> Bald and shiny, with pockets of wishes. ("Totem," A)

There is no rebirth. We imagine that the energy devoted to the autonomous rebirth of the self only materialized in the repetitive unfolding of the same suit from the same suitcase, and we feel the shock of seeing the same disfigured self metamorphosing in the mirror of words.

Our experience of Plath's poetry is suffused with scores of these repeated actions, some extraordinarily obscure and much less accessible than the drama of the dragged object or the drama of departure and destination.

We experience also a repeated act of using language intensely to embody what words might avoid or make bearable or distance. She seems more and more to exhibit what Kurt Goldstein called the "concrete attitude" of the schizophrenic for whom the distance between the use of metaphor and the recognition of it *as* metaphor collapses.[7] Words then become an equivalent of experience rather than mediating or reparative symbols. We see the kind of projection Roy Schafer calls "an emptying out of the subject's own impulse into the object."[8] Plath says she began writing poetry about external natural things, "all those subjects which are absolute gifts to the person who doesn't have any interior experience to write about."[9] Yet by the late 1950s and early 1960s the purpose changes; she would control what is exclusively catastrophic:

> I believe that one should be able to control and manipulate experiences, even the most terrifying, like madness, being tortured, this sort of experience. . . . it shouldn't be a kind of shut-box and mirror-looking, narcissistic experience. I believe it should be *relevant*, and relevant to the larger things, the bigger things, such as Hiroshima and Dachau and so on.[10]

We hear her speaking of an inner world *found* in history. The shut-box and the mirror of herself are denied, but the oven, in the end, was not in Dachau but in herself. History came home, because that is where it originated. It "shouldn't be" a mirror, but it was.

There is a terribly self-defeating circularity in a psychic activity like Plath's. Like the compulsive person Otto Fenichel describes, she turns from "the macrocosm of things to the microcosm of words," in an attempt to master frightening psychic realities, only to find that "the sober words do not remain sober but become emotionally overcathected; they acquire the emotional value which things have for other persons."[11] Plath could say, "It's like water or bread, or something absolutely essential to me. I find myself absolutely fulfilled when I have written a poem, when I'm writing one."[12] We suggest that her "fulfillment" became, paradoxically, a magical emptying out of unbearable inner conflict. Because magically conceived, it had to be repeated, until the magical strategy moved from words to things, because the difference was gone, and her project failed. When her inner world could no longer be ritualized in print she acted out the ritual. Plath's last poem in *Ariel*, written in the final weeks of her life, is called "Words."

> Axes
> After whose stroke the wood rings,
> And the echoes!
> Echoes travelling
> Off from the centre like horses.

And that poem ends not in fulfillment but deprivation, not motion outward but stasis:

> Words dry and riderless,
> The indefatigable hoof-taps.
> While
> From the bottom of the pool, fixed stars
> Govern a life.

In the following pages, we explore reasons for Plath's defeated project. If words failed her, they also revealed the purpose for which they were projected on the dream screen of the blank page.

In the title poem of *The Colossus*, Plath tries symbolically to reconstitute her father, the imago of a lost god. She begins in frustration: "I shall never get you put together entirely, / Pieced, glued, and properly jointed." In the role of a sculptress-housewife, she mocks the very process that claims her labor, dwarfs her presence before his intractible decomposition:

> Scaling little ladders with gluepots and pails of lysol
> I crawl like an ant in mourning
> Over the weedy acres of your brow
> To mend the immense skullplates and clear
> The bald, white tumuli of your eyes.

This imago is stone, monumentally distant from her human need:

> O father, all by yourself
> You are pithy and historical as the Roman Forum.

It is a labor of despair: "My hours are married to shadow."

The persistent, doomed effort to reconstruct father, to deny the vacant space left by his death, is a central theme in Plath's work. In "Daddy" (*A*) she writes:

> I was ten when they buried you.
> At twenty I tried to die

185

And get back, back, back to you.
I thought even the bones would do.

She imagines compulsive, ritualized suicide attempts as an effort to avoid an absence at the center of her being, a gap left by the father's loss, by identifying with the father's death. His death becomes, ironically, her first suicide, to be repeated at ten year intervals. In "Lady Lazarus" (*A*) she affirms the ritualistic nature of her efforts:

I am only thirty.
And like the cat I have nine times to die.

This is Number Three.
What a trash
To annihilate each decade.

To try to die every ten years is to identify with a father who died after the first nine years of her life. Living was laden with a guilty yearning that could only be undone by this brutal means. By focusing murderousness on herself rather than on the father who left her, she could have partially denied the magical idea that her bad feelings toward him caused his death.

We know of Otto Plath's startlingly precise and intellectualized prediction of the date of his son's birth two and a half years before the event.[13] In "Little Fugue" (*A*) she describes him as a "yew hedge of orders" and later poems see the father as a machine, emotionless and finally persecutory. The "Man in Black " (*C*), "fixed vortex on the far / Tip, riveting stones, air, / All of it, together," asks death as the price of his reclamation.

If the death of her father is illogically conceived but psychologically perceived as her own suicide we can understand this confusion if we regard the gap in Plath's self as the unfulfilled confirmation of her identity by her father. A crucial component of this identity is erotic, the need for a preadolescent girl of nine to have her womanliness accepted and confirmed by the first male in her life. When her father died the erotic component of Plath's identity, her sexuality as a woman, remained unconfirmed. The good libidinal attachment to the father could not realize itself and her subsequent fantasized relations with men confirm instead both her ambivalence toward her father's loss and her stuggle against that loss.

The need for a good libidinal attachment to men is continually upset by some bad one, and Plath's relation to the image of her father is characterized by intense erotic seductiveness and equally intense murderousness. In the first part of "Lady Lazarus" (*A*) she describes in specifically erotic terms the efforts to arouse her after a suicide attempt. Of being unwrapped in front of a crowd of spectators, she writes:

> What a million filaments.
> The peanut-crunching crowd
> Shoves in to see
>
> Them unwrap me hand and foot—
> The big strip tease.

Her contempt for her audience reflects the self-hatred impelling her self-exposure, yet it is autonomous others who unwrap her "resurrected" body. Then this prostitution fantasy of suicide changes into a confrontation with the persecutory doctor: "So, so, Herr Doktor. / So, Herr Enemy. // I am your opus, / I am your valuable, / The pure gold baby // That melts to a shriek." She becomes his child, a valuable possession, and the doctor fills the ambivalent model of the split father. In the final stanza we come full circle from the strip tease. Unable to gain the confirmation of sexual identity even by exhibiting the body in the bizarre manner of recovery from suicide, she voices her murderous rage toward this God father:

> Herr God, Herr Lucifer,
> Beware
> Beware.
>
> Out of the ash
> I rise with my red hair
> And I eat men like air.

Plath's response to her father's death was to become like her father. The compulsive aspect of Plath's ritual of self destruction mirrors the strongly obsessional nature of her personality. Hughes reports that she would sit with a thesaurus on her lap (it was her father's book), carefully going over the words, circling words of special significance (containing them with boundaries for further use) and writing each word in her poetry as if it were a hieroglyph, a separate entity of its own.[14] If she were unsatisfied with a poem, she would often scrap it altogether rather than rework it. She was ruthlessly self-critical and destroyed hundreds of her poems, but her determination was immense. We see a common obsessional root in the effort of composition and the inner need to recompose her father. Psychologically, she depends on the very imago she would murder for the means of murder itself; *she* drives the stake in the vampire's heart. Her aggression, in its verbal and phallic form, is inseparable from the fantasized aggression of the father, "the language obscene // An engine, an engine / Chuffing me off like a Jew." ("Daddy," *A*)

At the end of "Ocean 1212-W," a recollection of her childhood made mythical in retrospect, Plath writes:

> And this is how it *stiffens*, my vision of that seaside childhood. My father died, we moved inland. Whereon those first nine years of my life sealed themselves off like a ship in a bottle, beautiful, inaccessible, obsolete, a fine white flying myth. (Emphasis added.)

Her vision stiffened like the still corpse of her father. The death of the father became "the cold dead center // Where spilt lives congeal and stiffen to history" described in "A Birthday Present" (*A*). From the cold center of death where Plath's lives congealed emerged a phallic identification with the father. In *The Bell Jar* Esther gives Mrs. Willard's definition of man: "'What a man is is an arrow into the future and what a woman is is the place the arrow shoots off from'" (p. 74). But Esther does not want to be the "place an arrow shoots off from." "I wanted...to shoot off in all directions myself, like the coloured arrow from a Fourth of July rocket" (p. 87). Esther denies the arrowless, static definition of woman and instead imagines herself as the phallic man. She would be the penetrator of space, not the space itself. We think Plath experienced her father's death as a symbolic loss that she denied by becoming his masculine essence in a specific and primitive merger with his imagined capacity for endless self-celebration and self-extension.

The desire for the father also becomes a search for him in other men, what Plath calls "models" of him. After her suicide attempt in "Daddy,"

> I made a model of you,
> A man in black with a Meinkamf look
>
> And a love of the rack and the screw.
> And I said I do, I do.
> So daddy, I'm finally through.

Here the father is at once a negative ideal and an object of desire. In *The Bell Jar*, Esther's desire for "some flawless man" (p. 87) finds a more positive focus in Constantin, a simultaneous interpreter at the U. N. (a man of words). He is associated with sports and good food, and Esther fantasizes the loss of her virginity as the incorporation of his image: "Now I thought that if I looked into the mirror tomorrow I'd see a doll-size Constantin sitting in my eye and smiling out at me" (pp. 85-86). Yet when she wakes in the morning, still a virgin, his arm is "heavy as a dead man's" (p. 87), and the possibility of genuine, living intimacy is gone. Constantin's negative double, Marco, tries to rape her, vampirelike, and after she fights him off she rides the train home with the dried blood of their battle on her cheeks, "like the relic of a dead lover" (p. 119). Whether the other is positive or negative, Plath's search for images of the father in the external world metamorphoses to images of her lost love. When Plath writes, "Daddy, daddy, you bastard, I'm through," we hear a double echo of her frustrated desire, for she is done with murder, and she is "through," dead. Presence and absence, love and hate, can only be united in the suicidal act.

Unable to find daddy in the outside world, she will get back to him by dying. This raises the problem of location: where did daddy go after he died? In "Daddy" (A) this problem is stated in terms of origins: "So I never could tell where you / Put your foot, your root, / I never could talk to you." Daddy's image extends from the "freakish Atlantic" to Germany and Poland, as Plath's life ranged from the Atlantic shore to Europe and back, and then to England again. But the problem, although it may have been acted out geographically, is a psychological one. Where did daddy go after he died?

In "All the Dead Dears" (C) Plath gives us a hint of where she feels the father lies, and of the descent she must make to recover him:

> From the mercury-backed glass
> Mother, grandmother, greatgrandmother
> Reach hag hands to haul me in,
> And an image looms under the fishpond surface
> Where the daft father went down.

The father exists beneath the watery surface, where the generations of mothers in the mirror would haul her in after him. In *The Bell Jar*, Plath has Esther locate Constantin, who is explicitly associated with her father, also beneath the watery surface, "a bright, unattainable pebble at the bottom of a deep well" (p. 89). We find the lost and unattainable father symbolically enclosed in a maternal matrix, an area in Plath's mind where babies are born and which she frequently imagines to be the area of transformation from death to rebirth.

Father dead is in the sea. "Full Fathom Five" (C) her father lies, of his bones are poems made:

> I walk dry on your kingdom's border
> Exiled to no good.
>
> Your shelled bed I remember.
> Father, this thick air is murderous.
> I would breathe water.

In *The Bell Jar*, when Esther stands at the top of a ski slope and pushes herself off, she "aimed straight down," like an arrow. She would plummet to her "own past." Her destination becomes the mother:

> People and trees receded on either hand like dark sides of a tunnel as I hurtled on to the still, bright point at the end of it, the pebble at the bottom of the well, the white, sweet baby cradled in its mother's belly. (p. 102)

But identifying with the father in this fantasy of coital regression, she fills the gap left by his departure and travels a course that will lead into the mother's body where her speeding self will fuse with the inanimate stone and the pure, nurtured child. To identify with father is both to join in incestuous union with him (for he is unconsciously imagined to be in mother's body) and to be his child again free from maternal retribution. Even after this fantasy ends and her leg is broken in two places, Esther wishes to become "saintly and thin and essential as the blade of a knife." (p. 103)

Esther, like her creator, attempts suicide after a serious rejection, and she begins to experience her world as fluidly as the sea. The self aimed into her past in *The Bell Jar* becomes for Plath the train "screaming— / An animal / Insane for the destination" in "Getting There" (*A*). And like the phallic skier who aims for the mother's belly, the passenger in the "steaming and breathing" train with its "teeth / Ready to roll, like a devil's" seeks a stasis, a retreat from the fire of a war in Russia that dramatizes her conflict over catastrophic desires:

> I shall bury the wounded like pupas,
> I shall count and bury the dead.
> Let their souls writhe in a dew,
> Incense in my track.
> The carriages rock, they are cradles.
> And I, stepping from this skin
> Of old bandages, boredoms, old faces
>
> Step to you from the black car of Lethe,
> Pure as a baby.

When she has buried her father (pupas=papas=the dead father) she will have transformed the insane train into a cradle and will emerge from this "black car of Lethe," this body of death that is also the mother's body, reborn, a gift of herself to her father.

The price of entering the mother's body is death; one must die in order to begin again. In "Ariel" Plath concentrates the dynamics of her identification and regression in one brilliant passage:

> And I
> Am the arrow
>
> The dew that flies
> Suicidal, at one with the drive
> Into the red

Eye, the cauldron of morning.

At once rigid and diffuse, merged with and celebrating the suicidal drive, she would merge also with the red eye of the sun, the father who is also the cauldron, the mother, to die into morning (or is it really mourning?). "Stone, stone," she writes in "Lorelei" (C), "ferry me down there." And she ends "All the Dead Dears" (C) with the vision of going "to lie / Deadlocked with them, taking root as cradles rock."

Implicit in Plath's turning to suicide is the turning back to a maternal space to find the father when the sources of fatherhood in the outside world seem depleted. That is, the search for merger with the dead father who, in fantasy, resides inside mother's body is the last alternative. The dynamics of this fantasy bring us to Plath's fascination with sexual contact, and the violence to the body it involves in her psychic life.

In *The Bell Jar* Esther remarks: "I always had a terribly hard time imagining people in bed together" (p. 6). When she does confront this situation, its traumatic power is mirrored by the extremity of her defensive reactions. Doreen, Esther's ambivalently regarded double ("Everything she said was like a secret voice speaking straight out of my own bones," p. 7), engages in a mutual precoital seduction with Lenny, a stranger, as Esther herself, "as somebody in a side-show" (p. 10), agonizes in self-consciousness. She defends herself through specific schizoid maneuvers:

> I felt myself melting into the shadows like the negative of a person I'd never seen before in my life. (p. 10)

> I felt myself shrinking to a small black dot against all those red and white rugs and that pine-panelling. I felt like a hole in the ground. (p. 17)

Still, her scoptophilic fascination draws her to Lenny's apartment. "I wanted to see as much as I could" (p. 13). As the "thrashing" and "screeching" mounts, as Doreen's breasts "popped out of her dress" (p. 18), Esther suddenly leaves. Feeling weak, she decides to walk forty-three blocks to her hotel, compulsively "counting the blocks under my breath" (p. 19), only to find the face of a Chinese woman, "big, smudgy-eyed" (p. 19) in her mirror. Her ritual of undoing and her guilt for having witnessed the scene ends in the hot water of a bath, a withdrawal to aloneness in a healing space: "wrapped in one of the big, soft white, hotel bathtowels I felt pure and sweet as a new baby" (p. 22). Here the sin is washed away.

In "Ocean 1212-W" Plath ends her myth of seaside childhood with the description of a hurricane. "This was a monstrous specialty, a leviathan. Our world might be eaten, blown to bits. We wanted to be in on it." Here the pattern of scoptophilic and aural interest is followed by parental violence and her regression:

> We crept to a blind and hefted it a notch. On a mirror of rivery black our faces wandered like moths, trying to pry their way in. Nothing could be

seen. The only sound was a howl, jazzed up by the bangs, slams, groans and splinterings of objects tossed like crockery in a giant's quarrel. The house rocked on its root. It rocked and rocked and rocked its two small watchers to sleep.

Below, we will come more fully to the ramifications of the deep boundary confusion within Plath's imagination of violence and sexuality.

We find also at the source of Plath's anxiety over sexualized activity a competitive striving for the father at the oedipal level of organization. When Esther wakes up after her electric shock treatment she remarks: "I wondered what terrible thing it was that I had done" (p. 152). At that moment, "an old metal lamp" surfaces in her mind. The lamp was "one of the few relics of my father's study," she recalls. One day she "decided to move this lamp from the side of my mother's bed to my desk at the other end of the room" (p. 152). In the act of moving it,

> something leapt out of the lamp in a blue flash and shook me till my teeth rattled, and I tried to pull my hands off, but they were stuck, and I screamed, or a scream was torn from my throat, for I didn't recognize it, but heard it soar and quaver in the air like a violently disembodied spirit. (p. 152)

In the act of trying to take the sign of the father from the possession of the mother she receives a catastrophic shock, like the "punishment" for madness.

Catastrophe, shock, boundary loss — these experiences come together when Plath envisions sexual contact. Her imagination is suffused by a guilt so intense that every contact is unconsciously linked to the fantasy that she is stealing a look, or a symbolic phallus, or engaged in incest; and regression to the state of infancy, which in turn calls forth the very anxieties against which she seeks protection, becomes her double-bind. The pattern cannot be escaped. When Esther does lose her virginity to a professor of mathematics (a father again), the result is a torrent of blood, hemorrhaging as "after a difficult childbirth" (p. 244).

Readers familiar with psychoanalytic concepts will realize that Plath's intensity of guilt must go deeper than the oedipal level, that the dynamics of her relation to her father and her desperate conflicts over sexuality inherit the deeper conflicts with the mother. If suicide is an attempt to escape an intolerable vision of human contact and need, and a magical way of getting back to daddy by joining with him in mother's body, it also defends on the deepest levels against matricidal desires. In *The Bell Jar* Esther says of her suicidal urge:

> It was as if what I wanted to kill wasn't in that skin or the thin blue pulse that jumped under my thumb, but somewhere else, deeper, more secret and a whole lot harder to get at. (p. 156)

Suicide is a means of killing the other symbolically while killing the self literally. In "Lady Lazarus" (A) the murderous impulse is oral, "And I eat men like air," just as the violent fantasy in "Ocean 1212-W" is oral: "Our world might be eaten." But in Plath's rising out of the ash with red hair we see an identification with a multilative mother, the mother that is the "red stigmata," the Medusa-like center of the universe. On the deepest levels, Plath's murderousness is aimed at the mother. Esther, irritated by the piggish noise of her mother's snoring, feels a fleeting urge to kill her:

> for a while it seemed to me that the only way to stop it would be to take the column of skin and sinew from which it rose and twist it to silence between my hands. (p. 130)

To protect them both against this murderousness she

> crawled between the mattress and the padded bedspread and let the mattress fall across me like a tombstone. It felt dark and safe under there. (p. 130)

Buried under a weight that symbolizes her death, she is safe from her own matricidal impusles and from the mother's retaliation. Esther cannot mediate her desires without enacting talion punishments for their existence in fantasy.

Just as the father is perceived as cannibalistic, the vampire of "Daddy," so the mother imago shares Plath's voracious obsession with the mouth as the psychic representative of the whole person. In the labile world of her psychic style, the way back to the mother has the same anatomical location as the murderous wish; she would be reincorporated, back inside, like a piece of food. In one obvious way this seems a projection; it simply mirrors Plath's own cannibalism. Rather than consume, she will be consumed, rather than kill she will be killed. In *The Bell Jar* Esther focuses on mouths very often:

> Of Doreen: "a mouth set in a sort of perpetual sneer" (p. 5)
> Of a cab driver: "He had a big, wide, white toothpaste-ad smile." (p. 8)
> Of a poet: "I couldn't take my eyes off the pale, stubby white fingers travelling back and forth from the poet's salad bowl to the poet's mouth with one dripping lettuce leaf after another." (p. 28)

Later in the novel Esther watches Constantin and a buxom Russian interpreter from a distance. She experiences a wish to crawl inside the Russian lady and bark out her voice; then she focuses on the woman's mouth, working rhythmically with Constantin's. "I saw their mouths going up and down" (p. 78). She "felt dreadfully inadequate" (p. 80).

In "The Moon and the Yew Tree" (A) the moon, which is her mother, "is quiet / With the O-gape of complete despair." In "The Rival" (A) this moon mother appears again: "Her O-mouth grieves at the world." The O-mouth opens and becomes a cave, like the "grave cave" that eats the suicidal woman in "Lady Lazarus."

For the schizophrenic person, Searles writes, "sexual intercourse is reacted to as posing the threat that one will eat, or be eaten by, the sexual partner."[15] For Plath's *personae*, it is a short psychic distance from the obsessional interest in watching mouths to the psychotic wish to reenter the mouth. In *The Bell Jar*, Esther's suicide attempt enacts a return to a symbolic maternal space.

> The breezeway had been added to the house after the cellar was dug, and built out over this secret, earth bottomed crevice. . . . It took me a good while to heft my body into the gap, but at last, after many times I managed it, and crouched at the mouth of the darkness, like a troll. (p. 179)

The symbolic space seems both oral and vaginal. Obsessively rigid and taut, Esther, who wishes only to melt and be limp, seems to us to mime Plath's masculine self in the process of undoing itself. Like the father, Plath will be sucked beneath the surface, to reside finally in mother's body. In "The Stones," the last poem of *The Colossus*, a transition to the nightmare world of *Ariel*, this is where we find her:

> I entered
> The stomach of indifference, the wordless cupboard
>
> The mother of pestles diminished me.
> I became a still pebble.
> The stones of the belly were peaceable,
> . . . .
> Drunk as a fetus
> I suck at the paps of darkness.

Returning to the maternal matrix accomplishes several things. It resolves Plath's murderousness, her cannibalistic wish to take in others, by reversing the process, just as suicide reverses the wish to kill the other. It relocates her self in the landscape of the deepest oral regression; unlike a real one, this uterus has "paps"—the breasts are inside as well. Also, the maternal body is where siblings are born, specifically the envied terrain of the younger brother, whom she feels displaced her by destroying her beautiful fusion with the world. The body is also a space of death, where objects are mutilated or the dead return to existence. It is where daddy is, and her return is a union with the father. In "The Beekeeper's Daughter" (C) her father presides over "a queenship no mother can contest— // A fruit that's death to taste: dark flesh, dark parings." At this level of imagination we find no differentiation of mother and father.

Plath experiences separation from a nurturant matrix as a rejection of her being that makes her self close to nothing. She is thrust into "the city of spare parts" ("The Stones," *C*), or must "face the bald-faced sun." Consequently, all the world seems to give her yearning self is indifference, negation.

> All the night gave her, in return
> For the paltry gift of her bulk and the beat
> Of her heart was the humped indifferent iron
> Of its hills, and its pastures bordered by black stone set
> On black stone. ("Hardcastle Crags," *C*)

In "Ocean 1212-W" Plath's primary relatedness with the world and her myth of herself as an artist both go back to a profound interfusion of herself and her sea-mother. In the "motherly pulse of the sea" she knew the metamorphic quality of life. But this "beautiful fusion with the things of this world was over" when her brother's birth intruded on her private space.

> My mother was in hospital. She had been gone three weeks. I sulked. I would do nothing. Her desertion punched a smouldering hole in my sky. How could she, so loving and faithful, so easily leave me?

It was a baby, she realized, and "I hated babies." "I would be a bystander, a museum mammoth. Babies!" There is no transitional space for her between the oral-narcissistic world and absolute exclusion of herself from the world of the living. From metamorphosis she moves to a sense of imprisonment in separateness. "As from a star I saw, coldly and soberly, the *separateness* of everything. I felt the wall of my skin. I am I. That stone is a stone."

We suggest that for Plath this intolerable separateness marked a deep confusion between the sense of identity-as-separateness, the capacity to identify the boundary between self and other, and the loss of her own sense of identity as a person. If there are others and other things, then she is "a reject," thrown back from the sea. And her response again is murderous:

> Sometimes I nursed starfish alive in jam jars of sea water and watched them grow back lost arms. On this day, this awful birthday of otherness, my rival, somebody else, I flung the starfish against a stone. Let it perish. It had no wit.

But there is also a reversal of this act, and out of the intrusion of the rival comes the myth of the birth of the hero, her "chosenness." The world becomes her only when she becomes it. She turns to a universe of subjective objects, their existence being only for her. If mother deserted her, then she makes the mother-sea give her a "sign of election and specialness."

She finds a piece of wood washed on the shore, "a monkey of wood." It becomes for her a "totem," a "Sacred Baboon," a reparative object:

So the sea, perceiving my need, had conferred a blessing. My baby brother took his place in the house that day, but so did my marvellous and (who knew?) even priceless baboon.

She, too, would have a child, a narcissistic version of herself, yet a baboon (like her hated brother?). To reverse the pain of separation she reverses the separation in fantasy and once again restores the pretraumatic world. In "The Eye-Mote" (C) she writes:

What I want back is what I was
Before the bed, before the knife,
Before the brooch-pin and the salve
Fixed me in this parenthesis;
Horses fluent in the wind,
A place, a time gone out of mind.

The place and time could not be put in words without evoking the murderousness that makes her revert to it in fantasy. Beneath the driven-ness of her reparative brilliance is the childhood desire for symbiosis that makes separation an experience of unbirth, being nothing. "The sea sucks obsessively, / One hollow the whole sea's pivot." Until, finally, "The heart shuts, / The sea slides back, / The mirrors are sheeted." Sheeting the mirrors keeps the distorted images of the dead from returning to the mind. For Plath this means reversing the movement from loss to language. What she sees in mirrors, we see on the pages of her books.

Mirrors can kill and talk, they are terrible rooms
In which a torture goes on one can only watch.
The face that lived in this mirror is the face of a dead man.

("The Courage of Shutting Up")

Winnicott tells us that "the precursor of the mirror is the mother's face,"[16] the first reflector of the child's self. For Plath, the face in the mirror returns as a Chinese woman, or a sick Indian; it is transformed into the beaten face of a prisoner, or the horrible sight of her grotesque image after her suicide attempt recreated in *The Bell Jar*. Sometimes it is simply some-one else. Words, too, become "faces in a funhouse mirror" (p. 131) for Esther in her journey toward distintegration. Plath's mind hooks on to the mirror experience again and again, until it becomes another aspect of her coded psyche. Giving back only distortions, Plath's mirrors never offer a stabilizable image of the self; she cannot *relate* to them.

We suggest that Plath's weird mirror experiences indicate a failure in the early months of her life to find herself consistently reflected in the human environment. The sea then becomes the symbol of a mysterious and unpredictable maternal environment, at once fluid and static:

> Like a deep woman, it hid a great deal; it had many faces, many delicate, terrible veils. It spoke of miracles and distances; if it could court, it could also kill. When I was learning to creep, my mother set me down on the beach to see what I thought of it. I crawled straight for the coming wave and was just through the wall of green when she caught my heels.
>
> I often wonder what would have happened if I had managed to pierce that looking-glass. ("Ocean 1212-W")

The metamorphic aspect of the sea is contradicted by the images of the wall and the looking-glass. The symbolic mother she seeks is closed off by a barrier that must be pierced. The actual mother prevents her from crossing the barrier. But the symbolic mother is based on the actual mother for the child, and it seems to us that Plath could not reconcile her experience of maternal imperviousness with her experience of maternal change. It seems that the dialectical interaction of mother and child, in which the child could see that she was seen and therefore develop the capacity to establish a rhythm of symbolic relatedness alternating with recognized absence, was not firmly established. Plath's alternative was to attempt to repair this fault by making herself seen, by performing with courageous, yet always precarious brilliance.

In the final months of her life Plath's work was infused with extreme and contrary emotions about motherhood.[17] Her own childbearing seems to have amplified a fierce attempt to differentiate benign and malignant components of mothering, to find herself by ridding herself of horrid maternal images. In "The Moon and the Yew Tree" (A) she says:

> The moon is my mother. She is not sweet like Mary.
> Her blue garments unloose small bats and owls.
> How I would like to believe in tenderness.

In *Three Women*, a BBC broadcast of 19 August 1962, in which three aspects of a pregnant woman—Secretary, Wife, and Girl—speak a monologue, the malignant mother imago surfaces repeatedly. At one moment the Secretary thinks:

> She is vampire of us all. So she supports us,
> Fattens us, is kind. Her mouth is red.
> I know her, I know her intimately—
> Old winter-face, old barren one, old time bomb.
> Men have used her meanly. She will eat them.
> Eat them, eat them, eat them in the end.
> The sun is down. I die. I make a death.

The mother imago is replete with terrifying objects (small bats and owls) with a terrifying purpose (vampirism, oral incorporation). The child is part of the mother, a "red terrible girl," and its murderous needs suck the very life she is supposed to supply. For the Girl, the child's "cries are hooks that catch and grate like cats," and the Secretary represents childbirth as an amputation, the creation of a corpse. Plath seems helplessly enmeshed in a symbiotic mother-child matrix in which nurture is either inaccessible when needed or mutilative when feared, and the attempt to find tenderness leads inexorably to "the center of an atrocity."

This crisis of motherhood seems gradually to have overwhelmed Plath's resources. Her daughter was born in April 1960. By April 1961, she was in the midst of writing *The Bell Jar*. In 1961 she suffered a miscarriage, an appendectomy and became pregnant again. In the summer of 1961 she began keeping bees and horse-riding and described her life as "points of satisfaction separated by large vacancies." In January 1962, her son was born, and like her own mother she now had a daughter and a son. The birth of her son seems to have provided her both with new confidence and new access to her own rage. In the summer of 1962 she suffered flu and high fevers, and in June she was involved in a driving accident that she described to A. Alvarez as a suicide attempt. In the fall of 1962 she moved herself and her children from Devon to London, where she rented a house once occupied by Yeats. The move was probably a response to a triangular situation in which she felt abandoned by Ted Hughes. Early in the mornings, before the children awakened, she wrote at amazing speed many of the poems in *Ariel*. "I feel like a very efficient tool or weapon, used and in demand from moment to moment," she wrote. At night she felt "flat." In January 1963 *The Bell Jar* was published. In the early morning of 11 February 1963, in the midst of the coldest winter in London since 1813-14, she left bread and milk for her children in their room, wrote a suicide note, "Please call Dr. _____," and committed suicide by placing her head in an oven with the gas jets turned on. An *au pair* girl she had expected that morning gained entry to the apartment with the help of builders who had come to work in the house. They smelled gas. She was dead.[18]

We see a self-destructive trajectory that coincides with Plath's brilliant outpouring of poetry in this sequence of life crises. We suggest that the precipitating factor in her final self-destructive journey was her feeling of having been abandoned by Ted Hughes. Her separation from him seems to announce the loss of the protective stability that her marriage had made possible. But we also suggest that the ontogenetic factor was her inability to reconcile herself with a mother she conceived as a Medusa, a red stigmata. With the birth of her son her obsessional defenses, which seem to have become more useful than ever before, nevertheless failed to prevent her from being flooded by the fear that the destructive mother was herself.

She could not fill the horrible center of motherhood because her own rage now coincided with the sense of abandonment, and in her own role as a mother she could no longer maintain the boundary between the needs, aims, and fears of the mother and the needs, aims, and fears of the child without absolutely splitting her nurturant self from her incandescent inner world. For several months this split took the form of caring for her children when they needed her and confronting her murderous psychic reality alone. It seems to us that her actual suicide was an attempt to enact and to be rescued from an inner torment that she could no longer speak without intensifying her pain.

"A Life" (*UP*) tells its version of the whole story:

> A woman is dragging her shadow in a circle
> About a bald hospital saucer.
> It resembles the moon, or a sheet of paper
> And appears to have suffered a sort of private blitzkrieg.

This poem too ends in reversal:

> And a drowned man, complaining of the great cold,
> Crawls up out of the sea.

The private blitzkrieg, then the reversal of death. Is the rebirth merely a fantasy? The bald saucer, the moon, the blank paper — could they not be filled with something she could trust to remain good or life sustaining? Why did all the departures have to be undone by one final departure?

We see a great deal converging in her self-destruction. She would merge with father, with mother. She would murder them. She would act out their murderous wishes. She would cope magically with the burden of actual mothering. She would end her physical pain. She would stop performing. At once revenge on her introjected tormentors and fulfillment of her deepest regressive wishes, the poison in the oven was a gift of release and a confirmation that the mother is poisonous. In a macabre version of the mother-child dyad Plath negated the possibility of its continuity in herself and for herself. In a terrible personalization of the Nazi experience she became the Jew the Fascist in herself hated.

Must we conclude that the magical strategies of words and the fluidity of her mind could only end in the self-destroying performance? In *The Bell Jar* Plath began to articulate a process of "rebirth" in Esther's reentry to a world of human relationships. In spite of the dehumanizing and depersonalizing realities of the mental ward and the electric-chair terror of the shock treatments, something more occurs. Esther begins to emerge from the schizophrenic world in which fulfillment can only lead to depletion, like the terrible process of pregnancy and birth. She begins to form a trusting relationship with older women, drinking offered milk "luxuriously, the way a baby tastes its mother" (p. 213). After a shock treatment, Dr. Nolan asks Esther whether trust in her had been justified and Esther replies, simply, "Yes." In that moment she can say, "The bell jar hung, suspended, a few feet above my head. I was open to the circulating air" (p. 227).

Recovery, rebirth, depends on the maintenance of a relationship with one symbolic other. It can include hatred and rejection. *The Bell Jar* ends in a "ritual for being born twice" (p. 257), a physical and psychic contact between the two, "mother" and "child." Precarious as it is, it does exist for Esther, like an umbilical bond with another at a moment of positive magic. These are the last words of the novel:

> The eyes and the faces all turned themselves towards me, and guiding myself by them, as by a magical thread, I stepped into the room. (p. 258)

What Winnicott calls a "potential space" comes to exist for Esther for the first time:

> The potential space between baby and mother, between child and family, between individual and society or the world, depends on the experience which leads to trust. It can be looked upon as sacred to the individual in that it is here that the individual experiences creative living.
>
> By contrast, exploitation of this area leads to a pathological condition in which the individual is cluttered up with persecutory elements of which he has no means of ridding himself.[19]

Plath could imagine such a space for herself, as she could imagine tenderness, playfulness, wit. But in *The Bell Jar* Esther's incipient recovery is purchased at the price of splitting off her suicidal self. Joan, Esther's alter-ego ("Joan's room . . . was a mirror image of my own," p. 207), hangs herself, as Esther had contemplated hanging herself earlier in the book. Esther's ontological recovery is expressed as Joan is buried. "I am, I am, I am" (p. 256).

The aesthetic solution is not a psychological resolution. The price is the splitting of her self that Plath could neither sustain nor undo alone, by fantasy, or action, or the magic of words. Plath tried to go it alone and failed. Finally, she could not find a real opening out into actual relations with others on 11 February 1963, because her persecutory inner world and the cold, other, outer world had converged to produce an absence where she needed the space of a therapeutic relatedness. Perhaps she died with the delusion of a rebirth, "The upflight of the murderess into a heaven that loves her" ("The Bee Meeting"). But we are left with a feeling of emptiness and mourning.

Notes

1. A. Alvarez, "The Art of Suicide," *Partisan Review* 37 (1970): 357.
2. A. Alvarez, *The Savage God* (New York: Random House, 1972). In his book Alvarez comes much closer to describing the personal sources of Plath's obsession with death, and he recognizes some of the crucial determinants of her suicide, such as her identification of father and husband. We are indebted to Alvarez for his personal account, without which this essay would have been impossible. It is true, however, that his earlier dismissal of the significance of Plath's suicide remains, implicitly if not openly, the dominant attitude toward her work. More recent books, such as Eileen Aird's *Sylvia Plath: Her Life and Work* (New York: Harper and Row, 1973) and Ingrid Melander's *The Poetry of Sylvia Plath: A Study of Themes* (Stockholm: Almqvist and Wiksell, 1972) do not attempt to go beyond broad suggestions in explaining the dynamic relation between the content of her work and her suicide.
3. Elizabeth Hardwick, "On Sylvia Plath," in *Poetry Dimension 1: A Living Record of the Poetry Year* (London: Abacus, 1973), 13-21.
4. "R. D. Laing and the Death Circuit," *Encounter* 31 (July-December, 1968): 42.
5. Quotations from Plath's work follow the editions listed below. The title and the volume will be given either in the text or in parentheses following quotations, using the abbreviations indicated:
    The Bell Jar (London: Faber and Faber, 1963). Page references to this volume are included parenthetically in the text.
    "Ocean 1212-W" in *Writers on Themselves*, ed. Herbert Read (London: Cox and Wyman, 1964).
    Uncollected Poems (London: Turret Books, 1965). UP
    Ariel (New York: Harper and Row, 1966). A
    The Colossus (New York: Random House, 1968). C
    Three Women: A Monologue for Three Voices (London: Turret Books, 1968).
6. These crises are recounted in "Ocean 1212-W."
7. "Methodological Approach to the Study of Schizophrenic Thought Disorder," in *Language and Thought in Schizophrenia*, ed. J. S. Kazanin (Berkeley: University of California Press, 1944), p. 18.
8. Roy Schafer, "The Mechanisms of Defense," *International Journal of Psychoanalysis* 49 (1968): 56.
9. "Sylvia Plath," in *The Poet Speaks: Interviews with Contemporary Poets*, ed. Peter Orr (London: Routledge and Kegan Paul, 1966), p. 167.
10. Ibid., pp. 169-70.
11. Otto Fenichel, *The Psychoanalytic Theory of Neurosis* (New York: Norton, 1945), p. 295.
12. Orr, "Sylvia Plath," p. 168.
13. Lois Ames, "Notes Toward a Biography," *Tri-Quarterly* no. 7 (Fall, 1966): 95.
14. Hughes, "Notes on the Chronological Order of Sylvia Plath's Poems," *Tri-Quarterly*, no. 7 (Fall, 1966): 82.
15. Harold F. Searles, "The Sources of Anxiety in Paranoid Schizophrenia," in *Collected Papers on Schizophrenia and Related Subjects* (New York: International Universities Press, 1961), p. 484.
16. D. W. Winnicott, "Mirror-role of Mother and Family in Child Development," in *Predicament of the Family*, ed. Peter Lomas (New York: International Universities Press, 1967), p. 26.
17. The theme of motherhood is explored by Margaret D. Uroff in "Sylvia Plath on Motherhood," *Midwest Quarterly* 15 (October 1973): 71-90. Uroff does not seek to connect this theme with Plath's suicide. After this essay was completed, Shelley Orgel, M.D., published an interpretation of Plath's suicide that recognizes the centrality of her maternal fantasies, "Sylvia Plath: Fusion with the Victim and Suicide," *The Psychoanalytic Quarterly* 43 (1974): 262-87. The fullest theoretical justification for the maternal origins

of identity is Heinz Lichtenstein's "Identity and Sexuality: A Study of Their Interrelationship in Man," *Journal of the American Psychoanalytic Association* 9 (1961): 179-260.

18. We reconstruct this sequence out of reports given by A. Alvarez, "Sylvia Plath: A Memoir," *New American Review* 12 (1971): 21, 37, and Lois Ames, "Sylvia Plath," pp. 106, 107.

19. D. W. Winnicott, "The Location of Cultural Experience," in *Playing and Reality* (New York: Basic Books, 1971), p. 103.

Carole Ferrier

The beekeeper's apprentice

1

The American poet and writer Robin Morgan has commented in a poem that much criticism of Plath's work has been "a conspiracy to mourn [her] brilliance while / patronizing her madness, diluting her rage / burying her politics."[1] Critical attitudes to women's writing, as well as the conditions of its production, have been historically determined by the social and economic position of women, and the assumptions of the dominant male, white, middle-class group that has maintained control over literary taste and judgments are so pervasive that most critics can avoid the uncomfortable task of confronting them. Most critical approaches to Plath's work reflect rather than challenge the hegemonic ideology.

In attempting to develop a critical approach that will clarify the essentially *political* interrelationships of critic, society and audience, and author, as all relate to Plath's work, we might take from Kate Millett a definition of "politics" that attempts to develop a more relevant psychology and philosophy of power relationships beyond the simple conceptual framework provided by our traditional formal politics, . . . to define them on grounds of personal contact between members of well-defined and coherent groups: races, castes, classes and sexes. For it is precisely because certain groups have no representation in a number of recognized political structures that their position tends to be so stable, their oppression so continuous.[2]

My argument in this article is essentially about patriarchy, and therefore it is male hegemony and sexual politics in relation to Plath's work that will be focused upon. Direct confrontation of patriarchy and patriarchal values can lead, as generations of earlier women writers have discovered, to "rage" and "madness," though a controlled dialectic of liberation is the central pivot of much great art. But it is when the individual alienation is turned inward on the writer herself, rather than outward on its causes within society, that internalized "madness" and "rage" become destructive to the individual. Denise Levertov comments on this problem in an obituary for the poet Anne Sexton:

Alienation is of ethical value, is life-affirmative and conducive to creativity, only when it is accompanied by a political consciousness that imagines and affirms (and works toward) an alternative to the society from which it turns away in disgust. Lacking this, the alienated person, if he or she is gifted, becomes especially a prey to the exploitation that characterises capitalism and is its underlying principle.[3]

A continual dialectic embodying these two possibilities of self-destruction or motivation toward revolutionary social change is centrally present in Plath's work. It is expressed, for example, in the Jew/Nazi analogy for her own relation to patriarchy, the hegemony of which is embodied in a partly real, partly mythical father in various guises or disguises. The dialectic also emerges in the split female self or dual personality that figures in many of the poems — passive victim versus autonomous and triumphant "bitch goddess" (to borrow a phrase from Butscher).[4] In examining Plath's relationship to patriarchy as she perceives and expresses it, I will look at her treatment of the father figure, who variously appears as colossus, drowned man, assorted historical imperialists and tyrants from Napoleon to the Nazis, man in black, and beekeeper. In her later poems there is an attempt first to consciously realize and then to eliminate or exorcise the destructive or repressive aspects of dominating masculinity. A corresponding theme is the clarification of "femininity," and an attempt to develop an understanding of the self-destructive and negative aspects of this ideology.

The relatively large amount of biographical information that Plath herself (and others) has provided represents a potential critical problem. Much work, notably Butscher's recent "critical biography," illustrates snares into which an unwary critic supplied with biographical information can fall. We must remember that Plath maintains a persona (sometimes a dual one) in all her writing, even the most intimate and personal; it is ultimately unproductive to equate the persona with the poet, as critics like Oates and Holbrook with particular polemical purposes tend to do.[5] Clearly we cannot disregard the parallels between Plath's particular situation and the poetry she writes, but it is also generally true that her richest and most positive poetry (to use this term with a different thrust to that of Holbrook, whose predominant arguments are reminiscent of those of a conservative Christian social worker) expresses an attempt to broaden out from individual experience and apprehensions to generalizations about the wider group.

Bearing this in mind should save us, though it does not save Holbrook, from both crude reduction to the circumstances of Plath's personal biography and arrogant Freudian analysis. While it is certainly true that Plath makes use of para-Freudian categories in many poems, especially those dealing with her father, we must also be aware that she is using these ironically, saying, in effect, "yes, well, this is what patriarchal psychology, even the mainstream tradition of literature itself at certain points, makes of this." The recent vogue for Freud in radical circles frequently disregards the fact that, as Juliet Mitchell admits, in "popularized Freudianism . . .psychoanalysis is seen as a justification for the status-quo, bourgeois and patriarchal." Although Mitchell, arguing for the partial rehabilitation of Freud, may claim that "psychoanalysis is not a recommendation *for* a patriarchal society, but an analysis *of* one,"[6] critics willing to use not only Freud but Plath's own references to Freud against her are not centrally concerned with this debate, and the Freudian assumptions that biology is destiny and that men and women have definite and separate spheres of activity underlie much of their work.

Plath's poetry makes frequent use of myth and archetype, especially the figure of the moon goddess and various metaphors for the subconscious. The central position of her father in her subconscious is clear in such early poems as "Full Fathom Five," where he is depicted as drowned man (out of *The Tempest*):

> Old man you surface seldom.
> Then you come in with the tide's coming
> When seas wash cold, foam-
>
> Capped.

Plath herself nearly drowned when she was a child, and later constructed a personal mythology in which this was the first (accidental) one of a series of attempts to come to terms with her own inner self in which the father looms so large.[7] Later in the same poem she sees him as a kind of ruling deity of the underworld of the sea:

> I walk dry on your kingdom's border
> Exiled to no good.
>
> Your shelled bed I remember.
> Father, this thick air is murderous.
> I would breathe water.

The reference to incestuous desire here—"Your shelled bed"—is an at least partly ironic treatment of the Freudian framework and should be read as such. Critics who attempt to psychoanalyze Plath on the basis of this kind of material insult her intelligence; she quite frequently seeks the vantage point of "the stilts of an old tragedy," as she does in "Electra on Azalea Path."[8] Sometimes she images the dead father as a colossus, fallen beneath the surface of the water, but the possibility of being able to bring up and reassemble in her consciousness that "Ghastly statue with one grey toe / Big as a Frisco seal" ("Daddy") seems remote: "I shall never get you put together entirely, / Pieced, glued, and properly jointed" ("The Colossus").

The Bell Jar, Plath's semiautobiographical novel, is another fictional rendering of the beginning of her attempts to understand the role that her father played in her own early life:

> Then I saw my father's gravestone.
> It was crowded right up by another gravestone, head to head, the way people are crowded in a charity ward when there isn't enough space. The stone was of a mottled pink marble, like canned salmon, and all there was on it was my father's name and, under it, two dates, separated by a little dash.
> At the foot of the stone I arranged the rainy armful of azaleas I had picked from a bush at the gateway of the graveyard. Then my legs folded under me, and I sat down in the sopping grass. I couldn't understand why I was crying so hard.
> Then I remembered that I had never cried for my father's death.
> My mother hadn't cried either. She had just smiled and said what a merciful thing it was for him he had died, because if he had lived he would have been crippled and an invalid for life, and he couldn't have stood that, he would rather have died than had that happen.
> I laid my face to the smooth face of the marble and howled my loss into the cold salt rain.[9]

This pilgrimage is also the subject of "Electra on Azalea Path":

> The day I woke, I woke on Churchyard Hill.
> I found your name, I found your bones and all

> Enlisted in a cramped necropolis,
> Your speckled stone askew by an iron fence.[10]

The identification with Electra, whose life was destructively dominated by a sense of having lost her father, expresses a tendency to which women are prone because of their specific social oppression — becoming absorbed in a sense of hurt and rejection:

> The day you died I went into the dirt,
> Into the lightless hibernaculum
> Where bees, striped black and gold, sleep out in the blizzard
> Like hieratic stones, and the ground is hard.
> It was good for twenty years, that wintering.[11]

This kind of absoluteness about personal feeling means life is no longer acceptable; it is the position of Anouilh's Antigone: "I despise your idea of happiness! I despise your idea of life...I want everything of life, and I want it now! I want it total, complete, or nothing...I want to be sure of everything now, today: sure that everything will be as beautiful as it was when I was a little girl—or, if I am not, to die!"[12]

Joyce Carol Oates argues that on the basis of articulating this position Plath might be "diagnosed as one of the last Romantics.... reading [her poetry] is a kind of elegant 'dreaming back,' a cathartic experience that not only cleanses us of our personal and cultural desires for regression, but explains by way of its deadly accuracy what was wrong with such desires."[13] Oates here is unsympathetically patronizing Plath's "madness." She does not recognize that Plath, while describing such feelings, is not necessarily subject to or dominated by them. It is true that Plath's poems sometimes convey a state of masochistic self-abasement and self-abnegation —

> O pardon the one who knocks for pardon at
> Your gate, father — your hound-bitch, daughter, friend.
> It was my love that did us both to death.[14]

— and, as here, a wish that she could lose herself in being everything to another person, in this case her father. But Oates ignores both the crudity of her own critical method in reducing Plath's writing to biography and a thematic development in the poetry: as Plath gradually brings to light for herself the real nature of the feelings described and where they lead — up the Azalea Path to death — she begins to write of resistance to them and to fight back. Alvarez in *The Savage God*, which deals with suicide and self-destructive impulses in creative artists, develops a "romantic" attitude toward self-destruction on the part of poets, and proceeds to apply it to Plath: "[the arts] survive morally by becoming, in one way or another, an imitation of death in which their audience can share; to achieve this the artist, in his role of scapegoat, finds himself testing out his own death and vulnerability for and on himself."[15] Although Alvarez believes Plath did not mean to die on that February morning, that she achieved suicide only through poor luck, he tends to glamorize the masochistic and self-hating sentiments articulated in some of her work.

2

An activity that figures prominently in a number of Plath's poems, early and late, is beekeeping. Plath's father and, subsequently, the poet herself engaged in it, and in her poems on this subject beekeeping is invested with a various and complex symbolic significance. An early poem, "The Bee-keeper's Daughter," portrays a relationship between father and daughter in which the father is seen as moving about in a garden, "hieratical" among the "many-breasted hives," like a priest of Diana or Cybele. The "queen-ship no mother can contest" involves a relationship with the father that has sexual undertones: the scene of the poem evokes the Garden of Eden with its "fruit that's death to taste," and where the knowledge of death follows ritual initiation into certain mysteries:

> Father, bridegroom, in this Easter egg
> Under the coronal of sugar roses
>
> The queen bee marries the winter of your year.

These mysteries, however, lead toward a knowledge of sterility—"winter of your year." The bee stings can kill, and in another early poem, "Lament," they have a symbolic connection with death:

> The sting of bees took away my father
> Who walked in a swarming shroud of wings
> And scorned the tick of the falling weather.[16]

Plath took up beekeeping when she lived in Devon; it was both a natural occupation in the circumstances and an activity with considerable pos-sibilities of analogy with her own situation as wife, mother, and poet. In keeping bees, she seems to have at once identified with her father and assumed his former role (and with it his power). She frequently identifies herself also with the queen bee, this usually involving images of escape, freedom, fertility, and productiveness. Her later bee poems—"The Bee Meeting," "The Arrival of the Bee Box," "Stings," "Wintering," and "The Swarm"—are based upon her own experiences of the practical skills of beekeeping and the element of mystery in the appearance of the honey; in the poems beekeeping is a natural analogy for the craft of verse. In earlier bee poems, the presiding figure of the beekeeper is the father, but then the poet herself becomes beekeeper, thereby gaining symbolic control over her own life and actions.

The bee poems in *Ariel* chart a progress in consciousness that begins with the initiation ritual of "The Bee Meeting." The presence of the white goddess is indicated by various references.[17] Present as symbolic figures are the midwife (bringer forth of life) and the sexton (digger of graves), and also a mysterious "man in black," who in earlier poems was identified with the figure of Plath's father, the original beekeeper. Prominent in the ritual is a male figure in white, "the surgeon my neighbors are waiting for, / This apparition in a green helmet, / Shining gloves and white suit," who is also a kind of unidentified executioner. There is a sense that knowledge waits somewhere just beyond the limit of consciousness, but that to gain it could mean death. The persona feels threatened by the gorse, which seems to have a masculine aspect connected with the sun;[18] there is an identification of the speaker with the queen bee, who is also being hunted; and, in the connection of the hive with a coffin—the "long white box in the grove" —there is a clear threat of death.

The dual identification of the central character with both the woman who expects to be sacrificed and the queen bee suggests the two sides of the female personality as conceived of by patriarchal archetype—the victim and what Butscher calls the "bitch goddess"—that recur in Plath's work. It is not clear how far the man in the green helmet is identified with the figure in "Stings," the "third person" who "has nothing to do with the bee-seller or with me."[19] Butscher suggests that this figure is Ted Hughes and that the "rain / Tugging the world to fruit" is his writing. He sees the attack of the bees representing Plath herself and involving her desire for death and loss of self—"They thought death was worth it"—balanced by the concomitant desire to recover her own identity and power: "but I / Have a self to recover, a queen."

The ritual of the bee meeting leads to the delivery of the bee box in the next poem in the sequence. In this poem the box of bees becomes a metaphor for the fertile, swarming, and potentially destructive chaos that the poet senses within herself. The line "I have to live with it overnight" indicates that she is dealing with her own unconscious, in which she finds a mass of conflicting and incoherent messages that she is almost powerless to understand, let alone control (play Caesar to):

> It is the noise that appals me most of all,
> The unintelligible syllables.
> It is like a Roman mob, . . .

I lay my ear to furious Latin.

The evocation of incomprehensible disorder within recalls the earlier
account of the "colossus" who dominated her unconscious—"Mule-bray,
pig-grunt and bawdy cackles / Proceed from your great lips"—but instead
of the father, central here are the bees; and though they remain connected
with the father, they embody, through the queen bee especially, a sense of
the persona's separate female identity. Plath frequently uses metaphors of
a box, a windowless room, or a cellar as analogies for the unconscious, and
there is also a pervasive sense of the potential danger of breaking into, or
out of, this enclosed space. Sometimes the archetype represents the boundaries of the identity, threatened by what is outside; at other times it
represents the mysterious and frightening aspects of the inner, unconscious
mind, from which things intermittently rise up into consciousness. A sense
of the fear of this unknown is embodied in the powerful poem "A Birthday
Present":

> I know why you will not give it to me,
> You are terrified
>
> The world will go up in a shriek, and your head with it. . . .
>
> Only let down the veil, the veil, the veil.
> If it were death
>
> I would admire the deep gravity of it, its timeless eyes.
> I would know you were serious.
>
> There would be a nobility then, there would be a birthday.
> And the knife not carve, but enter
>
> Pure and clean as the cry of a baby,
> And the universe slide from my side.

In this poem the persona is portrayed in a curtained room surrounded by
"veils, shimmering like curtains" but with something beyond that "stands
at my window, big as the sky." The persona knows in "The Arrival of the
Bee Box" that she must set the bees free, but is afraid of what they will do
once they are loosed: "I am no source of honey / So why should they turn
on me?" The nature of the antinomy here comes through in "Stings." The
beekeeping activity threatens the beekeeper; she must organize and discipline her hive and attempt both to understand and master the craft of
beekeeping, which involves centrally the liberation of the queen into the
bride flight and subsequent fertility. The poet is both beekeeper, the
practising craftsperson, and the queen bee that soars into the sky. The
conclusion of "Stings" is an image of triumph and escape from constraint
and confinement:

> They thought death was worth it, but I
> Have a self to recover, a queen.
> Is she dead, is she sleeping?
> Where has she been
> With her lion-red body, her wings of glass?
>
> Now she is flying
> More terrible than she ever was, red
> Scar the sky, red comet
> Over the engine that killed her —
> The mausoleum, the wax house.

The imagery strongly recalls that at the end of "Lady Lazarus," where there is a phoenixlike rebirth:

> Out of the ash
> I rise with my red hair
> And I eat men like air.

The ominous conclusions of these two poems are not accidental. A familiarity with details of the life cycle of the bee (which we can be sure Plath possessed) clarifies her intentions and her irony in the poems.[20] The theme of repression and isolation building up a violence that turns on things outside rather than to self-destruction is central to the poem "Purdah," which ends:

> I shall unloose —
> From the small jewelled
> Doll he guards like a heart —
>
> The lioness,
> The shriek in the bath
> The cloak of holes.

Here we have a reference to the murder of Agamemnon by Clytemnestra. The figure of Clytemnestra contrasts strongly with the two famous daughters in Greek drama, Electra and Antigone, whose only course appears to be to resist and to refuse to say "yes": they are essentially passive female stereotypes who cannot take any positive action to free themselves (though Electra tries to work through Orestes). A patriarchy of family and possessiveness that turns women into "small jewelled dolls," Plath suggests, can sometimes only be adequately combated by the knife of Clytemnestra, and there is an increasing awareness in her poetry of the need to fight "the boot in the face," to abandon the passive and masochistic acceptance of authority. Her references to Greek drama give a wider context to the personally based material of her poetry and are also in some cases an incidental gloss on her use of Freudian categories.

To establish Plath's original order of the later bee poems it would be necessary to refer to her manuscripts, but in the American *Ariel* "The Swarm" follows next in sequence.[21] An awareness that Plath was beginning more deliberately to relate the personal to the wider historical context[22] is helpful to the interpretation of this, the most obscure of the bee poems. Napoleon's personal motif was the bee, and so there is a ready made connection that leads to a view of him in the poem as controlling figure—at once father, beekeeper, and empire-building dictator. In the poem, soldiers are transformed into bees and back again:

> How instructive this is!
> The dumb, banded bodies
> Walking the plank draped with Mother France's upholstery
> Into a new mausoleum,
> An ivory palace, a crotch pine.

In the final phrase of the poem—"O ton of honey"—the acquisitiveness of empire-building and the father as beekeeper come together. Plath is trying to broaden her frame of reference beyond the staple material of "confessional" poetry ("very serious, very personal emotional experience which...has been partly taboo"[23]), to its wider historical and societal context. A subsequently rejected line from "Lady Lazarus" after "I may be skin and bone" was "I may be Japanese" and introduced a reference to Hiroshima.[24] In "Fever 103°" there is a more extended passage:

> Such yellow sullen smokes
> Make their own element. They will not rise,
>
> But trundle round the globe
> Choking the aged and the meek,
> The weak
>
> Hothouse baby in its crib,
> The ghastly orchid
> Hanging its hanging garden in the air,
>
> Devilish leopard!
> Radiation turned it white
> And killed it in an hour.
>
> Greasing the bodies of adulterers
> Like Hiroshima ash and eating in.
> The sin. The sin.

Oates argues that this orientation leads to "a solipsistic and ironic and self-pitying art in which metaphors for [the artist's] own predicament are snatched from newspaper headlines."[25] But this trivializes Plath's attempt in these poems to break out of the isolation produced by, on the one hand, the privatized condition of life of most women under patriarchy and, on the other, the individualism that tends to deny the assertion of Adrienne Rich in her poem "Translations": "this way of grief / is shared, unnecessary, / and political."[26] In much of Plath's work, the persona *is* isolated and separate. The three characters in her radio play *Three Women* give their separate monologues but never act upon each other or share any feelings; there is little sense of a complex of relationships around each character and only one of the three even mentions the father of her child (and this in passing).

Plath's attempt to broaden her frame of reference is expressed in *Three Women* in an attack on the patriarchal institutions of state and church:

> And then there were other faces. The faces of nations,
> Governments, parliaments, societies,
> The faceless faces of important men.
>
> It is these men I mind:
> They are so jealous of anything that is not flat! They are jealous gods
> That would have the whole world flat because they are.
> I see the Father conversing with the Son.
> Such flatness cannot but be holy.

In the poem "Daddy" the forces of a repressive society, embodied in microcosm in the relationship between father and daughter, are imaged in the wider society in the Nazi repression of the Jews; the poet's love for her father—

> Every woman adores a Fascist,
> The boot in the face, the brute
> Brute heart of a brute like you

—or her husband—

> The vampire who said he was you
> And drank my blood for a year,
> Seven years, if you want to know

—is expressed in terms that imply a willing submission to violence. Joyce Carol Oates argues further about Plath: "Like many who are persecuted, she identified in a perverse way with her own persecutors, and not with those who, along with her, were victims."[27] But in fact in the poem "Daddy" the persona perceives that the only way to be free of what has become a destructive influence appears to be to resist it, to exorcise it by making a witch's doll: "I made a model of you, / A man in black with a Meinkampf look." After this act, the ghost who has been feeding on her life will be laid with "a stake" in his "fat black heart" so that his voice will no longer come through to her:

> The black telephone's off at the root,
> The voices just can't worm through.

The decision to make this break is in many ways a very painful one, for the father has long been a part of her subconscious, close to the source of the poems, the satisfaction in writing that is so central to her life.

In "Wintering," there is the sense of a new fortitude and individual endurance developed out of the new, deeper consciousness of the nature of the inner conflict that the earlier bee poems in *Ariel* had expressed. Plath had used before the metaphor of wintering for the state of mind that her father's death had induced. The poem "Electra on Azalea Path" opens with a reference to a wintering that was "good for twenty years." In the later poem "Wintering," the winter is symbolic as well as actual, a period of very little productivity as far as poetry is concerned. It is the time when the beekeeper has "whirled the midwife's extractor" and the honey has been collected.[28] The person extracting the honey is clearly, on a symbolic level, the poet herself who captures and stores in poems the essence of her perception of life. Now that winter—"the time of hanging on for the bees" —has come, no more honey will be collected for a while, and what has been gathered gleams in jars—"Six cat's eyes in the wine cellar"—shining into or from the darkness of the unconscious mind, the element of the poems. For Plath, that is "the room I have never been in," and it has a similar metaphoric force to that of the cellar where Esther in *The Bell Jar* makes her first suicide attempt. In the novel, Esther's attempt to kill herself with sleeping pills follows immediately after the account of the search for her father's grave, and clearly Plath's intention is to establish some connection between the meaning of the two situations. The episode in the cellar also recalls poems like "Full Fathom Five," in the evocation of an underwater atmosphere: "a dim undersea light filtered through the slits of the cellar windows . . . The silence drew off, baring the pebbles and shells and all the tatty wreckage of my life. Then, at the rim of vision, it gathered itself, and in one sweeping tide, rushed me to sleep" (*BJ*, 179).

Plath's last work attempts to break through to a generalization and universalization of her personal experiences—though I do not agree with Judith Kroll that what she was aiming to achieve was some sort of religious "transcendence" of her earthly condition.[29] What "Wintering" is about is withstanding a period of barrenness, attempting to achieve mental and physical control; the imagery expresses attempts to consolidate —

214

> Now they ball in a mass,
> Black
> Mind against all that white

—to hold on and survive like the woman who feels "Her body a bulb in the cold and too dumb to think." The potential for rebirth is conveyed in the repetition of the bulb image:

> . . .will the gladiolas
> Succeed in banking their fires
> To enter another year?

The persona is more clearly identified with the queen bee:

> The bees are all women,
> Maids and the long royal lady.
> They have got rid of the men.

There is a sense of life being hard but of having produced some results; the six jars of honey suggest a tangible poetic output. There is a shift away from the centrality of the father or indeed any male figure—the substitute, the "model" of the father—and toward an assertion of the persona's own separate identity independent of any 'other.'

Plath was in many ways a victim of the fifties and its ideology of the family. Women struggling to lead independent lives or pursue the ideal of being writers were under pressure to submerge themselves within monogamous marriage and create households straight out of the *Ladies' Home Journal*. Plath died just as the new wave of feminist theory began to surface with the rise of the women's movement and the publication of Betty Friedan's attempt to define "the problem that has no name" in *The Feminine Mystique*. Plath, in common with women grappling then with the problems of developing feminist theory, was fighting her way in those poems of the early sixties toward a definition of what life within the middle-class nuclear family does to its members. Her distinctive mediation of the ideology of the family and of love in the fifties and early sixties can tell us a great deal about patriarchal attitudes and how women in general, and women writers in particular, can find ways to resist and triumph over them.

It is not that Plath presents blueprints or role models; indeed, often what she portrays is the false directions into which her search led her. But her intellectual grasp of both crosscurrents and contradictions in the hegemonic ideology of this period and the new rising tide of women's resistance is what makes her work particularly valuable for us, and her search particularly important.

Notes

1. Robin Morgan, "Arraignment," in *Monster* (New York: Random House, 1972), p. 78.
2. Kate Millett, *Sexual Politics* (New York: Avon, 1971), p. 44.
3. Denise Levertov, "Light Up the Cave," *Ramparts* (December 1974/January 1975): 62.
4. Edward Butscher's "critical biography" of Plath, *Sylvia Plath: Method and Madness* (New York: Seabury Press, 1976), occasionally falls into biographical fallacy but contains interesting critical insights about some of the poems.
5. David Holbrook, in *Sylvia Plath: Poetry and Existence* (London: Athlone Press, 1976), tries to prove that he has caught Plath speaking as herself in *The Bell Jar*. Esther's reference to a baby, however, proves only that Plath's persona is portrayed as looking back on her experience from a vantage point in the future, not that "Esther 'is' Sylvia Plath, and that when she speaks of 'being all right again' she is speaking of her own breakdown and recovery: the baby was Mrs. Ted Hughes's" (p. 5). A similar assumption about poet and persona is made by Joyce Carol Oates in "The Death Throes of Romanticism: The Poems of Sylvia Plath," *Southern Review* 9 (Summer, 1973).
6. Juliet Mitchell, *Psychoanalysis and Feminism* (New York: Vintage, 1975), xiii.
7. The attempts are chronicled in the poem "Lady Lazarus":

   > I am only thirty.
   > And like the cat I have nine times to die.
   >
   > This is Number Three.
   > What a trash
   > To annihilate each decade.
   > . . . .
   >
   > The first time it happened I was ten.
   > It was an accident.
   >
   > The second time I meant
   > To last it out and not come back at all.
   > I rocked shut
   >
   > As a seashell.
   > They had to call and call
   > And pick the worms off me like sticky pearls.

8. This poem is collected in *Lyonnesse* (London: Rainbow Press, 1972), p. 12, and is dated 1958. The Azalea Path is part of Winthrop Cemetery, where Otto Plath is buried.
9. Sylvia Plath, *The Bell Jar* (New York: Bantam, 1972), pp. 136-37.
10. *Lyonnesse*, p. 12.
11. "Electra on Azalea Path," *Lyonnesse*, p. 12.
12. Jean Anouilh, *Antigone* (London: Harrap, 1960); my translation.
13. Oates, "The Death Throes of Romanticism," pp. 505, 510.
14. "Electra on Azalea Path," *Lyonnesse*, p. 13.
15. A. Alvarez, *The Savage God: A Study of Suicide* (London: Wiedenfeld and Nicholson, 1971), pp. 216-17.
16. "Lament" is collected in *Crystal Gazer* (London: Rainbow Press, 1971), p. 27. The poem is dated 1951-52.
17. Various plants referred to have connections with the White Goddess. The hawthorn is sacred to her, and further, "The flower of the bean is white and it blooms at the same season as the hawthorn. The bean is the White Goddess's . . . ; it seems that the reason for the Orphic taboo was that the bean grows spirally up its prop, portending resurrection" (Robert Graves, *The White Goddess* [New York: Farrar, Strauss, and Giroux, 1966], p. 69). See also Graves' account of the hawthorn on pp. 174-76. Judith Kroll, in *Chapters in a Mythology: The Poetry of Sylvia Plath* (New York: Harper and Row, 1976), discusses Plath's early interest in Graves and his account of Cardea, the White Goddess (pp. 37-79, passim).
18. According to Graves, the gorse or furze "typifies the young Sun at the Spring equinox . . . ; the religious importance of furze or gorse, which in Welsh folk-lore is 'good against

witches,' is enhanced by its flowers being frequented by the first bees of the year" (p. 192)

19. The precise force of the reference to the "green helmet" is unclear. We know that Plath reread Yeats's plays in 1962; she may have his play *The Green Helmet* in mind. If so, the figure could be identified with Cuchulain the sun hero. More information on Yeats's use of solar and lunar cycles in the Cuchulain plays can be found in P. Skene's *The Cuchulain Plays of W. B. Yeats* (New York: Columbia University Press, 1974), chap. 3.

20. It may be of interest to give here some references to the bride flight of the queen bee, as recounted by Maurice Maeterlinck in *The Life of the Bee*, trans. A. Sutro (London: George Allen, 1901):

> No sooner has the union been accomplished than the male's abdomen opens, the organ detaches itself, dragging with it the mass of entrails, the wings relax, and as though struck by lightning the emptied body turns on itself and sinks into the abyss (p. 252).

> She descends from the azure heights and returns to the hive, trailing behind her, like an oriflamme, the unfolded entrails of her lover (p. 260).

> She seats herself on the threshold and carefully strips away the useless organs that are borne far away by the workers, for the male has given her all he possesses and much more than she requires. She retains only in her spermetheca the seminal liquid where millions of germs are floating which, until her last day, will issue one by one as the eggs pass by, and in the obscurity of her body accomplish the mysterious union of the male and female element, whence the worker bees are born. Through a curious inversion, it is she who furnishes the male principle, and the drone who provided the female.... From that moment, possessed of a dual sex, having within her an inexhaustible male, she begins her veritable life (pp. 262-63).

21. "The Swarm" does not appear in the English edition of *Ariel*, and is there printed in *Winter Trees*. A bibliography of primary and secondary sources, including publication details for individual poems, can be found in *Hecate: A Woman's Interdisciplinary Journal* 1 (July, 1975): 94-112.

22. See her own comments in "Sylvia Plath," in *The Poet Speaks: Interviews with Contemporary Poets*, ed. Peter Orr (London: Routledge and Kegan Paul, 1966), p. 169.

23. Orr, *The Poet Speaks*, pp. 169-70.

24. This line was criticized by Alvarez when Plath read him the poem; see *The Savage God*, p. 15. For details of other rejected lines, see Eileen Aird, "Variants in a Tape Recording of Fifteen Poems by Sylvia Plath," *Notes and Queries* 19 (February, 1972): 59-61.

25. Oates, "The Death Throes of Romanticism," p. 516.

26. Adrienne Rich, *Diving into the Wreck* (New York: Norton, 1972), p. 41.

27. Oates, "The Death Throes of Romanticism," pp. 504-5.

28. This reference has basically an actual rather than symbolic force, since it was the local midwife who taught Plath to keep bees; the extractor referred to probably really was the midwife's.

29. The latter part of Kroll's *Chapters in a Mythology* is riddled with this term; it occurs, for example, seven times in two paragraphs on p. 172.

Jerome Mazzaro

Sylvia Plath and the cycles of history

1

Sylvia Plath told listeners of the B.B.C. shortly before her death that "I am not a historian, but I find myself being more and more fascinated by history and now I find myself reading more and more about history." The remark, make in October of 1962 in an interview commissioned by the Harvard Poetry Room, contrasts significantly with a statement that appeared in the February issue of *The London Magazine*. There she had written, "The issues of our time which preoccupy me at the moment are the incalculable genetic effects of fallout and...the terrifying, mad, omnipotent marriage of big business and the military in America." She claimed to be influenced by these issues only "in a sidelong fashion. ...My poems do not turn out to be about Hiroshima, but about a child forming itself finger by finger in the dark." On both occasions she cites the influence of Robert Lowell's *Life Studies* (1959) in helping her come to terms with her own emotional situation and craft, noting in the Harvard interview a belief "that personal experience is very important, but . . . it should be *relevant*, and relevant to the larger things, the bigger things such as Hiroshima and Dachau and so on."[1] No reader of *The Bell Jar* (1963) will mistake the impact of Lowell's "Memories of West Street and Lepke" (1958) on the structure of the novel. As that poem had seen his own breakdown, shock treatment, and recovery in terms of the electrocution of Czar Louis Lepke of Murder Incorporated, Plath's heroine sets her own breakdown, shock treatment, and recovery against the electrocution of Ethel and Julius Rosenberg.

Few readers, too, can avoid the coincidences of her interests in fallout, militarism, and concentration camps and the public discussions of militarism and the massive literature that attended the capture and impending trial of Adolf Eichmann. Atomic-bomb testing and radioactive fallout had been issues in the 1956 presidential campaign and continued as issues until 1963, when a test-ban treaty between the Soviet Union, the United Kingdom, and the United States was signed. The economy of the country seemed increasingly to owe its stability to what President Eisenhower called a "military-industrial complex," and the dependence was threatening not only to curb freedom in the United States but also to precipitate a new world war. Fred J. Cook had developed the history and implications of this "wedding" of arms and industry for an issue of *The Nation* (28 October 1961), and Plath cites the issue as important. She could not have missed the equally "sensational" capture of Eichmann in Argentina in June of 1960. At least three books on the capture and the life of the former Nazi were issued in 1961 from British publishers along with an account by Rudolf Hoess of his activities at Auschwitz. The year also saw the release of the motion picture *Judgment at Nuremberg*, in addition to lengthy controversies about the jurisdiction and legality of the upcoming Eichmann trial. Like others of her generation, Plath felt an era of noninvolvement ending. Her concern with these issues would mark an emergence from "silence" into an era of political and social activism. This new era would, in turn, require new attitudes toward both her surroundings and her self.

Some of the attitudes would be adopted from older, more politically involved poets like W. H. Auden, whom she told her interviewer she was "at one time . . . absolutely wild for" and imitated, and whose "age of anxiety" she appropriates in "General Jodpur's Conversion" (1961). Her allusion to "Daddy" and "Lady Lazarus" as "light verse" owes greatly to Auden's Introduction to *The Oxford Book of Light Verse* (1938), which had recently been reissued. Auden insists that "light verse can be serious," and he gives as its distinguishing characteristics its having been "written for performance" and its "having for its subject-matter the everyday social life of its period or the experiences of the poet as an ordinary human being." The poems of *The Colossus* (1960), she told her B.B.C. audience, were boring, "I didn't write them to be read aloud." She opposed their lack of flow to her "very recent work," which could be spoken and which, with its "stink of fat and baby crap," dealt intimately with everyday social life. Other attitudes would be derived from W. B. Yeats, whose poetry had already influenced such pieces as "Street Song" (pre-1957) and "Tinker Jack and the Tidy Wives" (1957) and whose tower at Ballylea the Hugheses had visited that summer. She had found the tower "the most beautiful & peaceful place in the world,"[2] and later that winter she would be excited by the coincidence of her moving into a flat in a house that Yeats had once lived in. But she also shared with contemporaries like W. D. Snodgrass views of having been socially conditioned, and Snodgrass's *Heart's Needle* (1959), detailing this conditioning, was then startling readers in England and the United States.

Nancy Steiner's *A Closer Look at Ariel* (1973) describes the torpid conditions from which the generation would be aroused. "The stereotyped Smith girl of the mid 1950's was a conformist, like thousands of undergraduates there and elsewhere, before and since." In this conformity, she was no different from her male counterparts in other universities who were being groomed to develop without radical innovations those vast programs that were started after the Second World War. The feeling Snodgrass expresses in "Returned to Frisco, 1946" (1957) that members of his generation were being conditioned to choose exactly what their elders wanted them to choose was general. David Riesman's *The Lonely Crowd* (1950) complained of "other directedness," and in certain circles, existential "bad faith" was cant and it was hoped that the outward conformity that was so visible might be offset by individual imaginative lives. In other circles, Auden's bleak predictions of "Tract for the Times" (1941) and "A Note on Order" (1941) had come to pass. His sense that if man "does not consciously walk in fear of the Lord, then his unconscious sees to it that he has something else, airplanes or secret police to walk in fear of" seemed to have been confirmed by the regimentation he feared would arise "when disorder is accepted as inevitable but has reached a point where it is felt as intolerable."[3]

Richard Wilbur's "Mind" (1954) tried to neutralize the seriousness of the situation by indicating that mind "in its purest play" is able through "a graceful error" to "correct" the physical limits of the world so as "not to conclude against a wall of stone." Discussions of André Gide's "gratuitous act" became fashionable, and Rainer Maria Rilke's "unicorn" (*Sonnets to Orpheus* 2.4), which "happened" because room was left for "the possibility that it might be," appeared in several new guises and contexts. "Reason" and "common sense," which had been the methods used to coerce acceptance by the "grey" organizational men who wander throughout Plath's poetry, were made to appear subversive. One placard of the times announced, "Be Reasonable. . . . Do it my way," and often in Plath's early poems, her speaker chooses an imaginative life to these forces of conformity. Yet, even in the dreamstates that typify the poems, Plath realizes that life without confirming objective correlatives is destined to end in either disappointment, insanity, or annihilation. Both the "clam-diggers" of "Dream with Clam-Diggers" (1957) and the "snowman" of "The Snowman on the Moor" (1957), for example, threaten the speaker's existence, and poems like "Recantation" (1957) advise one to "foreswear those freezing tricks of sight" just as Plath had foresworn her isolation during her sophomore year of college to "do good" at the People's Institute in Northampton "with [her] white hands." Much as Plath claimed to be little bothered by conformity, she still felt the need to "sneak in the rear door" if she was without a date on a Saturday night.

During this period of noninvolvement, Plath had chosen to submerge her political and social interest in the mythic method of James Joyce, the "vegetal radicalism" of Theodore Roethke, evolution, and the psychological oppositions of Fyodor Dostoevsky. Her senior honors paper at Smith was to be a study of the double in the works of Joyce, and the topic undoubtedly brought her into contact with the uses of paradigms from classical works to illuminate present circumstances and with T. S. Eliot's explanation of the method in "Ulysses, Order, and Myth" (1923). Joyce's view of history had presumed that events recur, if not exactly, with enough approximation that their patterns can be seen whole and their ends predicted by what had previously been ends. The determinism of such a view was supported by a curriculum of Great Books whose unexpressed justification was often an attempt to reduce faction by imposing a common regimen or to use history as a means to settle the future. For a student whose life seems to have been as sheltered as Plath's, these classics in translation could be deeply moving. Ted Hughes's "Notes on the Chronological Order of Sylvia Plath's Poems" (1966) asserts that, in fact, they were: "The mention of Oedipus, and the Greek Tragedians' figures elsewhere, may seem literary, but if one can take her dream life as evidence, those personalities were deeply involved in her affairs."[4]

"The Eye-Mote" (1960) and "The Colossus" (1960) affirm that her "manipulating a continuous parallel between contemporaneity and antiquity" as "a way of controlling, of ordering, of giving a shape and a significance" to contemporary history approximated something closer to the "lived myth" of Thomas Mann's "Freud and the Future" (1936) than the mechanical congruences of Eliot. The poems show her accepting what Rachel Bespaloff's *On the Iliad* (1943) terms "heroic" stature by having her speakers assume "total responsibility even for that which they had not caused." Both speakers confound classical necessity with individual choice in terms comparable to those that Auden's "The Dyer's Hand" (1955) had carefully distinguished, using *Oedipus Rex* and *Macbeth*. "Oedipus himself has no history, for there is no relation between his being and his acts. . . . In *Macbeth*, on the other hand, every action taken by Macbeth has an immediate effect upon him so that, step by step, the brave bold warrior we hear of in the first scene turns before our eyes into the guilt-crazed creature of the 'tomorrow and tomorrow and tomorrow' soliloquy."[5] The result in the first instance is pity that "it had to be this way," and in the case of *Macbeth*, "pity it was this way when it might have been otherwise." In "The Colossus," there is no sense of other alternatives as the speaker accepts the task of putting back together the greatness of the ancient world, symbolized by the *Oresteia*, the Roman Forum, and most importantly, the Colossus of Rhodes. The impossibility of reconstructing that bronze "wonder" of the ancient world, felled in 225 B.C. by an earthquake, foreshadows the poem's concluding failure.

In converting the actions of these poems from choice to necessity, Plath invents for herself a world where the sins of the fathers are visited on children. In "The Eye-Mote," the "sin" presumably is having been born. In "The Colossus" as in "Electra on Azalea Path" (1960), the "sin" is being overly attached to a dead father. The speakers gain by the attachment something like the curse of Atreus translated into psycho-analytic complexity. Both have lives arrested by accident and beyond reparation. In "The Colossus," the speaker decides to wait no longer for the ship that brings her release, and in "Electra on Azalea Path," she feels she and her father have been "undone" by the long, sterile attachment. These "necessary" actions contrast with the poet's earlier depiction of a father's death in "Lament" (1955). Here, "the sting of bees" takes the father away and, while he otherwise triumphs over nature, one has no sense that he is the destructive, hovering shade of the later poems. If these later poems are, as some critics have assumed, merely transcriptions and not artistic reworkings of material that has been augmented, cropped, and revised to suit the occasion, one is tempted to say that Plath has become so enamored of the mythic method that she is willing to accept its principles as determinative in life as well as art. Indeed, there is a sense in which, like the young St. Augustine, she seems in her work to be more deeply responsive to previous art than to life.

2

Much as Plath goes to Joyce for a comprehension of displaced events, she goes to Roethke for a concept of total pattern. *The London Magazine* includes mention of Roethke's "greenhouse poems" as being informative, and by the time Plath collected her work into the British edition of *The Colossus*, Anne Sexton could reproach the poet about the effects. Sexton recalls "saying something like...'if you're not careful, Sylvia, you will out-Roethke Roethke,'" and in "The Barfly Ought to Sing" (1966), she gives as Plath's response "that I had guessed accurately and that he had been a strong influence on her work." This "influence" settles most markedly in "Poem for a Birthday," five of whose seven sections were deleted from the American edition (1962) of the volume. Hughes places the start of the influence in the fall of 1959 when he and his wife were at Yaddo embarking on a combination of exercises and meditations. Plath began a serious study of Roethke then along with a reading of Paul Radin's *African Folktales and Sculpture* (1952), and Hughes believes the combination provided a break with her early style and "the first eruptions of the voice that produced *Ariel*." Eileen Aird's *Sylvia Plath* (1973) sees the transition from Plath's mythic poems to this vegetal radicalism as being more direct and evolutionary. "The reference to 'Mother Medea' [in "Aftermath"] may seem overliterary, but the figures of Greek mythology appear quite frequently in Sylvia Plath's early poetry, fulfilling in a more muted way the function of historical [natural?] references of the later poetry, by providing concrete examples of pain against which the personal experience of the poet can be projected."[6]

Some of what Plath derived from Roethke he had in turn adapted from Rilke. As early as "Rilke in English" (1939), Auden had proposed the direction of the German poet's "most immediate and obvious influence." In contrast to Shakespeare who "thought of the non-human world in terms of the human, Rilke thinks of the human in terms of the non-human, of what he calls Things." This thinking resembles not only that of children for whom "tables, dolls, houses, trees, dogs, etc., have a life which is just as real as their own or that of their parents" but also that of the African folktales Radin assembled, in which things and animals are given comparable reality. Roethke had converted to natural metaphors what was ostensibly in Rilke a notion that life and death form one complete cycle of existence and that any lesser view distorts life. For Roethke, the cycle becomes that of vegetal growth, harvest, and rebirth. In poems like "Weed Puller," the root life of plants (death) becomes the underside of "everything blooming above me" (life), and in the later poems of *The Lost Son* (1948), this vegetal cycle shapes an interior mind whose subsurface turns subconscious and oversurface, superego. Without relinquishing Rilke's belief that the function of poetry is praise, Roethke expresses a view of art that is a kind of fishing "patiently, in that dark pond, the unconscious" or a diving in "to come up festooned with dead cats, weeds, tin cans, and other fascinating debris." Each poem in *Praise*

223

to the End! (1951) was to be "in a sense . . . a stage in a kind of struggle out of the slime; part of a slow spiritual progress; an effort to be born, and later, to become something more."[7]

Both Roethke and Rilke had been able to tap into knowledges of these cycles through processes of meditation that resemble those described by Plath in "On the Plethora of Dryads" (1957) and "The Wishing-Box" (1957). Published two years before the interval at Yaddo, both works suggest that the exercises may themselves go back to efforts even earlier to recover her imagination after the attempted suicide and shock treatments of 1953. Nancy Steiner recalls how at the onset of the poet's return to Smith after the breakdown, she had fears that somehow the sharp intelligence that had made her an honors student was marred by electrotherapy. In the course of that final year, the fears quieted as more of Plath's memory returned and her control over the direction of her life solidified. "On the Plethora of Dryads" suggests that part of the exercises consisted in "starving my fantasy down / To discover that metaphysical Tree." "The Wishing-Box," which appeared in *Granta* shortly after her marriage to Hughes, tells of a wife whose present ability to dream in no way matches the imaginative drift she once had or that her husband presently exercises. In order to regain her "powers of imagination," she responds to his demands to "imagine a goblet" and describe the goblet for him. He asks her to elaborate on the description until he is satisfied that the image is palpable. She continues the recovery on her own until finally she manages to recapture in suicide the full powers she had as a girl.

The process of imagining objects as existing before one's eyes until they assume a reality of their own is similar to what Ignatius of Loyola makes basic to his *Spiritual Exercises* and Louis L. Martz's *The Poetry of Meditation* (1954) describes as obtaining for poets like John Donne and Gerard Manley Hopkins. For Plath as for Roethke, the "pond" or "slime" is created by associations that attach themselves to objects until the Sartrean-like "nausea" becomes an underworld of nightmares, and the individual psyche melts into a primal general sleep. "Johnny Panic and the Bible of Dreams" (1968) describes for readers the imaged "sewage farm of the ages," whose water "naturally stinks and smokes from what dreams have been left sogging around in it over the centuries. . . . Call the water what you will, Lake Nightmare, Bog of Madness, it's here the sleeping people lie and toss together among the props of their worst dreams, one great brotherhood, though each of them, waking, thinks himself singular, utterly apart." Ever "since the apes took to chipping axes out of stone and losing their hair," these dreams have been amassing.[8] In this story, they are burnt out in the worst nightmare of all — electrotherapy. The story suggests that the fear of relapse into chaos lingered far beyond that final year at Smith, and Nancy Steiner's report on the poet's hysteria on occasions when she lost control or the ability to think confirms Plath's own carefully expressed anxiety over the possible cosmetic nature of the recovery.

Poems like "Snakecharmer" (1959) suggest the probability of a direct influence from Rilke. Olwyn Hughes acknowledges that Plath was impressed by Rilke, whom she knew at least in German and had tried translating. Margaret Newlin's "The Suicide Bandwagon" (1972) cites "Black Rook in Rainy Weather" (1957) as containing overt echoes, and others have seen the recurrent "pure angels" of Plath's poetry as a second direct influence. Ostensibly based on Henri Rousseau's *The Snake Charmer* (1907), the Plath poem recounts a controlled meditation similar to that of Rilke's "Spanische Tänzerin." Both poems use performers to invoke moods that are eventually disrupted. Music is suggested as a control on the Dionysian worlds that the speakers' sense take over. The snakecharmer rules his snakedom and the snake-rooted bottom of his mind in much the same ways that the dancer controls, with her movements, the dangerous "consuming flames" and castanets' "snake" rattle and that myth in Eliot's review controls at a further remove the disorder of contemporaneity. Ignoring this aspect of Rilke's art, Ted Hughes is willing to compare the poem's vision to that "specific vision revealed to yogis at a certain advanced stage," but the "control" makes equally discernible Plath's hesitation in accepting the unmediated "invitation of her inner world" that both "Lorelei" and "Full Fathom Five" later represent.[9]

These two sea poems seem influenced not so much by Rilke as by Loren Eiseley's *The Immense Journey* (1957) and Eiseley's positing of the naturalist's analogue to Roethke's associative regressive meditation. Eiseley speaks of a lucky "once in a lifetime" when "one so merges with sunlight and air and running water that whole eons . . . might pass in a single afternoon without discomfort. The mind has sunk away into its beginnings among old roots and the obscure tricklings and movings that stir inanimate things." The book discredits the belief of Sir Charles Thomson's *The Depth of the Sea* (1873) that in the layers of the ocean "was the world of the past" where "down at the bottom . . . lay that living undifferentiated primordial ooze as deep in the sea as it lay deep in time."[10] Yet the very presentation of the view could have stimulated Plath's mind to accept its substance. The speakers of both lyrics wish to abandon the shore for the life-generating depths that have fathered all existence. They fear a lack of rapport with nature that "a well-steered country, / Under a balanced ruler" might bring about. In this fear, they resemble Ferdinand in Shakespeare's *The Tempest* (1611), who may have lost his father and his ties with the past but not his sympathy with water. Ariel's song on Alonso's suffering "a sea-change" allays Ferdinand's fury and passion and prepares him for the "rebirth" that will occur on the island. A similar rebirth may be suggested by the submerging and stone/seed imagery that figure in the poems.

The two lyrics are, according to Hughes, inspired by the same essay by Jacques-Yves Cousteau. The essay is most likely his *"Calypso* Explores an Undersea Canyon," which appeared in the March 1958 issue of *The National Geographic*. The article relates "fathom by fathom" the crew's dropping anchor and an undersea camera five miles beneath the ocean's surface into the Romanche Trench. Never before had man probed so deeply with anchor or camera, and the account seems specifically echoed in the title, "Full Fathom Five," as well as by the phrases "archaic trenched lines" and "labyrinthine tangle." The surprising calm that the marine biologists discovered existing at that depth may well have prompted the lines of "Lorelei": "They sing / Of a world more full and clear // Than can be," although one should not ignore the obvious sea/death and turret echoes of Edgar Allen Poe's "The City in the Sea" (1831, 1845). The biologists found several species of sea life that had not been known to exist before and other species, long believed to be extinct, whose recovery constitutes a kind of rebirth. Even without evidence of any "primordial ooze" further down, the existence of this more primitive world beneath the surface of the ocean invites a parallel to the human mind and the conscious/subconscious stratification of Roethke's vegetal landscape and supports the notion of the sea as an image for meditation.

The honors paper that Plath eventually did, on the double not in Joyce but in Dostoevsky, would have lent to these processes of meditation an almost psychoanalytic concept of the double. The concept would be based on opposition rather than congruence. The opposition would add up either to a third figure containing both or to a cancellation of what each half-figure represents. "Two Sisters of Persephone" (1957) demonstrates how the concept would be carried into Plath's poetry in terms of a nature myth. Here the Greek vegetation goddess, whose six months on earth and six months below earth embrace an explanation of the seasons, inspires the elaboration of the poem's two girls. One, who lives indoors "in the dark, wainscotted room," is finally "worm-husbanded" without ever becoming a wife. The second, who ventures outdoors, becomes "the sun's bride," grows quick with seed, and bears a king (Perseus?). More often, however, the opposition is divorced from these Joycean overtones of myth and left as a kind of split personality. "In Plaster" (1962), for instance, divides its speaker into a "new absolutely white person" and an "old yellow one," and it appears from what Nancy Steiner has written and from *The Bell Jar* that the poem's notion of alter-personalities was present in Plath's friendships as well.

A reading of *African Folktales and Sculpture* reinforces the sense that the eruption of Plath's mature voice was not quite so improvisational as her work later became. Both "Maenad" and "The Stones" from "Poem for a Birthday" use material out of Radin's anthology in much the same way that the wife of "The Wishing-Box" begins to recover her imagination by means of movies, alcohol, and television, and the heroine of "Johnny Panic and the Bible of Dreams" researches the dreams of other people in preparation for realizing history's consummate nightmare. In using tales like "The Bird That Made Milk" and "The City Where Men Are Mended," Plath reshapes their temporary disappearances of children (seeds) so as to discount Radin's warning that the stories not be looked at as a representation of a primitive society "belonging to the lower stages of man's development." Rather, as in the case of Thomson, she prefers to believe Charles Darwin's view of the continent as the place where apes first took on human characteristics. The view had recently been revived by prehistorians like Pierre Teilhard de Chardin and by finds like L. S. B. Leakey's *Sivapithecus* (1953) and *Zinjanthropus boisei* (1959); her acceptance of their work is not striking. Plath also seems to accept Robert Petsch's less provable position that the folktales of aboriginal peoples "are concerned exclusively with descriptions of what transpires before one's eyes and have as their ultimate purpose, primarily, the heightening of the sense of existence." The lessening of linear narrative in her writing for the present tense and the quick, associative dreamlike shifts that Ted Hughes terms "the improvisational nature" of the later poems owes much to the way that these folktales move. Like their narrative threads, these poems flow and turn at whim, never relinquishing their sense of immediacy and often assuming only the most subconscious links in joining incidents and images.

Nor does the stylistic influence of these tales stop merely with the matter of narrative. Plath's inability to accept institutional religions allows her to experiment with the view of man that Radin describes. "Contrary to the belief widespread throughout the world, man in aboriginal Africa is never thought of as having once possessed a portion of divinity and having subsequently lost it." The reverse is true. African myth is so geocentric that "the gods of native Africa...must lose their earthly constituent, their earthly adhesions, before they can become properly divine." Similarly, the tales allow her to merge the wish-fulfillment fantasies of the *Märchen* proper with the human heroes of these stories whose plots derive from purely human situations. Radin infers that this difference of folktales from *Märchen* results from an "economically and politically disturbed and insecure world." "Assuredly we have the right to infer that it is largely because these peoples are living in an insecure and semi-chaotic world, with its loss of values and its consequent inward demoralization, that cruelty and wanton murder loom so large in many of their tales.... Yet to judge from the very tales where cruelty and murder are the main themes, . . . the author-raconteur felt it necessary to attach to them a clear cut moral[:] . . . death is the inevitable fate of those who fail to resist disorganization, and that outward disorganization is followed remorselessly by inward disintegration."[11]

3

"The Manor Garden" and "Two Views of a Cadaver Room" open *The Colossus* and establish the ranges of the nature myth as it appears in that collection. Written while the poet was at Yaddo in the first months of her pregnancy, "The Manor Garden" opposes the harvest of nature to the growing foetus within the speaker. As the outer world comes to represent death, the child moves "through the era of fishes," reliving in its development the history of evolution. It will be born into a world whose sickness and dying will become "fits," and presumably, the child's life, like that existence described in "The Colossus," will be one of reconstruction. "Two Views of a Cadaver Room" repeats the message on a more personal plane. Using the image of a dissecting room that will reappear in *The Bell Jar*, Plath opposes the bodies of grown men that the medical students dissect to the foetuses that science has pickled for the same purpose of learning how to cure. By gaining knowledge from the dead, science comes to imitate in a dispassionate way the natural process of return that "The Manor Garden" describes. This imitation of nature extends to art in the second half of the poem as Pieter Brueghel's *The Triumph of Death* (c. 1562) replaces the cadaver room. The lust of the lovers in the painting's right-hand corner forms an oasis from the "panorama of smoke and slaughter" that comprises the rest of the panel. Their passion replaces the sterile atmosphere of the scientists, but not with any gentler feeling.

Plath's relegation of survival rather than suffering to a corner of the poems seems immediately to respond to Auden's famous "Musée des Beaux Arts" (1939) as well as to the poet's own earlier indecision about careers. She told her Harvard interviewer that "I think if I had done anything else I would like to have been a doctor." Hughes relates that "the chemical poisoning of nature, the pile-up of atomic waste, were horrors that persecuted her like an illness." Less immediately present are her responses to "the great civilized crime of intelligence" that Betrand Russell and others were enunciating. For them, civilization had reached a point where survival not comfort was its key accomplishment. Russell's "The Future of Mankind" (1950) presented three results of atomic war: "The end of human life, perhaps of all life on our planet"; "A reversion to barbarism after a catastrophic diminution of the population of the globe"; and "A unification of the world under a single government, possessing a monopoly of all the major weapons of war."[12] It appears that Plath had personally reduced the options to two: She subscribed to either a doomsday or a reversion to barbarism in which, as Radin states for Africa, an "outward disorganization" precedes the "inward disintegration." In both cases, the "progress" that a war would accomplish is a return of civilization to its "seed" form in much the manner that Plath describes for nature.

"The Thin People" (1959) embodies one of Plath's earliest efforts to move from this myth of nature to social and political concerns. The poem centers on an image of the famished that the speaker as a child saw in newsreels. These victims of "a war making evil headlines" had discovered "the talent to persevere / In thinness"; yet the "talent" remains expressed in the same terms that Plath's other protagonists embrace. Thinness becomes a "seed," and like seeds, the thin people go from darkness into "the sunlit room" where not even forests can arrest "their stiff battalions." "The Disquieting Muses" (1959) confirms this sense that human action is "necessary" rather than "willful." The poem presents its speaker in terms that Auden reserves for Oedipus. It confounds the wishes of the godmothers of "Sleeping Beauty" with the fate woven by the Norns. The mother who would have her daughter oppose like Oedipus the fate that she has been granted is asked to accept responsibility for the suffering that she has caused the speaker to bear. In making the request, the speaker — as she does in other poems — extenuates nothing and blames the parents for everything. Indeed, fixing blame seems to be the important process in the poems Plath wrote during and just after her classes with Lowell and may reflect not only his influence but the influence of Sexton as well. Yet, by the time Plath began "Getting There" (1963), fixing blame seems to be less important than purging guilt. The poem describes travel to a Nazi concentration camp in boxcars as a kind of Yeatsian "dreaming back." The trip is a purification rite, a stripping back of the shell of civilization until an infantile "purity" is reached. For Yeats, the process was necessary so that the spirit could separate from the passionate body and be reborn in a manner very much like that of plants.

One may associate this process of "dreaming back" in Plath's poems with psychoanalysis and what Auden calls Freud's major contribution to modern thought — treating neurosis historically — but to do so would be an error. Freud's process is a method by which the conscious comes to understand and purge itself of obsessive action; it does not promise innocence or, as "Lady Lazarus" (1963), superhuman status. It remains, as Auden indicates, in the area of human behavior. "Insomniac" (1961), which deals with "dream" in Freudian terms, has the night dissolve into "white disease" and "trivial repetitions" rather than the "celestial burning" of "obtuse objects" that "Black Rook in Rainy Weather" (1957) makes a forerunner of the ovens of "Mary's Song" (1963). There the heretics and Jews are viewed in language that deliberately recalls the "sages standing in God's holy fire" of Yeats's "Sailing to Byzantium" (1927). They burn until their being made translucent comes to be equated to Christ, and the speaker, like the Communion Host, is killed and eaten. The "meal" is possible, Plath maintains, because the world has not had its heart consumed away. The residual heart is the oven and holocaust through which the Jews and the poem's speaker must both proceed. If supported by a source other than Yeats, the process might derive from Radin's description of the loss of earthly constituents and adhesions that man undergoes in aboriginal Africa to become divine.

Plath's objections to Freud are lengthily expounded in "Johnny Panic and the Bible of Dreams," one of two stories she wrote based on her experiences as a secretary to a Boston psychiatrist during the summer of 1958. Opposed to the "dream-stopper," the "dream-explainer," and the "exploiter of dreams for the crass practical ends of health and happiness," Plath's narrator would be "that rare character, rarer, in truth, than any member of the Psychoanalytic Institute: a dream connoisseur." Dreams become her means for singling out people rather than classifying them, for as one typing dream transcriptions, she finds dreams more individualizing than "any Christian name." Yet, the very worst dreams collectively make up her single Lake Nightmare and turn the dreamers into "one great brotherhood" of those who have witnessed "unfinished messages from the great I Am." These deeper dreams force patients "to a place more permanent" than the clinic where the narrator works. Her "psyche-doctors" thrive on conformity as they labor daily "to win Johnny Panic's converts from him by hook, crook, and talk, talk, talk." They refuse to "forget the dreamer and remember the dream" or recognize that "the dreamer is merely a flimsy vehicle for the great Dream-Maker himself." They stand for proper social behavior and present rationally what the narrator would have remain a mystery, though one is perhaps not to accept as Plath's the bleakness of the narrator's final vision. The narrator sees herself as a Jeremiah willing to visualize "the slaughterhouse at the end of the track" and accept a love that is suicide.[13] One may suppose, instead, that like Lowell's "Skunk Hour" (1958), the emotions comprise "an Existential night" in which the writer reaches a point of final darkness at which the one free act is suicide, and she emerges from the experience stronger and less sure.

The Bell Jar continues in a more implicit way many of the arguments that begin in the story. Freud's formulaic allegorizing of human action into Ego and Id becomes part of the "shrinking everything into letters and numbers" that provokes Esther's revulsions to physics, chemistry, and shorthand. In the novel, Joan chatters about Egos and Ids with Doctor Quinn, whereas Esther "never talked about Egos and Ids with Doctor

Nolan." Since Doctor Nolan is a successful psychiatrist and Joan a lesbian and suicide, one presumes that Freud's use here is as negative coloring. This presumption is strengthened by Esther's own statement about analysis, "I had hoped, at my departure, I would feel sure and knowledgeable about everything that lay ahead—after all, I had been 'analyzed.' Instead, all I could see were question marks." Esther attributes to electrotherapy the purging of heat and fear that make up her "bell jar." Yet, however much these attitudes toward Freud are negative, they do not offset the excitement Plath reports feeling in the "emotional and psychological depth" of Sexton's poetry or her own view of poetry as "sensuous and emotional experiences . . . manipulated with an informed and intelligent mind." Her poems remain squarely in the psychological tradition of Auden and the generation of poets that emerged after him. Like Randall Jarrell, she believes art to be "the union of a wish and a truth" or a "wish modified by a truth," but because her "truths" often deal with obsessions, her poems appear open less to what Auden's "Squares and Oblongs" (1957) designates as "man's historical order of being" than to what he calls "the natural, reversible, necessary order." The effect is to give the poetry the appearance of being written by a writer who does not care much about book publication, reputation, critical accolades, awards, or whatever, but merely, as Stephen Spender asserts, about being able to express in her best poems "controlled uncontrolledness."[14]

4

A hiatus in Plath's development followed the Hugheses' return to England and the birth of their daughter before the poet began in early 1962 to recover her *"Ariel* voice" by writing "Elm" and "The Moon and the Yew Tree." Plath had already abandoned the methodical composition that she practiced at Smith, "plodding through dictionary and thesaurus searching for the exact word" to create her poetic effects. Now she wrote "at top speed, as one might write an urgent letter."[15] "Elm" shows her still caught up in the Roethkean systems of meditation and correspondence between the human and nonhuman. Based on an enormous tree that stood over the Hugheses' house in Devon, the poem presents associations whose intent is again to "know the bottom." The tree is "inhabited by a cry" that nightly flaps out, "looking, with its hooks, for something to love" and that daily terrifies the tree's existence with "its soft, feathery turnings, its malignancy." "Incapable of more knowledge," the tree/speaker identifies her fear as "the isolate, slow faults / That kill, that kill, that kill." Completed shortly afterward, "The Moon and the Yew Tree" already shows evidence of a Yeatsian influence with its conflict of religions.

Originally an exercise suggested by Hughes, the poem centers on the church and yew tree that stood opposite the front of their home and goes beyond the simple correspondences of Roethke to a tension between chthonic and Christian forces similar to that of Yeats's "The Unappeasable Host" (1896). In the Plath poem, color does most of the work of aligning forces. Those of nature are black whereas the "light of the mind," like Mary and the interior of the church, is "blue and mystical." Douglas Cleverdon recalls that early in 1962, Plath was asked by the B.B.C. to do a radio play, and her work on the verse play may well have set off a fresh reading of Auden, Eliot, and Yeats.

"Fever 103°" again takes up the Yeatsian image of purging fire, this time represented by the atomic destruction of Hiroshima. Al Alvarez ventures that the poem may well have been spawned by a viewing of *Hiroshima mon amour* (1959), but the popularity of John Hersey's *Hiroshima* (1946) and the ongoing discussion of the effects of atomic fallout in promoting the test-ban treaty cannot be ruled out. The title is meant to convey an enormously high body temperature, and the opening word "pure" immediately sets the work's theme. Fever is the body's method of "burning out" impurities. Here, the fever proves as inept as Cerberus at "licking clean . . .the sin, the sin." A vision of Isadora Duncan follows: rolls of smoke seem to surround the speaker much as scarves surrounded and strangled rather than cleansed the dancer. The image that seems to be set off superficially by an association of the smoke with scarves is cemented by Yeats's use of the dancer in his images of dreaming back. The smoke becomes a cloud of atomic radiation covering as it had the inhabitants of Hiroshima and eating away everything. The radiation becomes the speaker's sin as she turns from her own thoughts to address her love. Like Christs's descent into hell, her "purging" had lasted three days and made her "too pure . . .for anyone." She is a lantern, her skin "gold beaten"; she is "a huge camellia / Glowing"; in short, she is again one of Yeats's "dancers" or "sages burning in a holy fire." Her selves dissolve like "old whore petticoats" as she nears Paradise. Plath has identified the fires of the poem as "the fires of hell, which merely agonize, and the fires of heaven, which purify,"[16] but it is clear that rather than discrete fires, one has, as in Yeats, a single continuous fire that begins in the agony of burning off the world and ends in "flames that do not singe a sleeve."

"Candles" (1960) suggests that the "fires" of these poems may also go back to Walter Pater, from whom scholars conjecture Yeats derived his "purging fires." Pater's entreaty in the Conclusion to *The Renaissance* (1873) that one burn with "a hard, gem-like flame" is reversed as the birth of a child is seen as a hardening of lucent tallow into pearl. The hardening suggests the process of return or metempsychosis in Yeats. Metempsychosis is likewise a theme in Joyce's *Ulysses* and would figure in any study of the double in his writing; rebirth is a theme in both of the folktales that Plath takes from Radin. Certainly, the determinism and nature myth that underlie her work would encourage the concept of return, but "Cut" (1963) suggests that the "purging," as in the poetry of Rilke and Roethke, is more mystical than generative. The poem's recounting of a slip while slicing an onion, which ends in a cut thumb, defines the relationship between the personal and the racial as connatural rather than reincarnational. The plasmic structure of the blood contains within its chemical make-up a history of mankind, and the poem seems to say with its series of associations that Plath's Lake Nightmare is part of everyone's bloodstream instead of a recollection of previous existences. This statement would be consistent with Thomson's belief in a primordial ooze lying at the bottom of the sea from which all life evolved and with the use of that belief in "Full Fathom Five." The statement also suits with the view in "The Manor Garden" that, as proof of evolution, the human foetus reenacts the evolutionary process as part of its growth. Finally, the statement reinforces Plath's use of the heart as holocaust and oven in "Mary's Song."

"Cut" begins with a comparison of the hurt thumb to a little man. The severed tip is "a sort of hinge" or "a hat," the first implying entry into something and the second conveying that the "something" may be "the head." The second possibility produces the inaugural victimizer / victim pairing of "little pilgrim" and Indian. The speaker images a primal scalping whose streaming blood becomes a "turkey wattle." An application of Merthiolate / pink champagne changes the "crime" into a "celebration" and, just as one is about to deduce that the "celebration" is the first Thanksgiving, the speaker seizes on the fact that blood is made up of millions of red and white corpuscles to convert the occasion into the American Revolution. She now addresses the thumb as her "Homunculus," telling it that she has taken a pill—probably an aspirin—"to kill / The thin / Papery feeling." The "celebration" has thus become a "high" that must be treated before it turns into a hangover. Coevally, the juxtaposition of "homunculus" and "pill" sets off a sense of abortion that may have begun earlier with "turkey." *The Bell Jar* describes the male genital organ as "turkey neck and turkey gizzards," and in the history of medicine, homunculus preceded sperm as a theory of impregnation. Plath uses the word again in "Oregonian Original" (1962) to refer to Punch, and here she may simply mean "little man." From the remainder of the poem, however, one senses that if she does, she means a "little man" like that of "Gulliver" (1965) who comes with "petty fetters" and "bribes." The thumb becomes her "sabateur," a "kamikaze-man," and a member of the Ku Klux Klan. When it sees the pulp of its heart (life) is to become paper (art), the homunculus commits suicide, leaving only the "trepanned veteran" whose scar suggests a lobotomy. What remains at its departure becomes a Yeatsian husk, "dirty" with the numbness of a "stump."

At this point George Steiner's remarks about the poet's uses of concentration camps become relevant. Steiner's "Dying Is an Art" (1965) maintains that "perhaps it is only those who had no part in the events [of the death camps] who *can* focus on them rationally and imaginatively; to those who experienced the thing, it has lost the hard edges of possibility; it has stepped outside the real." Steiner marvels that "the dead men cry out of the yew hedge" and proposes that the poems constitute "an act of identification, of total communion with those tortured and massacred." But he wrongly supposes that the act of identification for Plath involves a radical rethinking of the whole question of "the poet's condition and the condition of language after modernism and war." Her adaptation of the strategies of Yeats's dreaming back does not constitute a response to "T. W. Adorno's dictim 'no poetry after Auschwitz.'" Rather, it suggests that the way her poetry handles "the politics of terror and mass-murder" is to return to her earlier mythic style.[17] She reaches an understanding of man's inhumanity not by looking directly at Auschwitz but by looking at its atrocities in a continuous parallel with Yeatsian myth. This myth had earlier led the Irish poet to a passive acceptance of fascism by seeing the movement as the next state in his cycles of history. Plath, too, is led in the poems to minimize the horror of the occasions by seeing the ovens as a place for moral tempering. The Jews emerge as passive victims of a Zeitgeist meant to be as coercive as the drug that *The Bell Jar* describes being administered to women about to give birth. As those women "would go straight home and start another baby," the victims, like Job, expect to "emerge as gold" from the testing (Job 23:10). Their suffering, as a Job's comforter might add, is proof of their guilt, and no other explanation need be given.

5

If these cycles of history are not determined by human choice, one may wonder exactly where Plath's activism begins. Her reviews, written at the same time as the poems, are militant. A General Jodpur can be thrown from a runaway horse, and in his walk back to camp, have a complete change of heart, tyrants can be tamed, and in *The Emperor's Oblong Pancakes*, an emperor can end his insistence on oblongity in the world. By analogy, Plath can strike out against the poisons "fisting themselves in the upper atmosphere," "the crisis of identity" that two "leaning Stonehenge shapes of parents" impose on "the ego-balls" of their children, and the self-righteous airs of Lord Byron's wife.[18] But as one nears the vision of the poetry, freedom becomes less apparent and one suspects a hierarchy at work similar to that which the narrator of "Johnny Panic and the Bible of Dreams" defines for dream. Political action is possible within Plath's cycles of history only insofar as one chooses what the Zeitgeist allows. As with Hegel, Auden, and Elizabeth Bishop, "Freedom is the knowledge of necessity," and necessity for both victimizer and victim is identical: the creation of a super race in an ongoing evolutionary process. The Nazis become "gods" by persecuting the Jews, and the Jews become "gods" by suffering the persecution. The two roles stand as thesis and antithesis in a relationship that Yeats describes as self and mask.

Thus, "Lady Lazarus," which begins the reversal from passivity, does not in any way alter the conditions of the cycle. Her admission that she has "done it again" may make her brushes with death seem willful, but the victim of her action is likewise herself. She may be "a walking miracle," but her sense of herself as a lamp recalls both the purging Yeatsian flames and the lampshades that Ilse Koch made from the skins of prisoners at Buchenwald. Hitler's purification may again initiate her dreaming back, but by the end of the poem she is equally Hitlerian. She promises "to eat men" in the same way that her selves have been consumed. Much as had the fasting of Franz Kafka's "hunger artist," her dyings have become a spectacle for "the peanut-crunching crowd," and one suspects that she is impelled toward death for the same reason that he is impelled toward hunger: she cannot find anything she wants to live for. Her art, nonetheless, has acquired commercial value. Although she is still "the same, identical woman," one must now pay "for a word or a touch / Or a bit of blood." Preserving the theme of Nazi persecution, she addresses her persecutors as "Herr Doktor" and "Herr Enemy," claiming to be their "opus," a "pure gold baby" ready to begin again. Powerful reminders of Hitler's "final solution"—"A cake of soap, / A wedding ring, / A gold filling"—have been left among the ashes from her dreaming back. Yet, the new purity that she gains has accomplished exactly what Alfred Rosenberg had imagined for the German race: a superman who can challenge "Herr God" and "Herr Lucifer" by having gained self-discipline. She has, in effect, undergone the dehumanization that Radin finds common in aboriginal African deities, although "Brasilia" (1963) once more binds the dreaming back to Nietzsche and Germany by referring to its survivors as "super-people."

The dialectic of wills that is implicit in "Lady Lazarus" is expanded in "Daddy." He is the "Herr Doktor" of the previous poem, but the speaker is far less willing to remain his "opus." Plath describes her condition as being that of "a girl with an Electra complex. Her father died while she thought he was God.... Her father was also a Nazi and her mother very possibly part Jewish." The two strains have married in the daughter into a kind of paralysis, and at the poem's beginning, she is rejecting the bonds that the father places on her, imaged as a shoe. By her resistance, the girl suggests that she may be rejecting Yeatsian history and its passivity as well, but Plath indicates an action like that of the father in Yeats's *Purgatory* (1939). Much as he murders his son in a reenactment intended to expiate a previous parricide, Plath's figure is compelled "to act out [her] awful little allegory . . . before she is free of it."[19] The paralysis, which has kept her infantile, is reflected in both the nursery-rhyme rhythms and her self-image as "The Woman in the Shoe." She has never been able to fix or speak to her father, and the poem begins by detailing the failures in Massachusetts, Germany, and Poland. The result has been an absence that the concentration-camp imagery converts to a guilt or torture. She finds herself bounded by barbwire and senses that she may have been brought into her present circumstances by some railway journey. There is no doubt that here and there Plath's own emotions have entered the poem, but what one has is not pure autobiography so much as another Yeatsian dreaming back to throw off the husk or passionate body for a pure existence.

The connection between the failure at communication and barbwire is explained in *The Bell Jar*, where Esther speaks of picking "up a German dictionary or a German book[;] the very sight of those dense, black, barbed-wire letters made my mind shut like a clam."[20] The poem's speaker admits to being "like a Jew" and having a "gypsy ancestress"—the two races signaled by Hitler for extermination. Her father turns Luftwaffe (Hermann Göring), bureaucrat (gobbledygoo), and panzer-man (Erwin Rommel). His brutishness becomes like Marco's "woman-hating" in *The Bell Jar*, a basis for attraction. The imagery again shifts as the poem becomes more confounded with the author's life and the father figure takes on the role of teacher. Clefts settle in the chin rather than his foot; nonetheless, he is the devil, as coercions of school and the speaker's attempt to get back to him at ten and twenty attest. His having reduced her to a nursery-rhyme character is now matched by her reconstructing this God-turned-superhuman as an imitation man. He is a voodoo doll to which the speaker has wedded herself. It is this wedding that is negated as the dreaming back ends and the speaker prepares for a final separation. She has disposed of two—the creator/father and the parasite/vampire —fused beneath a stake that she has driven into the creature's heart. Freed finally from these constrictions, she and the villagers relax, but it is a relaxation made possible by her assuming a brutality that equates her to him and thus makes her of one cycle with him, and superhuman as well.

Because of the reference to it in the Harvard interview, "The Swarm"

(1963) must be included among these other historical poems. Yet, it seems by any measure the least historical of Plath's final works. It depicts a struggle for survival between nature and the "men of business," variously imaged as a swarm of bees and beekeepers and as Napoleon's armies and the victors of Waterloo. The poem's equating bee swarms to swarming troops may be meant to convey the natural/cyclical process of the great events of history, managed because of their subconscious and impulsive character by the ontogenetic, exploitive superego. Nature produces hives and honey and the "grey" beekeepers who exploit them produce the "new mausoleums" of ivory. Nature, also, in the end promises to make temporary the reign of the mind in a teleology that echoes C. S. Lewis's *The Abolition of Man* (1947). There Lewis had explained man's attempts to control nature as deriving from his belief that he is the result of a natural accident and consequently may be destroyed by accident as well. To avoid this end, man has divorced himself increasingly from nature and the divorce has been dangerously injurious. The opposition in Plath's case seems less preoccupied than she normally is with "purging," and the tension may go back for its paradigm to either the double of Dostoevsky or the self and mask of Yeats. The selection of Napoleon may well have been provoked, as Plath indicates, by her reading. In April of 1962, she reviewed a life of Josephine by Hubert Cole and tended to see what was to become her own marital situation reflected in Josephine's separation from Napoleon and the comfort that her two children brought after the divorce.[21] Napoleon figures, too, in Lowell's *Imitations* (1961) and *Life Studies*.

Finished in the week before her death, "Edge" (1963) turns from these willful acts to "the illusion of Greek necessity." Clytemnestra's prophetic dream of her own destruction by Orestes seems to have inspired the imagery of Plath's "perfect," childless woman. "Perfection," as she noted in "The Munich Mannequins" (1965), is, like the angels of Rilke's *Duino Elegies*, "terrible[;] it cannot have children." Nor can it in Plath's mind allow even a possibility of things to exist and, consequently, for Rilkean unicorns to be. Rather, the woman folds possibility back into herself much as a rose closes its petals. The process is the reverse of that described by E. E. Cummings in "somewhere i have never travelled," read aloud by Esther to her boyfriend in *The Bell Jar*. The moon looks on, suggesting the cycles of its own waxing and waning as the menstrual cycle. The poem seems to be saying that one is killed as much by one's dreams of perfection as by any other means. In saying this, "Edge" echoes so many of the poems whose dreams of accomplishment terrorize the speaker, often as imagined father figures but as mother figures, too. As parents destroy possibility to live for their children and often destroy their children by trying to force them to live out parental aspirations, so also children destroy themselves in order to realize their parents' hopes or destroy their parents in order to be themselves. Technology has speeded up the process of change and made this "generational conflict" more visible and intense. There seems to be no way out of this "bad faith" that is recurrent and hence, natural, reversible, and nonhistorical.

Indeed, if one is to grant relevance to Plath's cycles of history, one grants it on the same terms that Auden grants history to Yeats—as a conflict between Reason and Imagination, objectivity and subjectivity, and the individual and the masses rather than between good and evil will, integrated and diffuse thought, and personality and the impersonal state. Without citing Auden directly or mentioning Yeats, Joyce Carol Oates's "The Death Throes of Romanticism" objects to Plath's work in exactly these terms. Oates finds Plath's battle between Reason and Imagination "a suicidal refusal to understand that man's intelligence *is* instinctive in his species." Plath's quarrel between objectivity and subjectivity becomes an "'I' that is declared an enemy of all others," and her preference for the individual over the masses is productive of "a limited vision" that believes itself unquestionably *the* correct "mirror held up to nature." Oates objects, too, to the passivity of Plath's victims, calling her "dreaming back" a regression into infantilism. Nevertheless, Oates is willing to see deeper than the visions of feminist critics who wish merely to make Plath a martyr for female oppression and who would limit the seriousness with which she undertook other areas of persecution and the total change that would be needed to offset her objections. Like Esther in *The Bell Jar*, once Plath realized the monotony of repetition, she "wanted to do everything once and for all and be through with it."[22] Part of the dilemma of her poetry is that, in sensing the repetitions of life, it could neither acquiesce nor provide alternatives for them.

6

Nancy Steiner remarks that Plath "could not guess that society would ever change; she seemed to see the taboos and tensions of her background as permanent conditions that could never be substantially altered." The sense is already present in the poems that Plath published as a high school student in *Seventeen* and the repetitious villanelles that seem to typify her undergraduate writing at Smith. Steiner opposes this attitude to other students who could flit "excitedly on the first wave of a new and radical movement, like a prophet who could see ahead into the '60's and '70's."[23] By accepting the backward glance of recurrence rather than the forward look of the industrial imagination, Plath could only move into a world that would become increasingly hostile to innovation. Nor could the psychological ideal that had sustained Auden and the generation of poets before her be any more comforting, for the very rationality of the Freudian approach had produced a conformism that threatened to destroy faction through coercion. Nonhistorical and nonrational approaches would have to be tried if poetry and politics were to recover some of the power to overcome the limitations of self that Freudian thinking had produced. It remained for other poets emerging in the mid-fifties to rediscover successful ways of opening up the closed world of the postmodernists with visions aided by surrealism, dada, deep imagery, technology, and the principles of natural science.

Notes

1. "Sylvia Plath," in *The Poet Speaks: Interviews with Contemporary Poets*, ed. Peter Orr (London: Routledge and Kegan Paul, 1966), pp. 169-70; Sylvia Plath, "Context," *The London Magazine* 11 (February, 1962): 45-46.
2. W. H. Auden, Introduction to *The Oxford Book of Light Verse* (Oxford: Oxford University Press, 1938; reprint ed. 1962), p. ix; Orr, *The Poet Speaks*, p. 170; quoted in Lois Ames, "Sylvia Plath: A Biographical Note," *The Bell Jar* (New York: Bantam, 1972), p. 213.
3. Nancy Steiner, *A Closer Look at Ariel* (New York: Harper's Magazine Press, 1973), p. 35; W. H. Auden, "Tract for the Times," *Nation* 152 (1941): 25; idem., "A Note on Order," *Nation* 152 (1941): 131.
4. Ted Hughes, "Notes on the Chronological Order of Sylvia Plath's Poems," in *The Art of Sylvia Plath: A Symposium*, ed. Charles Newman (Bloomington: Indiana University Press, 1970), p. 190.
5. T. S. Eliot, "Ulysses, Order, and Myth," *The Dial* 74 (1923): 483; Rachel Bespaloff, *On the Iliad*, trans. Mary McCarthy (New York: Harper Torchbooks, 1962), pp. 73-74; W. H. Auden, "The Dyer's Hand," *The Listener* 53 (1955): 1064.
6. Anne Sexton, "The Barfly Ought to Sing," in *The Art of Sylvia Plath*, p. 178; Hughes, "Notes," p. 192; Eileen Aird, *Sylvia Plath: Her Life and Work* (New York: Barnes and Noble, 1973), p. 27.
7. W. H. Auden, "Rilke in English," *New Republic* 100 (1939): 135; Theodore Roethke, "Open Letter," *Mid-Century American Poets*, ed. John Ciardi (New York: Twayne Publishers, 1950), pp. 67-68.
8. Sylvia Plath, "Johnny Panic and the Bible of Dreams," *Atlantic Monthly* 222 (September 1968): 55.
9. Margaret Newlin, "The Suicide Bandwagon," *The Critical Quarterly* 14 (1972): 376-77; Hughes, "Notes," p. 189.
10. Loren Eiseley, *The Immense Journey* (New York: Vintage, 1959), pp. 16, 31, 33.
11. Paul Radin, *African Folktales and Sculpture*, Bollingen Series 32 (New York: Pantheon Books, 1952), pp. 1, 12, 4, 9.
12. Orr, *The Poet Speaks*, p. 172; Hughes, "Notes," p. 190; Bertrand Russeell, "The Future of Mankind," in *Points of Departure*, ed. Arthur J. Carr and William Steinhoff (New York: Harper, 1960), p. 589.
13. Plath, "Johnny Panic," pp. 54-55, 58.
14. *The Bell Jar*, pp. 29, 183, 199, 176; Orr, *The Poet Speaks*, pp. 168-69; Randall Jarrell, *A Sad Heart at the Supermarket* (New York: Atheneum, 1962), p. 26; W. H. Auden, "Squares and Oblongs," *Language: An Inquiry*, ed. R. N. Anshen (New York: Harper,

1957), p. 174; Stephen Spender, "Warnings from the Grave," in *The Art of Sylvia Plath*, p. 200.

15. Nancy Steiner, *A Closer Look*, p. 43; Hughes, "Notes," p. 193.
16. Douglas Cleverdon, "On *Three Women*," in *The Art of Sylvia Plath*, p. 227; quoted in A. Alvarez, "Sylvia Plath," in ibid., p. 62.
17. George Steiner, "Dying Is an Art," in *The Art of Sylvia Plath*, pp. 217, 216; idem, "In Extremis," *Cambridge Review* 90 (1969): 247-48.
18. Sylvia Plath, "General Jodpur's Conversion," *New Statesman* 62 (1961): 696; idem., "Oregonian Original," ibid. 63 (1962): 660; idem., "Suffering Angel," ibid. 3 (1962): 828-29.
19. Quoted in Alvarez, "Sylvia Plath," p. 65.
20. *The Bell Jar*, p. 27.
21. Sylvia Plath, "Pair of Queens," *New Statesman* 63 (1962): 602-3.
22. W. H. Auden, "Yeats as an Example," *Kenyon Review* 10 (1948): 181-95; Joyce Carol Oates, "The Death Throes of Romanticism," *Southern Review* 9 (Summer, 1973): 502, 506, 508; *The Bell Jar*, p. 105.
23. Nancy Steiner, *A Closer Look*, pp. 78-79.

Sylvia Plath: a selected bibliography of primary and secondary materials

By Sylvia Plath

A. Books

A Winter Ship. Edinburgh: Tragara Press, 1960. Limited edition.
The Colossus
> London: William Heinemann, 1960.
> New York: Alfred A. Knopf, 1962. Published as *The Colossus and Other Poems*; contents differ slightly from Heinemann edition.
> London: Faber and Faber, 1967. Contents identical to Heinemann edition.
> New York: Random House, 1968 (paperback). Published as *The Colossus and Other Poems*; contents identical to Knopf edition.
> London: Faber and Faber, 1972 (paperback). Contents identical to Faber hardback.

The Bell Jar

> London: William Heinemann, 1963. Published under the pseudonym "Victoria Lucas."
>
> London: Faber and Faber, 1966.
>
> London: Faber and Faber, 1966 (paperback).
>
> New York: Harper and Row, 1971.
>
> New York: Bantam, 1972 (paperback).

Uncollected Poems. London: Turret Books, 1965. Limited edition.

Ariel

> London: Faber and Faber, 1965.
>
> New York: Harper and Row, 1966. Contents differ slightly from Faber and Faber edition.
>
> New York: Harper and Row, 1966 (paperback). Contents identical to Harper hardback.
>
> London: Faber and Faber, 1968 (paperback). Contents identical to Faber hardback.

Three Women: A Monologue for Three Voices. London: Turret Books, 1968. Limited edition.

Wreath for a Bridal. Frensham: Sceptre Press, 1970. Limited edition.

Million Dollar Month. Frensham: Sceptre Press, 1971. Limited edition.

Child. Exeter: Rougemont Press, 1971. Limited edition.

Fiesta Melons. Exeter: Rougemont Press, 1971. Limited edition.

Crystal Gazer. London: Rainbow Press, 1971. Limited edition.

Lyonnesse. London: Rainbow Press, 1972. Limited edition.

Crossing the Water

> London: Faber and Faber, 1971.
>
> New York: Harper and Row, 1971. Contents differ slightly from Faber and Faber edition.
>
> New York: Harper and Row, 1975 (paperback). Contents identical to Harper hardback.
>
> London: Faber and Faber, 1975 (paperback). Contents identical to Faber hardback.

Winter Trees

> London: Faber and Faber, 1971.
>
> New York: Harper and Row, 1972. Contents differ slightly from Faber and Faber edition.
>
> London: Faber and Faber, 1975 (paperback). Contents identical to Faber hardback.

Pursuit. London: Rainbow Press, 1973. Limited edition.

Letters Home: Correspondence 1950-1963. Selected and edited with commentary by Aurelia Schober Plath.

> New York: Harper and Row, 1975.
>
> New York: Bantam, 1977 (paperback).

The Bed Book (for children)

> London: Faber and Faber, 1976. Illustrations by Quentin Blake.
>
> New York: Harper and Row, 1976. Illustrations by Emily Arnold McCully.

Johnny Panic and the Bible of Dreams, and Other Prose Writings. London: Faber and Faber, 1977.

Sylvia Plath: A Dramatic Portrait. Assembled by Barry Kyle. New York: Harper and Row, 1977.

B. Uncollected Poems (Those poems not included in both the American and British editions of the four major collections; where several citations for a poem are available, the most accessible has been chosen.)

"Above the Oxbow." *Christian Science Monitor,* 4 May 1959, p. 8.

"Admonition." *Harvard Advocate* 101 (May, 1967): 2.

"Aerialist." *Cambridge Review* 90 (7 February 1969): 245.

"Alicante Lullaby." In *Crystal Gazer* (1971).

"Amnesiac." In *Winter Trees* (American edition, 1972).

"Apotheosis." *The Lyric* 36 (Winter, 1956): 10.

"Ballade Banale." In *Crystal Gazer* (1971).

"Battle-Scene from the Comic Operatic Fantasy 'The Seafarer.'" *Times Literary Supplement,* 31 July 1969, p. 855.

"The Beggars." *Critical Quarterly* 2 (Summer, 1960): 156.

"Bitter Strawberries." *Christian Science Monitor,* 11 August 1950, p. 17.

"Burning the Letters." In *Pursuit* (1973).

"Circus in Three Rings." *Atlantic* 196 (August, 1955): 68.

"Complaint of the Crazed Queen." *Times Literary Supplement,* 31 July 1969, p. 855.

"Crystal Gazer." In *Crystal Gazer* (1971).

"Danse Macabre." *Harvard Advocate* 101 (May, 1967): 2.

"Dark Wood, Dark Water." *Christian Science Monitor,* 17 December 1959, p. 12.

"The Death of Mythmaking." *Poetry* 94 (September, 1959): 370.

"Denouement." *Smith Review,* Spring, 1954, p. 23.

"The Detective." In *Winter Trees* (American edition, 1972).

"Dialogue en Route." *Times Literary Supplement,* 31 July 1969, p. 855.

"Doomsday." *Harper's* 208 (May, 1954): 29.

"Dream of the Hearse-Driver." *Times Literary Supplement,* 31 July 1969, p. 855.

"Dream with Clam Diggers." *Poetry* 89 (January, 1957): 232-33.

"Eavesdropper." In *Winter Trees* (American edition, 1972).

"Electra on Azalea Path." *Hudson Review* 13 (Autumn, 1960): 414-15.

"Ella Mason and Her Eleven Cats." *Poetry* 90 (July, 1957): 233-34.

"Epitaph for Fire and Flower." *Poetry* 89 (January, 1957): 236-37.

"Fable of the Rhododendron Stealers." In *Crystal Gazer* (1971).

"The Fearful." *The Observer,* 17 February 1963, p. 23.

"Fiesta Melons." In *Fiesta Melons* (1971).

"Go Get the Goodly Squab." *Harper's* 209 (November, 1954): 47.

"The Goring." In *Crystal Gazer* (1971).

"Green Rock, Winthrop Bay." In *Fiesta Melons* (1971).

"In Midas' Country." *London Magazine* 6 (October, 1959): 11.

"The Jailor." *Encounter* 21 (October, 1963): 51.

"The Lady and the Earthenware Head." In *Pursuit* (1973).

"Lament." *New Orleans Poetry Journal* 1 (October, 1955): 19.

"A Lesson in Vengeance." *Poetry* 94 (September, 1959): 371.

"Letter to a Purist." *Times Literary Supplement,* 31 July 1969, p. 855.

"Mad Girl's Love Song." *Mademoiselle* 37 (August, 1953): 358.

"Main Street at Midnight." *The Spectator* 202 (13 February 1959): 227.

"Mayflower." In *Lyonnesse* (1971).

"Memoirs of a Spinach Picker." *Christian Science Monitor*, 29 December 1959, p. 8.

"Metamorphoses of the Moon." In *Lyonnesse* (1971).

"Million Dollar Month." In *Million Dollar Month* (1971).

"Miss Drake Proceeds to Supper." In Newman, ed., *The Art of Sylvia Plath*.

"Natural History." *Cambridge Review* 90 (7 February 1969): 244-45.

"The Net Menders." *The New Yorker* 36 (20 August 1960): 36.

"Notes on Zarathustra's Prologue." In *Crystal Gazer* (1971).

"November Graveyard." *Mademoiselle* 62 (November, 1965): 134.

"Ode to a Bitten Plum." *Seventeen* 33 (January, 1974): 136.

"Old Ladies' Home." In *Lyonnesse* (1971).

"On the Decline of Oracles." *Poetry* 94 (September, 1959): 368-69.

"On the Difficulty of Conjuring Up a Dryad." *Poetry* 90 (July, 1957): 235-36.

"On the Plethora of Dryads." In Newman, ed., *The Art of Sylvia Plath*.

"The Other Two." In *Lyonnesse* (1971).

"Poem for a Birthday." In *The Colossus* (British edition, 1960).

"Prologue to Spring." *Christian Science Monitor*, 23 March 1959, p. 8.

"Pursuit." *Atlantic* 199 (January, 1957): 65.

"Recantation." *Accent* 17 (Autumn, 1957): 247.

"Resolve." *Cambridge Review* 90 (7 February 1969): 244-45.

"The Rival" (2). In *Pursuit* (1973).

"Second Winter." *Ladies' Home Journal* 75 (December, 1958): 143.

"A Secret." In *Pursuit* (1973).

"The Shrike." In *Pursuit* (1973).

"The Sleepers." *London Magazine* 7 (June, 1960): 11.

"The Snowman on the Moor." *Poetry* 90 (July, 1957): 229-31.

"Soliloquy of the Solipsist." *Granta* 61 (4 May 1957): 19.

"Song for a Summer Day." *Christian Science Monitor*, 18 August 1959, p. 8.

"Southern Sunrise." *Christian Science Monitor*, 26 August 1959, p. 8.

"Spider." In *Pursuit* (1973).

"Stars over the Dordogne." *Poetry* 99 (March, 1962): 346-47.

"Stings" (2). In *Pursuit* (1973).

"Street Song." *Cambridge Review* 90 (7 February 1969): 244.

"The Suitcases Are Packed Again." *Seventeen* 12 (March, 1953).

"Temper of Time." *The Nation* 181 (6 August 1955): 119.

"Tinker Jack and the Tidy Wives." *Accent* 17 (Autumn, 1957): 248.

"To Eva Descending the Stair." *Harper's* 209 (September, 1954): 63.

"Twelfth Night." *Seventeen* 11 (December, 1952).

"Two Lovers and a Beachcomber by the Real Sea." *Mademoiselle* 41 (August 1955): 52 and 62.

"Vanity Fair." *Gemini* 1 (Spring, 1957).

"White Phlox." *Christian Science Monitor*, 27 August 1952, p. 12.

"Whiteness I Remember." *Christian Science Monitor*, 5 March 1959, p. 12.

"A Winter's Tale." *The New Yorker* 35 (12 December 1959): 116.

"Words for a Nursery." *Atlantic* 208 (August, 1961): 66.

Bibliography

"Words Heard, by Accident, over the Phone." In *Pursuit* (1973).

"Wreath for a Bridal." *Poetry* 89 (January, 1957): 231.

"Yadwigha, on a Red Couch, among Lilies (A Sestina for the Douanier)." *Christian Science Monitor*, 26 March 1959, p. 8.

C. Uncollected Prose (work not included in *Johnny Panic and the Bible of Dreams*)

"An American in Paris." *Varsity*, 21 April 1956.

"And Summer Will Not Come Again." *Seventeen* 9 (August, 1950): 191, 275-76.

"As a Baby-Sitter Sees It." *Christian Science Monitor*, 6 November 1951, p. 19, and 7 November 1951, p. 21.

"B. and K. at the Claridge." *Smith Alumnae Quarterly* 48 (Fall, 1956): 16-17.

"Beach Plum Season on Cape Cod." *Christian Science Monitor*, 14 August 1958, p. 17.

"Eccentricity." *The Listener* 79 (9 May 1968): 607.

"Explorations Lead to Interesting Discoveries." *Christian Science Monitor*, 19 October 1959, p. 17.

"Kitchen of the Fig Tree." *Christian Science Monitor*, 5 May 1959, p. 8.

"Leaves from a Cambridge Notebook." *Christian Science Monitor*, 5 March 1956, p. 17, and 6 March 1956, p. 15.

"Mademoiselle's Last Word on College, '53." *Mademoiselle* 37 (August, 1953): 235.

"Mosaics—An Afternoon of Discovery." *Christian Science Monitor* 12 (October, 1959): 15.

"The Mothers' Union." *McCall's* 100 (October, 1972): 80 ff.

"Oblongs," *The New Statesman* 63 (18 May 1962): 724.

"Oregonian Original." *The New Statesman* 63 (9 November 1962): 660.

"Pair of Queens." *The New Statesman* 63 (27 April 1962): 602-603.

"The Perfect Setup." *Seventeen* 11 (August, 1952): 76 ff.

"Poets on Campus." *Mademoiselle* 37 (August, 1953): 290-91.

"Sketchbook of a Spanish Summer." *Christian Science Monitor*, 5 November 1956, p. 13, and 6 November 1956, p. 15.

"Smith College in Retrospect." *Varsity*, 12 May 1956.

"Smith Review Revived." *Smith Alumnae Quarterly* 45 (Fall, 1953): 26.

"Suffering Angel." *The New Statesman* 63 (7 December 1962): 828-29.

"Sylvia Plath Tours the Stores and Forecasts May Week Fashions," *Varsity*, 26 May 1956.

"A Walk to Withens." *Christian Science Monitor*, 6 June 1959, p. 12.

"Youth's Plea for World Peace." With Perry Norton, *Christian Science Monitor*, 16 March 1950, p. 19.

D. Interviews

"Four Young Poets." *Mademoiselle* 48 (January, 1959): 34 ff. Interviewed by Corinne Robins.

"Sylvia Plath." In *The Poet Speaks*, ed. Peter Orr. London: Routledge and Kegan Paul, 1966. Interviewed by Peter Orr.

"Sylvia Plath: A Reading and an Interview." Recorded at Springfield, Massachusetts, 18 April 1958. Washington, D.C.: Library of Congress, 1958.

"Two of a Kind." BBC: Poets in Partnership. Broadcast 31 January 1961 and 19 March 1961. Joint interview with Ted Hughes.

About Sylvia Plath

A. Books

Aird, Eileen. *Sylvia Plath: Her Life and Work*. Edinburgh: Oliver and Boyd, 1973; New York: Harper and Row, 1975.

Butscher, Edward. *Sylvia Plath: Method and Madness*. New York: Seabury Press, 1976.

————, ed. *Sylvia Plath: The Woman and the Work*. New York: Dodd, Mead, 1977.

Holbrook, David. *Sylvia Plath: Poetry and Existence*. London: Athlone Press, 1976.

Homberger, Eric. *A Chronological Checklist of the Periodical Publications of Sylvia Plath*. Exeter: Exeter University Press, 1970 (American Arts Pamphlet No. 1).

Kroll, Judith. *Chapters in a Mythology: The Poetry of Sylvia Plath*. New York: Harper and Row, 1976.

Lane, Gary, and Stevens, Maria. *Sylvia Plath: A Bibliography*. Metuchen, N.J.: Scarecrow Press, 1978.

Melander, Ingrid. *The Poetry of Sylvia Plath: A Study of Themes*. Stockholm: Almqvist and Wiksell, 1972.

Newman, Charles, ed. *The Art of Sylvia Plath: A Symposium*. Bloomington: Indiana University Press, 1970; London: Faber and Faber, 1970.

Steiner, Nancy Hunter. *A Closer Look at Ariel: A Memory of Sylvia Plath*. New York: Harper's Magazine Press, 1973; London: Faber and Faber, 1974.

Walsh, Thomas P. and Northouse, Cameron. *Sylvia Plath and Anne Sexton: A Reference Guide*. Boston: G. K. Hall, 1974.

B. Articles or book chapters (Where these have been reprinted, the most accessible appearance has been chosen.)

Adrich, Elizabeth. "Sylvia Plath's 'The Eye-mote': An Analysis." *Harvard Advocate* 101 (May, 1967): 4-7.

Aird, Eileen M. "Variants in a Tape Recording of Fifteen Poems by Sylvia Plath." *Notes and Queries* 19 (February, 1972): 59-61.

Alvarez, A. "The Art of Suicide." *Partisan Review* 37 (1970): 339-58.

————. "Beyond All This Fiddle." *Times Literary Supplement*, 23 March 1967, pp. 229-32.

————. "Sylvia Plath." In Newman, ed., *The Art of Sylvia Plath*.

————. "Sylvia Plath: A Memoir." In Alvarez, A. *The Savage God: A Study of Suicide*. London: Wiedenfeld and Nicolson, 1971; New York: Random House, 1972.

Bibliography

Ames, Lois. "Notes Toward a Biography." In Newman, ed., *The Art of Sylvia Plath*.

Arb, Siv. "Dikter nar förvananansvärt langt." *Ord och Bild* 83 (1974): 459-60.

Ashford, Deborah. "Sylvia Plath's Poetry: A Complex of Irreconcilable Antagonisms." *Concerning Poetry* 7, no. 1, pp. 62-69.

Bagg, Robert. "The Rise of Lady Lazarus." *Mosaic* 2 (Summer, 1969): 9-36.

Balitas, Vincent D. "On Becoming a Witch: A Reading of Sylvia Plath's 'Witch Burning.'" *Studies in the Humanities* 4 (February, 1975): 27-30.

Ballif, Gene. "Facing the Worst: A View from Minerva's Buckler." *Parnassus: Poetry in Review*, Fall/Winter, 1976, pp. 231-59.

Blodgett, E. D. "Sylvia Plath: Another View." *Modern Poetry Studies* 2 (1971): 97-106.

Boyers, Robert. "Sylvia Plath: The Trepanned Veteran." *Centennial Review* 13 (Spring, 1969): 138-53.

Buell, Frederick. "Sylvia Plath's Traditionalism." *Boundary* 2 (Fall, 1976): 195-211.

Burnham, Richard E. "Sylvia Plath's 'Lady Lazarus.'" *Contemporary Poetry* 1, no. 2 (1973): 42-46.

Butscher, Edward. "In Search of Sylvia: An Introduction." In Butscher, ed., *Sylvia Plath: The Woman and the Work*.

Campbell, Wendy. "Remembering Sylvia." In Newman, ed., *The Art of Sylvia Plath*.

Caraher, Brian. "The Problematic of Body and Language in Sylvia Plath's 'Tulips.'" *Paunch* 42-43 (December, 1975): 76-89.

Claire, William F. "That Rare, Random Descent: The Poetry and Pathos of Sylvia Plath." *Antioch Review* 26 (Winter 1966): 552-60.

Cleverdon, Douglas. "On *Three Women*." In Newman, ed., *The Art of Sylvia Plath*.

Cluysenaar, Anne. "Post-culture: Pre-culture?" In *British Poetry since 1960*, edited by M. Schmidt and G. Lindop, pp. 215-32. Oxford: Carcanet Press, 1972.

Cooley, Peter. "Autism, Autoeroticism, Auto-da-fe: The Tragic Poetry of Sylvia Plath." *Hollins Critic* 10 (February, 1973): 1-15.

Corrigan, Sylvia Robinson. "Sylvia Plath: A New Feminist Approach." *Aphra* 1 (Spring, 1970): 16-23.

Cunningham, Stuart. "Bibliography: Sylvia Plath." *Hecate* (Australia) 1 (July, 1975): 95-112.

Davis, Robin Reed. "The Honey Machine: Imagery Patterns in *Ariel*." *New Laurel Review* 1 (Spring, 1972): 23-31.

_____. "Now I have Lost Myself: A Reading of Sylvia Plath's 'Tulips.'" *Paunch* 42-43 (December, 1975): 97-104.

Davis, Stuart A. "The Documentary Sublime: The Posthumous Poetry of Sylvia Plath." *Harvard Advocate* 101 (May, 1967): 8-12.

Davis, William V. "Sylvia Plath's 'Ariel.'" *Modern Poetry Studies* 3 (1972): 176-84.

Donovan, Josephine. "Sexual Politics in Sylvia Plath's Short Stories." *Minnesota Review* 4 (Spring/Summer, 1973): 150-157.

Dyroff, Jan M. "Sylvia Plath: Perceptions in *Crossing the Water*." *Art and*

Literature Review 1: 49-50.

Dyson, A. E. "On Sylvia Plath." In Newman, ed., *The Art of Sylvia Plath*.

Efron, Arthur. "Sylvia Plath's 'Tulips' and Literary Criticism." *Paunch* 42-43 (December, 1975): 69-75.

_____. "'Tulips': Text and Assumptions." *Paunch* 42-43 (December, 1975): 110-122.

Ellmann, Mary. "*The Bell Jar:* An American Girlhood." In Newman, ed. *The Art of Sylvia Plath*.

Eriksson, Pamela Dale. "Some Thoughts on Sylvia Plath." *Unisa English Studies* 10 (1972): 45-52.

Ferrier, Carole. "The Beekeeper and the Queen Bee." *Refractory Girl*, Spring, 1973, pp. 31-36.

Fraser, G. S. "A Hard Nut to Crack from Sylvia Plath." *Contemporary Poetry* 1 (Spring, 1973): 1-12.

Gordon, Jan B. "'Who Is Sylvia?': The Art of Sylvia Plath." *Modern Poetry Studies* 1 (1970): 6-34.

Hakeem, A. "Sylvia Plath's 'Elm' and Munch's 'The Scream.'" *English Studies* 55 (December, 1974): 531-37.

Hardwick, Elizabeth. "Sylvia Plath." *New York Review of Books* 17 (12 August 1971): 3-4, 6.

Hardy, Barbara. "The Poetry of Sylvia Plath: Enlargement or Derangement?" In *The Survival of Poetry*, edited by Martin Dodsworth. London: Faber and Faber, 1970.

Himelick, Raymond. "Notes on the Care and Feeding of Nightmares: Burton, Erasmus, and Sylvia Plath." *Western Humanities Review* 28 (Autumn, 1974): 313-26.

Holbrook, David. "Out of the Ash: Different Views of the 'Death Camp' —Sylvia Plath, Al Alvarez, and Viktor Frankl." *The Human World* 5 (November, 1971): 22-39.

_____. "R. D. Laing and the Death Circuit." *Encounter* 31 (August, 1968): 35-45.

_____. "Sylvia Plath and the Problem of Violence in Art." *Cambridge Review* 90 (7 February 1969): 249-50.

_____. "The 200-Inch Distorting Mirror." *New Society* 12 (11 July 1968): 57-58.

Hosbaum, Philip. "The Temptations of Giant Despair." *Hudson Review* 25 (Winter, 1972/73): 597-612.

Howard, Richard. "Sylvia Plath: 'And I Have No Face, I Have Wanted to Efface Myself....'" In Newman, ed., *The Art of Sylvia Plath*.

Howe, Irving, "The Plath Celebration: A Partial Dissent." In Butscher, ed., *Sylvia Plath: The Woman and the Work*.

Hoyle, James F. "Sylvia Plath: A Poetry of Suicidal Mania." *Literature and Psychology* 18 (1968): 187-203.

Hughes, Ted. "Notes on the Chronological Order of Sylvia Plath's Poems." In Newman, ed., *The Art of Sylvia Plath*.

_____. "Sylvia Plath's *Crossing the Water:* Some Reflections." *Critical Quarterly* 13 (Summer, 1971): 165-72.

Bibliography

_____. "Winter Trees." *Poetry Book Society Bulletin* 70 (Autumn, 1971).

Jones, A. R. "Necessity and Freedom: The Poetry of Robert Lowell, Sylvia Plath, and Anne Sexton." *Critical Quarterly* 7 (Spring, 1965): 11-30.

_____. "On 'Daddy.'" In Newman, ed., *The Art of Sylvia Plath*.

Kamel, Rose. "'A Self to Recover': Sylvia Plath's Bee Cycle Poems." *Modern Poetry Studies* 4 (1973): 304-18.

Kenner, Hugh. "Ariel—Pop Sincerity." *Triumph* 1 (September, 1966): 33.

Kinzie, Mary. "An Informal Check List of Criticism." In Newman, ed., *The Art of Sylvia Plath*.

_____, Conrad, Daniel Lynn, and Kurman, Suzanne. "Bibliography." In Newman, ed., *The Art of Sylvia Plath*.

Kissick, Gary. "Plath: A Terrible Perfection." *The Nation* 207 (16 September 1968): 245-47.

Kopp, Jane. "'Gone, Very Gone Youth': Sylvia Plath at Cambridge." In Butscher, ed., *Sylvia Plath: The Woman and the Work*.

Krook, Dorothea. "Recollections of Sylvia Plath." In Butscher, ed., *Sylvia Plath: The Woman and the Work*.

Lameyer, Gordon. "The Double in Sylvia Plath's *The Bell Jar*." In Butscher, ed., *Sylvia Plath: The Woman and the Work*.

_____. "Sylvia at Smith." In Butscher, ed., *Sylvia Plath: The Woman and the Work*.

Lane, Gary. "Sylvia Plath's 'The Hanging Man': A Further Note." *Contemporary Poetry* 2 (Spring 1975): 40-43.

Lavers, Annette. "The World as Icon: On Sylvia Plath's Themes." In Newman, ed., *The Art of Sylvia Plath*.

Levy, Laurie. "Outside the Bell Jar." In Butscher, ed., *Sylvia Plath: The Woman and the Work*.

Libby, Anthony. "God's Lioness and the Priest of Sycorax: Plath and Hughes." *Contemporary Literature* 15 (Summer, 1974): 386-405.

Lindberg-Seyersted, Brita. "Notes on Three Poems by Sylvia Plath." *Edda* 74 (1974): 47-54.

_____. "On Sylvia Plath's Poetry." *Edda* 72 (1972): 54-59.

Lowell, Robert. "Foreword." *Ariel* (American editions, 1966).

Lucie-Smith, Edward. "A Murderous Art." *Critical Quarterly* 6 (1964): 355-63.

_____. "Sea-Imagery in the Work of Sylvia Plath." In Newman, ed., *The Art of Sylvia Plath*.

Martin, Wendy. "'God's Lioness'—Sylvia Plath, Her Prose and Poetry." *Women's Studies* 1 (1973): 191-98.

McClatchy, J. D. "Staring from Her Hood of Bone: Adjusting to Sylvia Plath." In *American Poetry since 1960*, edited by R. B. Shaw. Oxford: Carcanet Press, 1973.

McKay, D. F. "Aspects of Energy in the Poetry of Dylan Thomas and Sylvia Plath." *Critical Quarterly* 16 (Spring, 1974): 53-67.

Meissner, William. "The Opening of the Flower: The Revelation of Suffering in Sylvia Plath's 'Tulips.'" *Contemporary Poetry* 1 (Spring, 1973): 13-17.

_____. "The Rise of the Angel: Life Through Death in the Poetry of Sylvia Plath." *Massachusetts Studies in English* 3 (Fall, 1971): 34-39.

Melander, Ingrid. "'The Disquieting Muses': A Note on a Poem by Sylvia

Plath." *Research Studies* 39 (March, 1971): 53-54.

_____. "'Watercolour of Grantchester Meadows': An Early Poem by Sylvia Plath." *Moderna Sprak* 65 (1971): 1-5.

Mollinger, Robert N. "A Symbolic Complex: Images of Death and Daddy in the Poetry of Sylvia Plath." *Descant* 19, no. 2, pp. 44-52.

_____. "Sylvia Plath's 'Private Ground.'" *Notes on Contemporary Literature* 5, no. 2, pp. 14-15.

Newman, Charles. "Candor Is the Only Wile: The Art of Sylvia Plath." In Newman, ed., *The Art of Sylvia Plath*.

Nims, John Frederick. "The Poetry of Sylvia Plath: A Technical Analysis." In Newman, ed., *The Art of Sylvia Plath*.

Oates, Joyce Carol. "The Death Throes of Romanticism: The Poems of Sylvia Plath." In Butscher, ed., *Sylvia Plath: The Woman and the Work*.

Oberg, Arthur K. "The Modern British and American Lyric: What Will Suffice?" *Language and Literature* 7 (Winter, 1972): 70-88.

_____. "Sylvia Plath: 'Love, love, my season.'" In Oberg, Arthur, *The Modern American Lyric: Lowell, Berryman, Creeley, and Plath*. New Brunswick, N.J.: Rutgers University Press, 1978.

_____. "Sylvia Plath and the New Decadence." In Butscher, ed., *Sylvia Plath: The Woman and the Work*.

Oettle, Pamela. "Sylvia Plath's Last Poems." *Balcony* 3 (Spring, 1965): 47-50.

O'Hara, J. D. "An American Dream Girl." *Washington Post Book World*, 11 April 1971, p. 3.

Oliva, Renato. "La Poesia di Sylvia Plath." *Studi Americani* (Roma) 15 (1969): 341-81.

Oshio, Toshiko. "Sylvia Plath no Shi." *Oberon* 14 (1973): 45-59.

Ostriker, Alicia. "'Fact' As Style: The Americanization of Sylvia." *Language and Style* 1 (Summer, 1968): 201-12.

Perloff, Marjorie. "Angst and Animism in the Poetry of Sylvia Plath." *Journal of Modern Literature* 1 (1970): 57-74.

_____. "Extremist Poetry: Some Versions of the Sylvia Plath Myth." *Journal of Modern Literature* 2 (November, 1972): 581-88.

_____. "On Sylvia Plath's 'Tulips.'" *Paunch* 42-43 (December, 1975): 105-9.

_____. "On the Road to *Ariel*: The 'Transitional' Poetry of Sylvia Plath." In Butscher, ed., *Sylvia Plath: The Woman and the Work*.

_____. "'A Ritual for Being Born Twice': Sylvia Plath's *The Bell Jar*." *Contemporary Literature* 13 (Autumn, 1972): 507-22.

Phillips, Robert. "The Dark Funnel: A Reading of Sylvia Plath." In Butscher, ed., *Sylvia Plath: The Woman and the Work*.

Pratt, Linda Ray. "'The Spirit of Blackness Is In Us. . . .'" *Prairie Schooner* 47 (Spring, 1973): 87-90.

Roche, Clarissa. "Sylvia Plath: Vignettes from England." In Butscher, ed., *Sylvia Plath: The Woman and the Work*.

Roland, Laurin K. "Sylvia Plath's 'Lesbos': A Self Divided." *Concerning Poetry* 9 (1976): 61-65.

Romano, John. "Sylvia Plath Reconsidered." *Commentary* 57 (April, 1974):

Bibliography

47-52.

Rosenblatt, Jon. "'The Couriers.'" *Explicator* 34 (December, 1975), item 28.

Rosenstein, Harriet. "Reconsidering Sylvia Plath." *Ms* 1 (September, 1972): 44 ff.

Rosenthall, M. L. "Sylvia Plath and Confessional Poetry." In Newman, ed., *The Art of Sylvia Plath.*

Salamon, Lynda B. "'Double, Double': Perception in the Poetry of Sylvia Plath." *Spirit* 38 (1970): 34-39.

Scheerer, Constance. "The Deathly Paradise of Sylvia Plath." In Butscher, ed., *Sylvia Plath: The Woman and the Work.*

Schrickx, W. "De Dichtkunst van Sylvia Plath." *Dietsche Warande en Belfort* 116 (1971): 191-210.

Sexton, Anne. "The Barfly Ought to Sing." In Newman, ed., *The Art of Sylvia Plath.*

Sigmund, Elisabeth. "Sylvia in Devon: 1962." In Butscher, ed., *Sylvia Plath: The Woman and the Work.*

Smith, Pamela. "Architectonics: Sylvia Plath's *Colossus.*" In Butscher, ed., *Sylvia Plath: The Woman and the Work.*

————. "The Unitive Urge in the Poetry of Sylvia Plath." *New England Quarterly* 45 (September, 1972): 323-39.

Smith, Stan. "Attitudes Counterfeiting Life: The Irony of Artifice in Sylvia Plath's *The Bell Jar.*" *Critical Quarterly* 17 (Autumn, 1975): 247-60.

Spendal, R. J. "Sylvia Plath's 'Cut.'" *Modern Poetry Studies* 6 (Autumn, 1975): 128-34.

Spender, Stephen. "Warnings from the Grave." In Newman, ed., *The Art of Sylvia Plath.*

Stade, George. "Introduction." In Steiner, Nancy Hunter. *A Closer Look at Ariel: A Memory of Sylvia Plath.*

Stainton, Rita T. "Vision and Voice in Three Poems by Sylvia Plath." *Windless Orchard* 17 (Spring 1974): 31-36.

Steiner, George. "'Dying Is an Art.'" In Newman, ed., *The Art of Sylvia Plath.*

————. "In Extremis." *Cambridge Review* 90 (7 February 1969): 247-49.

Stilwell, Robert L. "The Multiplying Entities: D. H. Lawrence and Five Other Poets." *Sewanee Review* 76 (July-September, 1968): 520-35.

Sumner, Nan McCowan. "Sylvia Plath." *Research Studies* 38 (June, 1970): 112-21.

Talbot, Norman. "Sisterhood Is Powerful: The Moon in Sylvia Plath's Poetry." *New Poetry* (Sydney) 21 (June, 1973): 23-36.

Taylor, Andrew. "Sylvia Plath's Mirror and Beehive." *Meanjin* 33 (September, 1974): 256-65.

Uroff, Margaret D. "Sylvia Plath on Motherhood." *Midwest Quarterly* 15 (October, 1973): 70-90.

————. "Sylvia Plath's 'Tulips.'" *Paunch* 42-43 (December, 1975): 90-96.

————. "Sylvia Plath's Women." *Concerning Poetry* 7, no. 1, (1974): 45-56.

Vendler, Helen. "La Poesia de Sylvia Plath." *Plural* 33 (1974): 6-14.

Yoshida, Sachiko. "Incense of Death: Sylvia Plath no Sonzai no Kaku." *Eigo Seinen* 120: 488-89.

Zollman, Sol. "Sylvia Plath and Imperialist Culture." *Literature and Ideology* 1 (1969): 11-22.

Contributors

Calvin Bedient is professor of English at the University of California at Los Angeles. His articles and reviews appear in numerous magazines and journals. His most recent book is *Eight Contemporary Poets*.

Richard Allen Blessing is professor of English at the University of Washington. In addition to poems and critical essays, he is the author of *Wallace Stevens's "Whole Harmonium"*; *Theodore Roethke's Dynamic Vision*; and *Winter Constellations*.

Christopher Bollas practices psychoanalysis and teaches literature in London. He has worked as a therapist at the Tavistock Clinic, and he writes on Melville, the psychoanalysis of character, and aesthetic theory.

Carole Ferrier lectures in women's studies and modern literature at Queensland University in Australia. She is an activist in the Australian left and feminist movements and has published widely in the field of women's studies.

Barnett Guttenberg is associate professor of English at the University of Miami (Florida). He edits *Faulkner Studies* and, in addition to critical essays, has published *Web of Being: The Novels of Robert Penn Warren*.

Gary Lane is associate professor of English at the University of Texas at San Antonio. In addition to poems and critical essays, he has published

I Am: A Study of E. E. Cummings' Poems. He is completing a book to be called *Sulphur Loveliness: The Poetry of Sylvia Plath.*

Hugh Kenner is Andrew Mellon Professor of the Humanities at The Johns Hopkins University. His numerous books include *The Poetry of Ezra Pound; Wyndham Lewis; Dublin's Joyce; The Art of Poetry; The Invisible Poet: T. S. Eliot;* and *The Pound Era.*

Jerome Mazzaro, professor of English at The State University of New York, Buffalo, is presently Visiting Professor of English at San Diego State University. He edits *Modern Poetry Studies,* is the author of *The Poetic Themes of Robert Lowell,* and has edited *Modern American Poetry: Essays in Criticism.*

J. D. McClatchy teaches at Yale University. His poems, essays, and reviews appear regularly in such journals as *Poetry,* the *Nation, Yale Review, American Poetry Review,* and the *Georgia Review.* He is the editor of *Anne Sexton: The Artist and Her Critics.*

J. D. O'Hara is professor of English at the University of Connecticut. He is the author of *Poetry,* and his essays, poems, and reviews appear regularly in magazines and journals.

Marjorie Perloff is Florence R. Scott Professor of English at the University of Southern California. She has written numerous essays on modern poets from Yeats and Pound to Ammons and Ashbery and is the author of *The Poetic Art of Robert Lowell* and *Frank O'Hara: Poet Among Painters.* She is completing a book to be called *The Other Tradition: Toward a Postmodern Poetry.*

Sister Bernetta Quinn, O.S.F., a member of the faculty at the College of St. Teresa, Winona, Minnesota, is currectly Visiting Professor of English at Norfolk State University. She is the author of *The Metamorphic Tradition in Modern Poetry; Ezra Pound: An Introduction to the Poetry;* and a forthcoming book on Randall Jarrell.

Murray M. Schwartz is a professor in the English Department and the Center for the Psychological Study of the Arts at the State University of New York at Buffalo. His writings on theoretical and applied psycho-analysis include interpretations of Freud, Erikson, William Carlos Williams, and D. H. Lawrence and essays on critical self-definition. He is completing a book on Shakespeare derived from his lectures as a Senior Fellow at the Center for the Humanities at Wesleyan University in the spring of 1978.

David Shapiro teaches at Columbia University. His books of poems include *January; Poems from Deal; A Man Holding an Acoustic Panel* (nominated for a National Book Award); and *The Page-Turner.* His art criticism appears in *Art News* and *Craft Horizons*, and two new books, a volume of poems and a critical study of John Ashbery, are forthcoming.

Index of Sylvia Plath's works

General index